School-Based Management

An International Perspective

School-Based Management

An International Perspective

Edited by

Ami Volansky
Isaac A. Friedman

State of Israel
Ministry of Education

Graphic Design: *Shoshana Shahar*
Printed by: *Scorpio 88*
Published by: *Publication Department, Ministry of Education, Devora Ha-Niviah 2,*
                     Jerusalem, Israel
                     ISBN: 965-444-031-8
                     © 2003 All Rights Reserved.

No part of this book may be reproduced, stored in or introduced into a retrieved system or transmitted in any form or by any means, electronic, mechanical, photocopying, recording or otherwise, without the prior written permission of the publisher.

CONTENTS

Contributors

Ronit Bogler is a lecturer in the Department of Education and Psychology at Israel's Open University. Her research interests include educational leadership as well as job satisfaction for school teachers. Her most recent publications include "The Influence of Leadership Style on Teacher Job Satisfaction" in *Educational Administration Quarterly* (2001) and "Two Profiles of School Teachers: A Discriminant Analysis of Job Satisfaction" in *Teaching and Teacher Education* (in press).

Brian J. Caldwell is a professor and the Dean of Education at the University of Melbourne, Australia. His international work over the last decade includes presentations, projects and other professional assignments in 28 countries, with several assignments for OECD, UNESCO, UNICEF, World Bank and the Asia Development Bank. He is co-author of books that have helped guide educational reform in a number of countries. He was President of the ACEA from 1990 to 1993, and was awarded its Gold Medal in 1994.

Yin Cheong Cheng is a professor and the Director of the Center for Research and International Collaboration of the Hong Kong Institute of Education. He is also the head of the Asia-Pacific Center for Educational Leadership and Educational Quality, and the founding vice-president of the Asia-Pacific Educational Research Association. His major research interests include educational effectiveness, school-based management, educational reforms, teacher education and paradigm shifts in education. Prof. Cheng has published eight books and nearly 150 book chapters and academic journal articles all over the world, and his research has won him numerous international awards.

Isaac A. Friedman is the Director of the Henrietta Szold Institute, the National Institute for Research in the Behavioral Sciences, and serves as one of its senior researchers. He teaches education and organizational psychology at the School of Education of the Hebrew University of Jerusalem. His major research interests include psychological and organizational aspects of teaching, the school climate and culture, principal training, measurement and evaluation.

Michael W. Kirst is a professor of Education at Stanford University. He was president of the California State Board of Education, and staff director of the U.S. Senate Committee on Manpower and Poverty. Kirst is a member of the American National Academy of Education, and is on the management board of the Consortium for Policy Research in Education.

Rosalind Levačić is a professor of Economics and Finance of Education at the Institute of Education, University of London. Her research deals with the allocation of resources to and within schools, and the management of finance and resources in schools. She is research associate at the DfEE-funded Center for the Economics of Education, where she is working on projects concerning the relationship between school resources and student outcomes.

Adam E. Nir is a lecturer and head of the Educational Administration and Planning Program at the Hebrew University of Jerusalem. His current interests and research are in school-based management, educational planning and human resource management. Among his most recent works are "The Impact of School-based Management on School Health" in the *Journal of School Leadership* (in press).

Ami Volansky is the Deputy Director for Policy Planning and Assessment in Israel's Ministry of Education. Dr Volansky is an adjunct lecturer at the School of Education of Tel Aviv University, specializing in the processes of centralization and decentralization in education systems. He initiated and led the transition to school-based management in Israel's school systems, as well as other system-oriented changes, and has served as consultant for higher education under five education ministers.

Vivian J. Williams is the Director of the Norham Center for Leadership Studies and Emeritus Fellow, St. Peter's College, University of Oxford. The research projects she has conducted were generously funded through awards from the Leverhulme Trust, London, and the Norham Center for Leadership Studies, Oxford.

8

PREFACE

In April 2001, a conference was held in Israel on the topic of School-based Management. Participants at this conference were principals, policy-makers, scholars and experts from Israel and abroad. Some of the lectures presented at that gathering have been compiled into this book, in the hope of adding to the ever-increasing wealth of information in the field of education on this method of school management, which perceives the school as a source of authority and accountability for educational outcomes.

This book is aimed at those who formulate educational policy, holders of key positions in educational institutions and local authorities, researchers, lecturers and education students. They may find this book to be a source of both theoretical and practical information on questions pertaining to advanced and innovative school administration, changes in management culture, and ways to empower schools as a source of decision-making authority.

But primarily, this book is dedicated to the leaders of the education systems – the school principals. They are the ones who bear the main burden and stand at the forefront of the educational enterprise on a day-to-day basis. Expectations for pupil achievement – and criticism when those expectations are not met – are aimed at them, while they attempt to lead a complex, human system in a changing environment. Principals create an educational experience for the thousands of pupils in their charge, and what they do determines, for good or bad, the quality of their education and consequently, the quality of society as well.

During one of our school visits we met a principal who had been head of a school for 26 years. In essence, some 20,000 pupils passed under his baton, equivalent to a mid-sized sports stadium. No other societal role enables us to have a greater qualitative and quantitative impact upon the future of so many thousands of young people than that of the school principal and his teachers. It is to them that we dedicate this book in recognition and appreciation of their efforts, with hope for their continued success.

ACKNOWLEDGEMENTS

Publication of this book was made possible through the assistance of many individuals. First and foremost, we express our thanks to the authors, both from Israel and from abroad. Their expertise in this field has helped us convey to readers the knowledge that continues to develop throughout the world. Based on their extensive understanding, we were able to present both theoretical and research advances, thereby helping to formulate educational policies to improve the quality of our teaching, and make our schools the focus of authority and accountability for educational outcomes.

This book is being published in both English and in Hebrew, and the process of bringing the book to press was more complex than anticipated. Special thanks go to Sagir International Translations, Ltd. - to Penina Arbit and Michele Sagir for linguistic editing of the English edition and to Raya Cohen for linguistic editing of the Hebrew version. Puah Shai was enlisted to prepare the book for press, and her competence and unfailing professionalism allowed us to overcome the many obstacles involved in preparing the book. Shoshana and Yochanan Shahar created the tasteful layout and design, and worked on the actual printing. Last but not least, thanks to Naomi Eyal, director of the Publications Department of the Ministry of Education, for her devoted and continuous supervision throughout the publishing process in both languages.

Many within the Ministry of Education are involved in the transition to school-based management in Israel and the struggle for its implementation. Without the faith of district superintendents, administration directors and department heads, and without their understanding that certain powers must be relinquished, this process of change would never have become a reality and this book would not have seen the light of day. To them, and to many other leaders within the education system, the Ministry of Education and local authorities, we express our gratitude and appreciation.

Special thanks are due to the small staff at the Ministry who have had to bear with the day-to-day burdens, crises and numerous difficulties of implementing the transition to self-management, headed by Dr. Chaim Rubinstein and Nili Biron. Thanks as well to Asher Lichtenberg for his dedication in preparing the material contained in this book, and to Annette Hazut, executive secretary for the Planning Division, whose proficiency in handling the endless details were a help to all of us in publishing this book.

Above all, special appreciation goes to Ronit Tirosh, Director-General of the Ministry of Education, who encouraged the printing and publication of this book from the day she took office.

Without the contribution of all these individuals, neither the English edition nor the Hebrew edition of this book would have been possible.

INTRODUCTION

Ami Volansky and Isaac A. Friedman

Education systems throughout the world are undergoing a period of tension and conflict surrounding two approaches to school management, between the centralized, hierarchical, authoritative model of school management, and an administrative model based on a new system of parities along the path from centralization to decentralization, while viewing the school itself as a source of authority, accountability and responsibility for educational outcomes.

Although in some cases the centralized model is deeply rooted within the organizational culture of education systems, the model that delegates to and empowers the schools and underlies the theory of decentralization of authority is relatively new, both in terms of its theoretical conception and in how it is practically applied. Another element behind the tension is the difficulty in finding a new equilibrium, as centralized systems are finding it hard to give up the power they enjoy and surrender to the school, as the end unit that provides educational services, the full credit needed for a new management system.

Beginning in the 19th century and until the last quarter of the 20th century, preference was given to the centralized management of education systems. Gradually it became clear that education should not be a privilege afforded to only a minority of the population but rather must be established as a right to which everyone is entitled. Toward the end of the 19th century the requirement to provide elementary school education as "education for all" was formulated; at a later stage, during the first half of the 20th century, this requirement was extended to secondary school education as well. The early 20th century also marked the birth of the "welfare state," inspired by movements for social equality. These movements reinforced the trend toward "education for all." They called for equality for all social strata, and were the driving force behind processes of legislation and reforms, offering basic services to citizens with regard to income supplements, unemployment benefits, pensions, housing and health, and education. This policy was intensified in the wake of World War I, and even more so after World War II. At that point, many countries appropriated the authority for organizing educational services from private or semi-official organizations – including the church, communities, local authorities, and various corporations – and reorganized them in such a way as to guarantee both uniform administrative procedures and the principle of equality in the provision of educational services. These procedures, supervised by the state, were organized differently from country to country, but the basic trend was the same – greater centralization of educational services. Thus, for example, in England, educational organization was concentrated under the authority of LEAs (Local Education Authority), in North America education was organized by school districts, while in France, Sweden and Israel operational authority was concentrated in the hands of the central government.

Beginning in the 1960s, two elements of criticism were being leveled against the process of centralization. One element, which doesn't relate exclusively to education, resulted from the claim that the variety of services offered as part of welfare policies led to the formation of bureaucratic mechanisms and organizational monoliths that were controlled and run by the state. These centralized systems generated an increasing sense of unwieldiness and lack of control, excessive public spending and a need for organizational efficiency. There was a growing feeling that, instead of serving the citizens, these mechanisms were making them feel alienated, angry and rejected. Another aspect that came under criticism was the claim that the citizen's dependence upon bureaucratic and hierarchical mechanisms neutralizes the feeling of initiative and creativity among organization employees, to the point where it could jeopardize the organization's ability to achieve its goals (Friedman, 1962; Gamble, 1985; Hayek, 1960).

In the field of education, two principal arguments were raised concerning the impact of centralization. One had to do with the complexity of the organization; the other concerned the state's inability to effectively supervise the quality of education, the proof of this being the schools' failure to bridge the gaps in academic achievement among different ethnic and social groups.

In the organizational sphere, the claim was that the centralized structure was burdensome for the schools, to the point that it reduced their ability to achieve the educational objectives established by the state. Critics argued that the larger and more complex the organization became, the greater was the internal inconsistency involved in its management. Different units within the organization overlapped and often clashed in terms of timetables or aspects of official and unofficial policy and even acted in conflict with one another, although this was generally limited to complex organizations. The tendency of the centralized system toward fragmentation burdens the curriculum the schools are supposed to be implementing and makes it difficult for the school to realize established educational objectives. Political pressure for the rapid implementation of programs, recommendations by the professional and public committees that are established periodically, expectations of officials at the national, district or local, as well as the legislative level, to improve achievement, all conspire to make the school's job more complex. The result is a "project-oriented mentality" among schools, which threatens to make the education system a victim of its own method. In a democratic government, particularly one with an unstable coalition, every new term of office brings with it new programs and initiatives: new banners are run up the flagpole while others are taken down, new slogans replace the old ones, rhetoric is replaced by different rhetoric, and the schools are required to respond to meet the expectations and pressures from outside agencies. The result is that the pupil and his needs, the school and the community it serves, are all pushed aside. In this type of organizational structure the pupil is not at the center; rather, the instructions from on high are at the center, and teachers are expected to respond and carry them out (Hallak, 1991; Hill & Bonan, 1991; OECD, 1989; Volansky, 1999).

The second argument was the lack of effective state supervision of the education system and its outcomes. This criticism went hand in hand with the education systems being expanded and being opened to everyone. The Crowther Report, published in England in 1959, stated that, "Among the families of manual workers it is still the exception for a child to stay at school after he is legally free to go" (UK Department for Education, 1959).

In the wake of the Crowther Report, England appointed a commission to examine the factors that prevented the lower socio-economic sectors of the population from enjoying significant benefit from educational services. The commission's report, entitled *Half Our Future* and published in 1963, 19 years after passage of the Secondary School Education for All Act, begins as follows:

> Approximately one-half of our secondary school pupils, [from the weaker sectors of the population] will become one-half of the citizens of this country, half of the workers, half of the mothers and fathers, half of the consumers... . Therefore, they are half our future (UK Department for Education, 1963, p. viii).

In analyzing the causes underlying the difficulties these pupils experienced in school, it was found that:

> The evidence of research increasingly suggests that linguistic inadequacy, disadvantages in social and physical background, and poor attainments in school, are closely associated. Because the forms of speech which are all

they ever require for daily use in their homes and the neighborhoods in which they live are restricted, some boys and girls may never acquire the basic means of learning and their intellectual potential is therefore masked (ibid., p. 15).

Criticism regarding the quality of education and the lack of national objectives grew in the United States, too. In 1983 a report entitled *A Nation at Risk* was submitted to the US federal government. The findings contained in this report indicated that:

- 23 million American adults are illiterate;
- 13% of 17 year-olds are functionally illiterate;
- In minority groups, the rate of illiteracy reaches as high as 40%;
- The USA placed last on achievement tests seven times, compared with other industrialized nations.

The expansion of education systems, the economic crises of the 1970s and 1980s and their impact on education systems, and the dissatisfaction with the state's ability to guarantee effective mechanisms for supervision and control, together with criticism concerning the effect of centralized control in those countries where it was the norm, brought various countries to the limits of their ability to stand up to public criticism and expectations to improve education. It became clear to education systems that existing management methods did not enable them to withstand the stress and organizational difficulties that had been discovered, and they were no longer equipped to operate such a large-scale education system. Moreover, the nature of education is such that it fosters involvement and multiple centers for decision-making, making the reality even more complex. Parents' organizations, teachers' organizations, districts, locally elected school boards, and the schools themselves – all have an impact that may result in the definition of priorities that sometimes differ from those established by the central authority.

As a result of the criticism, many countries over the past two decades have attempted to implement far-reaching mechanical changes in the structure of education system authority and organization. Thus, for example, the achievements of the education system in England and Wales have been the subject of ongoing monitoring since the early 1970s. The transition to "secondary school education for all" and the opening of the gates to higher education following the Robbins Report, resulted in a sweeping attack on the quality of public education in professional, public and political circles, which finally ended in a comprehensive legislation in 1988. This legislation led to a redistribution of responsibilities and accountabilities. While the government focused on defining curricula and monitoring achievement, the schools themselves were given expanded responsibilities and, in practical terms, switched over to school-based management (Smyth, 1993; Volansky, 2003).[1] The education system in Canada underwent a significant process aimed at merging districts in order to achieve increased equity and equality. This process of merging school districts led to the reorganization of education into large-scale, centralized operational units, which fostered a sense of unwieldiness and the feeling that proper attention was not being paid to the individual within the organization – either the pupil or the teacher (Gue, 1985). As a result of various processes, some provinces encouraged their schools to switch to self-management, while the curriculum remained the responsibility of the province.

Beginning in 1973, the federal government of Australia started to become more involved in what was happening in the different states by establishing a federal education commission. The purpose of the government's involvement was to increase equality between schools, as well as with regard to curricula and the assessment of achievement. At the same time, the schools in three Australian states switched over to school-based management (Caldwell & Spinks, 1998; OECD, 1989). France has been famous for its centralized policies since the days of Napoleon. In 1982-84 the authority of the secondary school councils was expanded in several spheres, the ideology underlying this reform being the school in the center. Since World War II, the Swedish education system had been characterized by a high degree of centralization, but beginning in 1974, Sweden instituted a process of serious decentralization for the purpose of guaranteeing a modern curriculum, reinforcing principles of equality and ensuring a relatively unified administrative system. The decentralization was carried out by delegating authority to both the schools and local authorities, while dismantling the administrative machinery of the central government (OECD, 1989). The education system in the United States underwent three waves of changes, in the wake of a series of publications warning about the status of the American education system. First, in the early 1980s, federal involvement in education was coordinated with the state leadership. In 1989, President Bush, Sr., and the state governors agreed on six national goals for education that were to be achieved by 2000. At the same

---

1   The inspiration for this major legislation in England and Wales in 1988 led to the adoption of "market principles in education" and included additional components beyond school-based management.

time, a gradual process was instituted for empowering schools in some states and their transition to school-based management (Volansky, 1995). The Israeli education system is also characterized by a high degree of centralization, whose roots go back to the waves of immigration following the establishment of the state in 1948. As a result of mounting criticism from teachers' organizations and other parties within the system, a process of educational autonomy was introduced in the mid-1970s. This process became more powerful in the 1990s, with schools gradually moving to a system of school-based management.

In all of the processes taking place in different countries, both those characterized by a high degree of centralization and those typified by a high degree of decentralization, there emerged a broad common denominator for agreement – the separation of the central authority of the state or federal government from the responsibilities delegated to the schools. Generally speaking, the trend that is becoming a world-wide phenomenon is to have government authority and involvement in three main areas. These are:

- defining curricula and educational objectives;

- defining budgetary criteria, *inter alia,* to reduce educational gaps;

- defining standards and assessing achievement.

While the state tends to define the "what" – What should be taught? What will be achieved? What steps are to be taken in order to reduce gaps? – there is a growing movement to expand the operational authority of the schools regarding how to realize its goals and, in practical terms, schools define "how" to achieve the objectives defined by the state. This is an integrated management approach, which enables the state to determine national values and goals through curricula and by monitoring achievement while being liberated from ongoing bureaucratic management, and by granting a greater level of operating freedom to those who are closest to the pupils – the schools.

This new management system has two primary sources of inspiration. One source of inspiration is business organizations. As the environment of business organizations became more complex and more competitive, the more often these organizations were faced with crisis. Studies by Argyris (1982), Drucker (1977), Gamble (1985), Peters & Waterman (1982), and Srivasta & Barrent (1988) found that under certain circumstances, organizations that excel are those that succeed in infusing their employees with a shared vision; defining a (limited) number of organizational values that can motivate workers; defining shared operating goals; defining mechanisms of control; and undertaking widespread decentralization that leaves the organization's secondary units with plenty of maneuvering room, in terms of both discretion and initiative and innovation. It was clear that organizations that were able to grow, even during times of crisis, had adopted the operating principles described above. Underlying the change was the adoption of a new approach regarding the position of the individual within the organization as a source of energy and motivation for success (Handy, 1988; McGregor, 1985).

The second inspiration for education reform was the findings of research conducted on effective schools. These studies resulted from disappointment in the results of efforts to increase equality of educational opportunity. In the 1970s, findings began to mount from studies that examined the impact of factors such as community, family, school and class on differences in educational achievement. These studies consistently showed that such disparities were primarily explained by the cultural assets of the pupil's family. The work conducted by Coleman (1966) in the US had a significant influence. The report findings point out that:

> Home environment variables were the most important in explaining the variance in achievement levels for all racial and regional groups, and school facilities and curriculum were the least important variables (Coleman et al., 1966, p. 325).

The findings of the Coleman report set off a series of professional discussions and motivated many other research studies. Jencks (1973), like Coleman, found that a pupil's scholastic achievements are influenced by and contingent upon his family background more than the school as an educational organization and social institution. Kerensky (1975) summarized the two reports as follows:

> The school has much smaller role in a child's total education than most teachers and parents have assumed.... What the child brings to school is more important than what happens in the classroom in determining the kind of person he will become... (Kerensky, 1975, p. 44).

The findings of these studies, along with additional studies conducted by Bernstein (1961) and Halsey et al. (1980), which concluded similar findings, motivated educational researchers to find an answer to the question, Were there schools whose organizational and administrative methods enabled scholastic success even for pupils from low socio-economic backgrounds? Was it possible to neutralize the family background of these pupils so that it would not serve as a factor preventing positive achievement?

Indeed, during the 1970s and 1980s, research findings showed that under certain organizational conditions schools were found to be "effective," "excellent" and "outstanding." The main thesis of this movement toward effective schools was based on research findings indicating that under certain operational and management conditions schools could raise standards significantly, achieve better results and be more efficient (Bashi et al., 1990; Caldwell & Spinks, 1988, 1998; Chen, 1995; Cheng, 1996; Cuttance, 1985; Friedman, Horowitz, & Shaliv, 1988; Hopkins, 1987).

Despite differences in the issues examined, these studies appeared to share a fundamental common denominator, that schools that have a collective educational vision; define clear objectives; operate a monitoring and feedback system for assessing goals; have a shared and supportive management style; encourage initiative, creativity and individual responsibility; can make decisions in real time; and focus their efforts on the curriculum and promoting the needs of their pupils – these schools are more effective and boast higher scholastic achievement.

The findings spearheaded the formulation of new management theories and methods for schools. The theory essentially turned the management pyramid upside down. From now on, instructions would come not from the top down, but rather by focusing on addressing the pupils' needs, on the assumption that those who were closest to the pupil were better equipped to assess his needs. According to the new approach, encouragement was given to enterprising, creative solutions to problems, solutions devised by the school faculty using, perhaps, unconventional methods that didn't necessarily follow the paths and instructions that until now had been established by supervisory personnel or the central authorities. No longer would officials outside the school be seen as responsible for educational outcomes, rather – for better or worse – outcomes would depend upon the actions of the individual teacher or the school's teaching staff. A teacher's image and achievements, the success of his pupils, the pupils' affect for their school, and the school's status within the community now rested in the teachers' own hands and sense of self-efficacy, commitment and accountability.

Such an approach cannot be carried out unless most of the means which until now had been in the hands of central authorities outside the school, are handed over to the educational institution itself and its teachers. They are the ones who must make decisions based on their professional judgment in order to maximize pupil achievement. This change is part of the process to restructure the education system that is presently underway in a number of countries around the world. In order to turn the school into an organizational unit that can provide for its own needs and make decisions in real time, a comprehensive organizational change must take place within all of the organizational units that have been the source of managerial and financial authority until now. Such a reform and change is based on delineating all those who are part of this interaction – districts, local authorities, personnel from the Ministry's head office, and school principals. The essence of the change sometimes operates in opposition to "human nature", in that certain officials outside the school must transfer their authority and power to the schools. This process of change can empower the school and weaken those who have relinquished their authority, and therefore, in many countries around the world, the process is fraught with difficulty and tension.

The theory being developed in the field of self-management is based on fundamental research conducted in other disciplines. These include motivation theories, which draw on the field of psychology; the subfield in psychology that deals with people's resistance to change; research with regard to locus of control and self-efficacy; the field of organizational behavior in an environment of change, based on the new science of chaos and disorder; the field of feedback which is based on systems theory; the sphere of decision-making, taken from organizational theory; the area of resource management, derived from economic theories. This knowledge, which focuses on the school as an organizational unit, is one side of the coin. The information presented in this book is part of the ongoing, growing process that is likely to shed light on the school's capacity to become more effective by improving educational achievements. The more knowledge we acquire about school management, the more we become aware of the complexity involved in running the individual school, a complexity that takes form as part of an extensive, multi-faceted management theory exposing the intricacies of working in and managing an educational institution. This book does not deal with the other side of the coin – the management of education systems from the perspective of the center – nor does it discuss the role of state, district or local educational authorities. This book focuses on the "how" – how to manage schools, emphasizing an internal examination of the school's work processes. To enable implementation of school-based management theory, we must formalize and expand theories and practices concerning the role of the central authority (state, district, local education authorities) into a comprehensive management theory, thereby constituting both sides of the coin, two integrated management systems that rely on each other.

This book is divided into three parts. The first section focuses on formulating theoretical perspectives on school-based management. The second section of the book concentrates on the meaning of this new leadership perspective and the conditions for making it effective. The third section presents some of the things taking place in various countries, including the tension involved in the reciprocal relations between the central authority and schools undertaking self-management. This book is the result of the first international conference on this subject held in Israel in 2001. Most of the authors featured in this publication presented their work and research findings to the conference.

The first article by Yin Cheong Cheng contributes to both our theoretical and the practical understanding of school-based management in the new era of globalization, while comparing it with several other new, important aspects of education, such as localization and individualization. School-based management, which has become a major international trend in the last ten years, is a major means of promoting effective decision-making and resource use to meet the diverse school-based needs in education. This line of thinking maintains that school restructuring is necessary, in the author's view, but not sufficient for facing the challenges of the era of globalization and information technology. Accordingly, school-based management should aim to facilitate a new paradigm of education that emphasizes the development of students' contextualized multiple intelligences (CMI). Through globalization and localization, with the help of information technology and networking, the school can bring in a variety of resources and intellectual assets from the local community and different parts of the world to support world-class teaching and learning in each classroom, for every teacher and pupil. Through individualization, the human initiative and motivation of all pupils can be encouraged so they can develop their economic, social, political, cultural, and learning intelligences more effectively. Finally, Cheng argues that the new school-based management should aim not only to improve internal school processes but also to create new educational goals and enhance the relevance of education to the future through triplization. Such a school can support each student in becoming a contextualized multiple intelligence citizen who will be engaged in life-long learning and will creatively contribute to building up a multiple intelligence society and global village.

Isaac Friedman presents the self-managed school as an intelligent school. With this in mind, he defines two concepts: organizational intelligence and the intelligent organization, both of which rely upon the concept of human intelligence. An intelligent organization is one that formulates for itself clear thinking and behavior patterns and follows them in order to achieve its objectives. The behavior of an intelligent organization is expressed by properly assessing the present, learning from the past and from changes in the present, and by correctly anticipating and preparing for the future and, in particular, preparing for the future based on the findings of these assessments. The intelligent behavior of the organization's members is expressed via the changes they make, of their own free will, in response to a changing reality. Friedman defines five types of intelligence: reflective intelligence (which includes task-oriented behaviors, professionalism and improvement); strategic intelligence (which involves formulating a mission statement, defining objectives and deciding how to carry them out); contextual intelligence (which includes community-orientation, thinking big and a system-oriented perspective); collegial intelligence (which involves shared management within a school, cooperation with parents and the community, support, mutual assistance and giving credit where it is due); and ethical intelligence, which is based on human, spiritual and moral values. In addition, Friedman surveys the research that has dealt with the processes that typify the self-managed school and points to the fact that these processes reflect a high level of several organizational intelligences. Friedman's article contributes to both our theoretical understanding and practical application. At the applied level, the intelligence approach towards studying organizations can serve as a powerful analytical tool for assessing self-managed schools, defining their level of school-based management and indicating directions for improvement, if needed.

Brian J. Caldwell opens his article with a description of the decentralization and devolution of authority introduced in 1,600 government schools in Victoria, Australia, which constitute some 70% of all the schools in this state. The decentralization policy involved transferring 93.7% of the budget to schools, defining curriculum standards in eight subjects, teacher hiring policies, and requiring of every school a framework of accountability to the community from which the pupils come. The article focuses on the relationship between the self-managed school and learning outcomes, by surveying three generations of research in this field. The first generation of studies found that there was little evidence to support the notion that self-management is effective in increasing pupil performance. The second generation of studies was conducted at a period of time when the self-management reform had become more entrenched, when budgets were given to the schools, a framework for standards of accountability were defined, and the curriculum was defined by the central government. Findings from this phase were not so clear-cut and again, no actual basis was found to support the argument that self-managed schools were effective in increasing scholastic achievement.

The third generation of studies, published at the end of the 1990s, indicated a connection between the self-management of schools and their effectiveness with regard to learning, performance and curriculum. Caldwell's explanation for the development in this generation of studies as compared with the previous generations is that policies toward schools were more clearly defined and expectations regarding the connection between self-management and academic performance were spelled out. Furthermore, at this point in time the researchers now had available to them a broader spectrum of performance data and indicators concerning scholastic achievement. The principal findings, obtained in a series of studies, indicate that personnel and professional benefits, improved curricular planning based on pupil performance and adapting teaching to pupil needs, increased confidence in raising the level of self-management, school-based planning of resource allocations, and an increased sense of direction and purpose, together with enhanced accountability and responsibility – that all of these factors pointed to the connection between self-management and scholastic performance. The author concludes his article with a recommendation to policy-makers and claims that a precondition for improving performance is structural rearrangement in the direction of decentralization at various levels throughout the education system, with change focused around the children and the class if there is to be an impact on the improvement of pupil performance.

The article written by Vivian J. William deals with the concept of effective school culture within the context of the 1988 Education Reform Act in England and Wales. A key element of this reform was the devolution of financial and personnel control to the individual school level, which was called "Local Management of Schools" (LMS). The most significant outcome of the reform has been the gradual acceleration of cultural change within the schools. Research findings concerned with school leadership demonstrate that older, more traditional organizational models for the effective working of schools are neither appropriate nor fully able to engage the talent, abilities and experience of graduate and skilled professionals who work in schools – not least because they are unenthusiastic about positively contributing as subordinates. According to Williams, as schools become increasingly more complex organizations, there is persuasive evidence that the majority of teachers in them would always choose to contribute fully to the development of more effective schools within a culture of collective purpose that valued them and the quality of their contributions. Head teachers and other teachers are being required to "manage" and "lead" schools within cultures that are fundamentally different from those of a decade earlier. Recent trends, in the author's view, are for leadership in schools to increasingly emphasize the benefits of cultures for collective educational purposes rather than ordered control through hierarchical management roles. The main research finding is that leaders earn their status from others who elect to follow, which means that earned leadership is an accorded status, not an appointed one, gained through mutual trust and a recognition of professional commitment to education and consideration of their attitudes, values and comprehension.

Adam Nir and Ronit Bogler discuss the role of vision as a key element for effective leadership of school-based management. Organizational vision is directed not only inward, to serve as a compass for school personnel, but also outward, toward people in the school's local community. This duality may produce conflicts of interest under certain circumstances, especially for leaders in self-managing schools. The authors argue that a vision of school-based management should be conceived as a blend of the qualities of the school's environment, the qualities of the school's leader, and the attributes of the school staff. The article discusses likely consequences of disregarding these three essential leadership components. Furthermore, it is argued that in reality, a discrepancy is likely to exist between a school's inner qualities and the expectations directed at it from external agencies. The greater the discrepancy, the higher the chances that school leaders will articulate an illusionary vision that will mostly serve populist purposes rather than educational ends. The authors claim that when articulating a vision, the emphasis that is placed on the need of self-managing schools to respond to local expectations should be moderated, depending on the different types of interaction between schools and their communities.

Rosalind Levačić considers the development of school-based management in England and Wales and examines the efficiency of this reform and the policy of allocating resources to schools. The main driving force behind school-based management in England was, and remains, improving efficiency and raising educational standards. A further reason is the political appeal of giving parents broader scope in expressing school choice. The development of school-based management in England was followed by a considerable extension of the power of the central government over school and a diminution of the powers of local education authorities which, prior to 1988, had managed local school systems with little interference from the central government. Decision-making power, particularly with respect to resources, including private sponsorship and personnel, has been decentralized from Local Education Authorities (LEAs) to head teachers and school governing bodies. Thus, the net result of the reform is that the Ministry of Education determines the strategy and manages the performance of its sub-units (LEAs and schools) by setting performance goals, monitoring them against these goals and applying sanctions and rewards accordingly. Schools are given managerial discretion over how to utilize the resources allocated to them, including determining how to spend the allocated budget; curriculum matters such as time allocations, textbooks, some choice of syllabus at the secondary school level; or other matters such as defined performance goals, review of payment awards, monitoring teachers' performance, admissions policy, and having a "school development plan." In conclusion, the author examines performance indicators since the implementation of school-based management.

The article by Michael Kirst includes both a historical analysis and a current view of school-based management in the United States. The historical section stresses that the basic unit of US school organization was the school district, not the school. This historical structure has hindered and limited the spread and effectiveness of school-based management. The US school system was formed from the bottom up, with over 120,000 school districts (now reduced to 14,000). The elected school board governs the district, and most school boards resist school-based management in its pure form. From 1900-1920, US cities created centralized districts that established uniform policies and direction for all schools. This "one best system" ended much of the autonomy within each school and introduced standardized budgets, personnel, curriculum, etc. School-based management was lost in this centralized efficiency model that persists to this day in large and small cities and suburbs. School-based management has also been hampered by a lack of confidence in the ability of site-level educators to manage well. Opponents contend there is not a lot of site-level talent waiting to be unleashed by school-based management. Rather, extensive capacity building is needed before school-based management can begin. But few districts have been able or willing to invest in this site capacity, including information systems and rethinking principals' ubiquitous role. Kirst argues that US scholars do have good plans on how to make school-based management work. But there is a lack of agreement on who should control these self-managed schools – teachers, parents, administrators, or all three? Although there have been many successful cases of school-based management in the United States, the amount of school improvement has not been overwhelming. This is partly due to the fact that it is difficult to measure change. Kirst concludes that without a political coalition and commitment, SBM will not be implemented on a large scale.

Ami Volansky's article describes the background underlying the transition to school-based management in Israel. Teachers' organizations were the first, in the early 1970s, to call upon the Ministry of Education to liberate schools from extreme centralization because under the existing management conditions teachers were avoiding personal responsibility for the quality of education, and exhibited a lack of interest and initiative. As a result, a process was introduced to delegate authority to the schools in pedagogic matters. During the 1980s, it became clear that the statement of intent issued by the Ministry of Education did not pass the test of reality, the result being that the Ministry's policy to grant operational authority to schools remained theoretical, a "right with no opportunity." On the basis of these findings, the Ministry of Education decided to adopt new implementation principles. Beginning in 1996, the transition to school-based management was introduced, through which the operating authority in terms of budgeting and performance evaluation was transferred to schools. From now on, every school was expected to define a work plan that included clear pedagogic goals, obtaining feedback regarding the defined goals, and striving toward decision-making processes that would lead to increased commitment and accountability for educational outcomes. Despite increased efforts by the Ministry to transfer the locus of decision-making power from the Ministry and the local authorities to the schools, by the year 2002 only some 700 schools have become self-managing schools. The article describes severe opposition to delegating authority to the schools and the unwillingness of key personnel to relinquish their own power in favor of the schools, to the point that the Israeli education system has not yet passed the point of no return to traditional centralized management patterns.

In his second article included in this book, Yin Cheong Cheng develops a theoretical perspective concerning the complexities of managing school effectiveness and the link between school effectiveness and school-based management. The author argues that most past educational reforms, which focused on fragmentary improvement and remedial treatment, are insufficient to bring about holistic school development and long-term effectiveness and inevitably many of them resulted in serious frustration, if not failure. The author explains that the failure of past international school reforms is often due to (1) ignoring the relevance of school goals to the rapidly changing environment, and (2) the lack of understanding with regard to internal school processes. Therefore, the relevance of school goals and the improvement of internal school processes should be considered the two key elements for implementing school-based management and improving school effectiveness. Cheng offers a necessary knowledge base for practicing school-based management in the pursuit of school effectiveness, which should include the theory of school-based management, knowledge about healthy school profiles, the technology of strategic management, the dynamic concept of maximizing multiple effectiveness, the idea of layer management, the theory of congruence in school, the knowledge of total home-school cooperation and community support, and the new paradigm of school leadership. Moreover, in order to assess and monitor school effectiveness as a whole, certain models are developed, such as the goal model, resource-input model, and total management model. These comprehensive theoretical, as well as practical, multiple models can, in the author's view, contribute to the practice of school-based management for greater school effectiveness.

REFERENCES

Argyris, C. (1982). *Reasoning, learning and action - Individual and organizational.* London: Jossey-Bass.

Bashi, J. et al. (1990). *Effective schools: From theory to practice.* Jerusalem: Van Leer Institute.

Bernstein, B. (1961). Social structure, language and learning. *Educational Research,* 3(3).

Caldwell, B. J., & Spinks, M. J. (1988). *The self-managing school.* London: Falmer Press.

Caldwell, B. J., & Spinks, M. J. (1998). *Beyond the Self-managing School.* London: Falmer Press.

Chen, M. (1995). The effective school and the integrative class. *Studies in Administration and Educational Organization, 20,* 47-88 (in Hebrew).

Cheng, Y. C. (1996). *School effectiveness and school-based management - A mechanism for development.* London: Falmer Press.

Coleman J. S., Campbell, E. Q., Hobson, C. J., McPartland, J., Mood, A. M., Weinfeld, F. D., & York, R. L. (Eds.). (1996). *Equality of educational opportunity (The Coleman Report).* Washington, DC: US Government Printing Office.

Cuttance, P. (1985). Framework for research on the effectiveness of schooling. In D. Reynolds (Ed.), *Studying school effectiveness.* London: Falmer Press.

Drucker, P. (1977). *People and performance: The best of Peter Drucker on management.* London: Heinemann.

Friedman, I. A., Horowitz, T., & Shaliv, R. (1988). *School effectiveness, culture and climate.* Jerusalem: Henrietta Szold Institute (in Hebrew).

Friedman, M. (1962). *Capitalism and freedom.* Chicago: University of Chicago Press.

Gamble, A. (1985). *Britain in decline.* London: Macmillan.

Gue, R. L. (1985). *An introduction to educational administration in Canada.* Toronto: McGraw-Hill.

Hallak, J. (1991). *Managing schools for educational quality and equity: Finding the proper mix to make it work.* Paris: UNESCO, International Institute for Educational Planning.

Halsey, A. H. et al. (1980). *Origins of destinations.* Oxford, England: Clarendon.

Handy, C. B. (1988). *Understanding organizations.* London: Penguin.

Hayek, F. A. (1960). *The constitution of liberty.* London: Routledge & Kegan Paul.

Hill, P. T., & Bonan, J. (1991). *Decentralization and accountability in public education.* New York: Rand Corparation.

Hopkins, D. (1987). Implications for school improvement at the local level. In D. Hopkins (Ed.), *Improving quality of schooling.* London: Falmer Press.

Jencks, C. (1973). *Inequality: A reassessment of the effect of family and schooling in America.* London: Allen Lane.

Kerensky, V. M. (1975). The educative community. *National Elementary Principal, 54*(3).

McGregor, D. (1985), *The human side of enterprise.* New York: McGraw-Hill.

OECD - Office of Economic Cooperation and Development (1989). *Decentralization and school improvement: New perspectives and conditions for change.* CERI.

Peters, T., & Waterman, R. (1982). *In search of excellence.* New York: Harper.

Smyth J. (Ed.). (1993). *A socially critical view of the self-managing school.* London: Falmer Press.

Srivastva, S., & Barrent, F. (1988). Foundations for executive integrity: Dialogue, diversity, development. In S. Srivastva (Ed.), *Executive integrity.* London: Jossey-Bass.

UK Department for Education (1959). *Fifteen to eighteen (the Crowther Report).* London: Central Advisory Committee for Education.

UK Department for Education (1963). *Half our future (the Newsom Report).* London: Central Advisory Committee for Education.

Volansky, A. (1995). *Development trends in the American education system.* Jerusalem: Ministry of Education (in Hebrew).

Volansky, A. (1999). The dialectic between decentralization and centralization. In E. Peled (Ed.), *Ministry of Education Jubilee Publication.* Tel Aviv: Ministry of Defense Publications (in Hebrew).

Volansky, A. (2003). *The "Pendulum Syndrome" of centralization and decentralization processes in education - The case of England and Wales.* Tel Aviv: Ramot Publishing, Tel Aviv University.

Part I

Theory

NEW VISION OF SCHOOL-BASED MANAGEMENT: GLOBALIZATION, LOCALIZATION, AND INDIVIDUALIZATION

Yin Cheong Cheng

INTRODUCTION

International Trends Towards School-based Management

To cope with the challenges from the rapidly changing environment in 1990s and the 21st century, numerous educational reforms and school restructuring movements have been implemented to pursue educational effectiveness and school development not only in Canada, the USA and the UK in the West, but also in the Asia-Pacific regions such as Australia, New Zealand, Mainland China, Singapore, Malaysia and Hong Kong (Cheng & Townsend, 2000). The search for effective schools, the shift to school-based management, the emphasis on development planning in school, the assurance of school education quality, the implementation of new curricula and the application of information technology in education are typical examples of efforts towards educational reform (Caldwell & Spinks, 1992, 1998; Cheng, 1996, 2001a, 2001b; Hargreaves & Hopkins, 1991; MacGilchrist, Mortimore, Savage, & Beresford, 1995; Murphy & Beck, 1995; Reynolds & Cuttance, 1992; Stringfield, Ross, & Smith, 1997).

Among all these reforms, school-based management (SBM) is one of the most salient international trends of school reform, which emphasizes decentralization down to the school level as the major means for promoting effective decision-making, improving internal processes, and utilizing resources in teaching and learning to meet the diverse school-based educational needs. Even though there have been different types of challenges, difficulties and problems in implementing SBM, numerous opportunities have been created for the schools, teachers, parents, educators, education officers and even educational leaders engaged in such school reform to rethink educational practices, develop themselves, modify roles, formulate innovations, and improve the educational outcomes of their schools (Cheng & Chan, 2000; Cheng & Cheung, 1999).

School-based management and improvement of internal process

In the past decade of implementation of SBM, a key issue has often been how to improve or even re-engineer the internal school process so that the school as a whole can add value through school effectiveness. The answer to this issue requires a new knowledge base regarding internal school processes, indicating how a school can maximize use of its internal resources to achieve optimal conditions for operation and continuous development in management, teaching and learning, within the changing environment of the new century.

Integrating from my previous research on school effectiveness and school-based management (Cheng, 1996, 1998), a new knowledge framework of internal school processes can be proposed to guide the implementation of school-based management for internal improvement and development. This new framework includes the following types of knowledge, as summarized in Table 1:

1. Principles of school-based management

2. Knowledge of school healthy-functioning profile

3. Knowledge of strategic management

4. Knowledge of multi-level self management in school

5. Knowledge of dynamic process

6. Knowledge of layer management

7. Knowledge of congruence in school

8. Knowledge of total home-school collaboration and community support

9. Knowledge of transformational leadership

It is hoped that through the implementation of SBM within this framework, schools can facilitate continuous learning and development of pupils, personnel and the schools themselves; increase support from parents and the community; improve technology in education and management; and meet the needs and challenges in the rapidly changing educational environment.

Table 1
A knowledge framework of internal school process for SBM

The new knowledge framework of internal school processes		**Key elements to be achieved in school re-engineering**
1. **Principles of school-based management**	• Principle of Equifinality • Principle of Decentralization • Principle of Self-managing system • Principle of Human initiative	• **School autonomy and self-initiative**

2. **Knowledge of healthy school profile**	• A Positive profile on:
	  • school mission
	  • nature of school activities
	  • management strategies
	  • use of resources
	  • roles
	  • human relations
	  • quality of administrator
	  • evaluation of effectiveness
	• Monitoring educational quality in school
		• **Healthy and smooth school functioning**

3. **Knowledge of strategic management**	• Including critical components:
	  • Environmental analysis
	  • Planning and structuring
	  • Staffing and directing
	  • Implementing
	  • Monitoring and evaluating
	  • Participation and leadership
	• A cyclical process of continuous learning, action, and development
		• **Continuous organizational learning and school development**

4. **Knowledge of multi-level self-management**	• School self-management • Group self-management • Individual self-management • Self-learning and development of individuals and groups • Mutual influence and support among individuals, groups, and the school	• **Human initiative of individuals, groups, and the school**
5. **Knowledge of a dynamic process for multiple school effectiveness**	• Awareness of unbalanced situation • Adaptability and flexibility to set up priority • Maximizing long-term effectiveness of multiple functions	• **Multiple effectiveness of five school functions**
6. **Knowledge of layer management**	• Matrix of school process • Layers: administrator, teacher and pupil • Layer as comprehensive unit • Management, teaching, and learning as holistic processes • Development cycles on layers	• **Holistic school education and maximum opportunity for teaching and learning**

Table 1 (continued)

The new knowledge framework of internal school processes		Key elements to be achieved in school re-engineering

7. **Knowledge of congruence in school process**	• Congruence in school process:
	    • Across actors, domains, and levels
	    • Between-layer
	    • Within-layer
	• Congruence in technology:
	    • Between-types
	    • Within-type
	• Congruence in culture:
	    • Between-types
	    • Within-type
		• **Reducing internal wastage, increasing synergy and maximizing effectiveness**

8. **Knowledge of home-school cooperation and community support**	• Total parental involvement in school education • Total family education as a strong partner • Community support	• **Provision of necessary resources, ideas, and legitimacy in education and management**
9. **Knowledge of transformational leadership**	• Shift to transformational leadership • Shift to multi-dimensions of leadership: structural, human, political, cultural, & educational	• **Driving force for developing members and re-engineering school**

Challenges to SBM in a new era

The dramatic impact of the new information technology, economic globalization, international market competition, worldwide concerns for pollution and peace, as well as increasing local social-political demands, have generated rapid changes and developments in nearly every society throughout the world (Cheng & Townsend, 2000). In such a fast-changing era, schools and teachers are faced with numerous new problems, uncertainties, and challenges rising from their internal and external environments. They are often expected to perform a wide range of new functions to support the rapid advances in individuals, local communities, societies, and international relations (Cheng, 1996; Tsui & Cheng, 2000).

In the last decade, policy-makers and schools had implemented numerous initiatives in education with aims to improve school performance. Although a great deal of effort has been invested in this aspect, people, if not disappointed, still doubt very much whether the performance of teachers and schools can meet the challenges and needs of the new century, even though schools and teachers have already worked very hard.

Recently, there has been a rapid, worldwide economic transformation towards an information-based or knowledge-based economy. The new generations are expected to be more self-learning, creative and adaptive to the changing environment with multiple intelligences and a global outlook. People are beginning to be aware of the limitations of the traditional paradigms and efforts regarding educational quality, and are increasingly concerned with the relevance of existing educational aims and practices on the future in a new era of globalization and information technology (Cheng, 2000a, 2000b). In these few years, paradigm shifts in education are strongly urged through educational reforms in some countries and areas, for example, the USA, UK, Australia, Hong Kong, and others (Cheng, 2001a, 2001b).

Undoubtedly, the current efforts of SBM are necessary and important for improving and enhancing the internal school process. To a great extent, SBM represents the advancement and application of human knowledge to school management and educational practice. When considering the tremendous impact of globalization and information technology on every aspect of human life in the new century, we believe a paradigm shift in education is necessary. We believe SBM should have a new vision that aims to facilitate such a paradigm shift in education, to establish a new educational paradigm and develop new educational aims and practices for future generations. Therefore, this paper aims at presenting a new vision of SBM, which can further support all ongoing efforts of SBM in the challenging new millennium.

NEW EDUCATIONAL PARADIGM

Different parts of the world are now in the process of globalization in technological, economic, social, political, cultural, and learning spheres (Cheng, 1999). The world is quickly becoming a global village, in which different parts of the world are rapidly being networked and globalized through the Internet and different types of IT, communications, and transportation (Albrow, 1990; Naisbitt & Aburdence, 1991). Most countries and regions are finding they share more common concerns. Moreover, the interactions between nations and people have become unlimited, multi-dimensional, multi-level, fast, and frequent. People have become more and more mutually dependent through international collaboration, exchange, and interflow. According to Cheng (1999), human nature in the social context of the new millennium will be a multiple person – a technological person, economic person, social person, political person, cultural person, and learning person – in a global, multi-cultural village of information and high technology. Both individuals and society need multiple developments in the technological, economic, social, political, cultural, and learning spheres. Life-long learning and a learning society (or knowledge society) are necessary to sustain the continuous multiple development of individuals and society in a changing new century (Drucker, 1993, 1995). Society must move towards becoming a multiple intelligence and learning society that can provide the necessary knowledge and intelligence base and serve as a driving force to support multiple developments. What's more, the individual must move towards becoming a multiple intelligence citizen who can contribute to the development of a multiple intelligence society.

In such a context, there is an emerging paradigm shift in education. According to Cheng (1999, 2000a), the paradigm should be shifted from the traditional *site-bounded paradigm* to a new triplization paradigm. The new paradigm will emphasize the development of students' *contextualized multiple intelligences* (CMI) including technological, economic, social, political, cultural, and learning intelligences; and the processes of *triplization* including globalization, localization and individualization in education. (For a detailed description of contextualized multiple intelligences, please see the Appendix).

Triplization in education

Globalization: This refers to the transfer, adaptation, and development of values, knowledge, technology and behavioral norms across countries and societies in different parts of the world. The typical phenomena and characteristics associated with globalization include the growth of global networking (e.g., Internet, worldwide e-communications, and transportation); global transfer and interflow in technological, economic, social, political, cultural, and learning spheres; international alliances and competitions; international collaboration and exchange; the concept of the global village; multi-cultural integration; and use of international standards and benchmarks.

Implications of globalization for education should include maximizing the global relevance, support, intellectual resources, and initiative in schooling, teaching, and learning (Caldwell & Spinks, 1998; Daun, 1997). Some examples of globalization in education are: web-based learning and learning from the Internet; international visit/immersion programs; international exchange programs; international partnerships in teaching and learning at the group, class, and individual levels; interactions and sharing through video-conferencing across countries, communities, institutions, and individuals; and new curriculum content on technological, economic, social, political, cultural, and learning globalization.

Localization: This denotes the transfer, adaptation, and development of related values, knowledge, technology, and behavioral norms from/to the local contexts. It has two types of meanings: First, it can mean the adaptation of all related external values, initiatives, and norms to meet local needs at the society, community, or site levels. Second, it can also mean the enhancement of local values, norms, concerns, relevance, participation, and involvement in related initiatives and actions. Some characteristics and examples of localization include: local networking; adaptation of external technological, economic, social, political, cultural, and learning initiatives to local communities; decentralization to the community or site level; development of indigenous culture; meeting community needs and expectations; local involvement, collaboration, and support; local relevance and legitimacy; and concern for school-based needs and characteristics, social norms and ethos (Cheng, 1998; Kim, 1999; Tam, Cheng, & Cheung, 1997).

Localization in education means maximizing local relevance, community support, and initiative in schooling, teaching, and learning. Some examples of implementing localization include community and parental involvement in school education; home-school collaboration; ensuring school accountability; implementing school-based management, school-based curriculum, and community-related curriculum; and developing new curricular content with regard to technological, economic, social, political, cultural, and learning localization.

Individualization: This suggests the transfer, adaptation, and development of related external values, knowledge, technology, and behavioral norms to meet individual needs and characteristics. The importance of individualization to human development and performance is based on the concerns and theories of human motivation and needs (e.g., Alderfer, 1972; Manz, 1986; Manz & Sims, 1990; Maslow, 1970). Some examples of individualization are: providing individualized services; emphasizing human potentials; promoting human initiative and creativity; encouraging self-actualization, self-management and self-governance; and concern for special needs. The major implication of individualization in education is maximizing motivation, initiative, and creativity of pupils and teachers in schooling, teaching, and learning through such measures as implementing individualized educational programs; designing and using individualized learning targets, methods, and progress schedules; encouraging students and teachers to be self-learning, self-actualizing, and self-initiating; meeting individual special needs; and developing students' contextualized multiple intelligences.

Using the concepts of triplization, pupils, teachers, and schools can be considered to be *globalized, localized, and individualized through the process of triplization*. Or, simply, they are triplized. The major features of the new triplization paradigm with regard to learning, teaching and schooling are completely different from the traditional site-bounded paradigm. In order to facilitate development of SBM towards a new paradigm of education, these features are described below in figure 1.

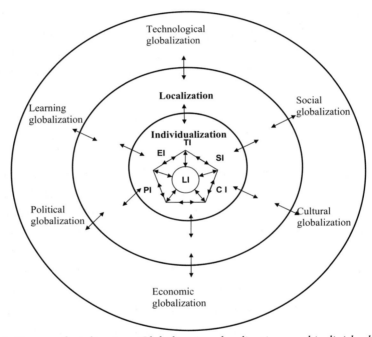

Figure 1. Process of triplization: Globalization, localization, and individualization

New paradigm of learning

In the new paradigm of school education, students and their learning should be individualized, localized, and globalized (Cheng, 2000a) (see Table 2).

Individualized learning: This assumes that the pupil is at the center of education. Pupils' learning should be facilitated in a way such that all types of transfer, adaptation, and development of related values, knowledge, technology, and norms during the learning process can meet their needs and personal characteristics. Their potential, particularly their contextualized multiple intelligences (CMI), can develop in an optimal way. Different students can learn in different styles. Individualized and tailor-made programs (including targets, content, methods, and schedules) for different students are necessary and feasible. Pupils can be self-motivated and self-learning with appropriate guidance and facilitation, and learning becomes a self-actualizing process of discovery, experience and reflection. Since information and knowledge are accumulated at an astonishing rate but are outdated very quickly, it is nearly impossible to make any sense of it all if the purpose of education is mainly to deliver skills and knowledge, particularly when pupils can find the knowledge and information easily with the help of information technology and the Internet. Therefore, the paradigm for the new century emphasizes that the focus of learning is on learning how to learn, think, and create. In order to sustain life-long learning, it should be enjoyable and self-rewarding.

Localized and globalized learning: Students and their learning should be facilitated in such a way such that local and global resources, support, and networks can be utilized to maximize the opportunities for their development during the learning process. Through localization and globalization, there are multiple sources of learning for students, both inside and outside their schools, locally and globally, rather than being limited to a small number of teachers in their schools. Participation in local and international learning programs can help them achieve the related community and global outlook and experiences beyond schools. Additionally, their learning is a type of networked learning. They will be grouped and networked locally and internationally. Learning groups and networks will become a major driving force to sustain the learning climate and multiply the learning effects through sharing and mutual motivation. We may expect that each pupil can have a group of life-long partner-students in different corners of the world to share their learning experiences.

It is expected that learning happens everywhere and is life-long. School education is just the start or preparation for life-long learning. Learning opportunities are unlimited. Students can maximize the opportunities for their learning from local and global exposures through Internet, web-based learning, video-conferencing, cross-cultural sharing, and different types of interactive and multi-media materials (Education and Manpower Bureau, 1998). Students can learn from world-class teachers, experts, peers, and learning materials from different parts of the world. In other words, they can experience world-class learning.

Table 2
Two paradigms of learning

New triplization paradigm	Traditional site-bounded paradigm
Individualized learning	**Reproduced learning**
□ Pupil as the center	□ Pupil as the follower
□ Individualized programs	□ Standard programs
□ Self-learning	□ Absorbing knowledge
□ Self-actualizing process	□ Receiving process
□ How to learn	□ How to gain
□ Self-rewarding	□ External rewards
Localized and globalized learning	**Site-bounded learning**
□ Multiple sources of learning	□ Teacher-based learning
□ Networked learning	□ Separated learning
□ Life-long and everywhere	□ Fixed period and within school
□ Unlimited opportunities	□ Limited opportunities
□ World-class learning	□ School-bounded learning
□ Local and international outlook	□ Mainly school experiences

Traditional paradigm of learning

In traditional thinking, pupils and their learning are part of a process for reproducing and perpetuating the existing knowledge and manpower structure to sustain the society's development, particularly in the social and economic spheres (Blackledge & Hunt, 1985; Cheng & Ng, 1992; Hinchcliffe, 1987; McMahon, 1987). It is no surprise, then, that education is perceived as a process for pupils through which their learning is reproduced to meet the needs of the society. The traditional profiles for students and their learning are clearly different from those in the new paradigm (see Table 2).

Reproduced learning: In school education, students are the followers of their teacher. They go through standard programs of education, in which pupils are taught in the same way and at the same pace, even though their abilities may be different. Individualized programs seem to be unfeasible. The learning process is characterized by absorbing certain types of knowledge: students are "students" of their teachers, and they absorb knowledge from their teachers. Learning is a disciplinary, receiving, and socializing process, such that close supervision and control on the learning process is necessary. The focus of learning is on how to gain knowledge and skills. Learning is often perceived as hard work, for the purpose of achieving external rewards and avoiding punishment.

Site-bounded learning: In the traditional paradigm, all learning activities are school-bounded and teacher-based. Pupils learn from a limited numbers of school teachers and their prepared materials. Therefore, teachers are the major source of knowledge and learning. Pupils learn the standard curriculum from their textbooks and related materials assigned by their teachers. Students are often arranged so that they learn in a separated way and are made responsible for their individual learning outcomes. They have few opportunities for mutual support or to learn from one another. Their learning experiences are mainly school experiences, alienated from the rapidly-changing local and global communities. Learning happens only in school within a given time frame. Graduation tends to be the end of students' learning.

New paradigm of teaching

In the new triplization paradigm, teachers' teaching should be triplized: individualized, localized, and globalized (see Table 3).

Individualized teaching: Teachers and their teaching are facilitated to take full advantage of their potential to maximize student learning. Teaching is considered a process for initiating, assisting, and sustaining students' self-learning and self-actualization; therefore, teachers should play the role of a facilitator or mentor who can support the pupils' learning. The focus of teaching is to arouse pupils' curiosity and motivation to think, act, and learn. In addition, teaching is about sharing with students the joy of the learning process and its outcomes. For teachers themselves, teaching is a life-long learning process involving continuous discovery, experimenting, self-actualization, reflection, and professional development. Teachers should be multiple intelligence teachers who can set an example for students in developing their multiple intelligences. Each teacher has his/her own potential and characteristics, and different teachers can teach in different styles to maximize their own contributions.

Localized and globalized teaching: The new paradigm emphasizes that teachers and their teaching should be facilitated in such a way that local and global resources, supports and networks can be brought in from local communities and different parts of the world to maximize the opportunities for their development in teaching and their contributions toward students' learning. Through localization and globalization there are multiple sources of teaching, for example, self-learning programs and packages, web-based learning, outside experts, and community experiential programs – inside and outside their schools, locally and globally. Teachers can maximize the opportunities to enhance the effectiveness of their teaching from local and global networking and exposure through Internet, web-based teaching, video-conferencing, cross-cultural sharing, and different types of interactive and multi-media materials (Education and Manpower Bureau, 1998). With their help, pupils can learn from world-class teaching materials, experts, peers, and teachers in different parts of the world, so that their teachers' teaching can become world-class teaching. By participating in local and international development programs, teachers can achieve a global and regional outlook and engage in experiences beyond the schools. Furthermore, their teaching is a type of networked teaching. Teachers are grouped and networked locally and globally to develop and sustain a new professional culture, and to multiply the effects of their teaching through sharing and mutual motivation. They become world-class and networked teachers through localization and globalization. It is not a surprise that each teacher can have a group of life-long partner-teachers in other parts of the world to continuously share and discuss experiences and ideas relating to their professional practice.

Traditional paradigm of teaching

As discussed in the traditional site-bounded paradigm of learning, teaching is often perceived as part of the process for reproducing and perpetuating the existing knowledge and manpower structure to sustain the society's development (table 3).

Reproduced teaching: Teachers are the center of education. They have some technical, social, and professional competencies to deliver knowledge to pupils. Teachers teach using a few standardized styles and patterns to ensure that standardized knowledge is taught to pupils, even though teachers' potentials and personal characteristics may be different. Their main task is to transfer some of the knowledge and skills they have to pupils, and therefore teaching is often a disciplinary, delivery, training, and socializing process. What's more, teaching is often perceived as hard work for the purpose of achieving some external standard in examinations.

School-bounded teaching: In the traditional paradigm, teachers and their teaching are bounded within the school. Schools are the major venue for teaching and teachers are the major source of knowledge. Teachers are often arranged to teach in a separated way and are made responsible for their teaching outcomes. They have few opportunities for mutual support and to learn from one another. Their teaching is bounded such that they teach the standard curriculum with textbooks and related materials assigned by their schools and the education authority. The teachers and their teaching are often alienated from the fast-changing local communities or international contexts. From this traditional perspective, teachers are clearly school-bounded and separated, and will rarely have any global and regional outlook to develop a world-class education for their pupils in the new century.

Table 3

Two paradigms of teaching

New triplization paradigm	Traditional site-bounded paradigm
Individualized teaching	**Reproduced teaching**
☐ As facilitator	☐ As center
☐ Multiple intelligence teacher	☐ Partially competent teacher
☐ Individualized teaching style	☐ Standard teaching style
☐ Arousing curiosity	☐ Transferring knowledge
☐ Facilitating process	☐ Delivery process
☐ Sharing joy	☐ Achieving standard
☐ As life-long learning	☐ As a practice of previous knowledge
Localized and globalized teaching	**School-bounded teaching**
☐ Multiple sources of teaching	☐ School-bounded
☐ Networked teaching	☐ Separated teaching
☐ World-class teaching	☐ Bounded teaching
☐ Unlimited opportunities	☐ Limited opportunities
☐ Local and international outlook	☐ Mainly school experiences
☐ As world-class and networked teacher	☐ As school-bounded and separated teacher

New paradigm of schooling

Similarly, the characteristics of schooling in the new triplization paradigm are also contrastingly different from those of the traditional paradigm, as shown in Table 4 (Cheng, 2000a). School is perceived as a facilitating place to support students' learning. School itself should be a contextualized multiple intelligence environment, supporting students to develop their multiple intelligences. Each school has its own strengths, potential, and characteristics. Based on their strengths, different schools can conduct and manage schooling in different styles to maximize their own contributions to students' learning. The focus of schooling is to encourage curiosity and motivate both pupils and teachers to think, act, and learn in a multiple intelligence way. Schooling is also an open process to initiate, facilitate, and sustain self-learning and self-actualization of pupils and teachers. It provides opportunities to share the joy of learning and teaching among teachers and pupils. In order to face the challenges of the new century and pursue contextualized multiple intelligences, school must be a continuously learning and developing organization, involving continuous discovery, experimenting, actualization, reflection, and development on an institutional level.

Schools and their schooling should be managed and facilitated in a way that brings in local and global resources, supports, and networks to maximize opportunities for their development and contributions to their pupils' learning and teachers' teaching. In addition to the school itself, there are multiple sources of teaching and learning, such as self-learning programs and packages, web-based learning, outside experts, community experiential programs, etc. – both inside and outside the school, locally and globally. Parents and communities, including social services, business, and industry, are actively involved in schooling. The partnership with them is necessary to support effective networked schooling and multiple sources of learning. Locally and globally networked schooling can provide a wide spectrum of learning experiences and maximize opportunities for teachers and students to benefit from various settings and cultures. With the help of globalized schooling, students can learn about world-class experiences from different parts of the globe. Schools can maximize the opportunities for teachers and pupils to enhance the quality of teaching and learning from local and global networking and exposure. Schools in the new paradigm are conceptualized as world-class and networked schools.

Traditional paradigm of schooling

Traditionally, school is perceived as a place for reproducing and perpetuating the existing knowledge and structures, and therefore schooling is a process for "being reproduced or reproducing." It is reproduced on the basis of existing key social elements such as traditional values, beliefs, knowledge and structures in the society. And, the school itself is reproducing or perpetuating these social elements to the next generation through teaching and learning. A school is assumed to be the central place for education and a source of knowledge and qualifications, which delivers some knowledge and skills to pupils, socializes them into given norms, and qualifies them to meet the specified standards. Schools should be organized and managed in some standardized styles and patterns to ensure standardized knowledge and norms to be delivered to pupils, even though schools' characteristics and strengths may be different. The main task of schooling is to transfer certain knowledge and skills to students, and teachers are the ones who perform this transfer. Therefore, schooling is a disciplinary, delivery, training, and socializing process aimed at qualifying pupils to satisfy the manpower needs of the society. Inevitably, schooling is hard work for both students and teachers for the purpose of achieving some external standards in examinations. It is no surprise, then, that a school is a stable bureaucracy equipped with a designed structure, policies, and procedures to ensure the standards of teaching and learning outcomes.

From the traditional perspective, a school is almost like an isolated island bounding all activities of schooling, teaching, and learning in a very narrow way. There is no clear need to have strong community linkage and parental involvement, as the school is the major source of knowledge and qualifications. Parents and communities are just recipients of educational outcomes. Schools are often arranged to manage in a separated way in order to be kept accountable for their schooling outcomes. Schools, even within the same community, have few opportunities for mutual support or to learn from one another. Schools can provide a standardized environment, curriculum, textbooks, and related materials for teachers and pupils to teach and learn. The opportunities for learning are quite limited. School life and its activities are alienated from the rapidly changing external "real" environment or local communities. Schools are bounded and separated from the outside world.

Table 4
Two paradigms of schooling

New triplization paradigm	Traditional site-bounded paradigm
Individualized schooling	**Reproduced schooling**
□ A facilitating place	□ A central place
□ Multiple intelligence school	□ Source of knowledge and qualifications
□ Individualized schooling style	□ Standard schooling style
□ Place for curiosity	□ Place for transfer
□ Open process	□ Qualifying process
□ Sharing joy	□ Achieving standard
□ As a learning organization	□ As a bureaucracy
Localized and globalized schooling	**Bounded schooling**
□ Coupled with multiple sources	□ Isolated school
□ Community and parental involvement	□ Weak community linkage
□ Networked schooling	□ Separated schooling
□ World-class schooling	□ Site-bounded schooling
□ Unlimited opportunities	□ Limited opportunities
□ Local and international outlook	□ Alienated experiences
□ As a world-class and networked school	□ As a bounded and separated school

NEW VISION OF SCHOOL-BASED MANAGEMENT

Decentralization, school autonomy, site-based decision-making, and flexible use of resources themselves are the means but not the final aims of school-based management. The above paradigm shift in education inevitably demands that ongoing school-based management efforts have a new vision in the new millennium, in addition to the existing targets at improving internal school processes.

If we believe that in the new millennium, our world is moving towards multiple globalization and becoming a global village with boundless interactions among countries and areas, our new generation should be expected to act as multiple intelligence (MI) persons in a rapidly-changing and interacting global village. The development of society should be towards a multiple intelligence (MI) society. SBM should embrace a new vision to provide a learning environment for developing students as MI citizens who will creatively contribute to the formation of an MI society and an MI global village with multiple developments in the technological, economic, social, political, cultural, and learning spheres.

Therefore, the new vision of SBM should facilitate a paradigm shift from the traditional site-bounded education towards the new triplization education and to provide a triplized (i.e., globalized, localized, and individualized) learning environment, with the support of information technology and various types of local and global networking, for developing pupils' triplized self-learning ability and their multiple intelligences.

SBM should help our schools, teachers, and pupils become triplized in the new century. Our learning, teaching, and schooling will finally be globalized, localized, and individualized with the help of the information technology and boundless multiple networking. We will have unlimited opportunities and multiple global and local sources for life-long learning and development for both pupils and teachers. New curriculum and pedagogy should facilitate triplized learning and make it an interactive, self-actualizing, enjoyable, and self-rewarding process of discovery. New curriculum and pedagogy should be triplized, as well as multiple intelligence-based, so they can provide world-class learning for pupils. Pupils can learn from world-class teachers, experts, peers, and learning materials from different parts of the world in any time frame and obtain a local, regional, and global exposure and outlook as an MI citizen. The new vision of SBM will help transform education into triplized and world-class learning for pupils to meet the challenges and needs of the new millennium.

With this new vision, the success of school-based management implementation in schools will be assessed through the following key questions:

1. How well can learning, teaching, and schooling be triplized through SBM? (This question aims to ensure that SBM can support pupil learning, teacher teaching, and schooling in a globalized, localized, and individualized environment.)

2. How thoroughly will pupils' learning opportunities be maximized through the IT environment, networking, teachers, and schools under SBM? (This question intends to ensure that SBM can maximize opportunities for pupils' learning and development in a triplized MI environment.)

3. How well can the pupils' self-learning be facilitated and sustained as potentially life-long learning, with SBM? (This question aims to ensure that maximized opportunities for pupils' self-learning are sustainable throughout their lives.)

4. How well can pupils' multiple intelligences and their ability to triplize their self-learning be developed through SBM? (This question focuses on ensuring the relevance of SBM on the outcomes of pupil learning in terms of multiple intelligences and their ability to triplize their self-learning.)

CONCLUSION: VALUE ADDED AND CREATED BY SBM

The new vision of SBM brings important implications for policy formulation and implementation at both the school and system levels. SBM in the new millennium aims not only to improve internal processes for achieving some given school goals, but also to ensure the relevance of educational practice and the new paradigm of education for the future, and to create new school goals for their pupils.

Value added through SBM: To improve the internal process through SBM, we can use the new knowledge framework of internal process including: principles of school-based management, knowledge of school healthy functioning profile, knowledge of strategic management, knowledge of multi-level self-management in school, knowledge of dynamic process, knowledge of layer management, knowledge of congruence in school, knowledge of total home-school collaboration and community support, and knowledge of transformational leadership. With the improvement of the internal school process through SBM, the school can achieve more of its given school goals such that it adds value in terms of school effectiveness from time t1 to time t2, as shown in area A in Figure 2. This is what we call value added in school effectiveness in current education reforms.

Value created through SBM: To ensure and enhance the relevance of educational practice for the future through the new vision of SBM, we should facilitate a paradigm shift in school education to the new paradigm, with emphasis on the development of students' multiple intelligences and capacity for life-long self-learning and the process of triplization in schooling, teaching and learning. We believe the processes of globalization, localization and individualization in education can bring in international and local resources and intellectual assets to each classroom, each teacher and each student, to create new educational goals relevant to the future and maximize opportunities for learning and development. While the school improves its internal process and enhances the relevance of school goals or creates new education goals, the school can create new values (that differ from the given school goals) in school effectiveness from time t1 to time t2, shown in area B in Figure 2. This is value created in school effectiveness through the new vision of SBM. (Here, it is assumed that enhancement of goal relevance or the development of new goals will only occur through the improvement of internal process.)

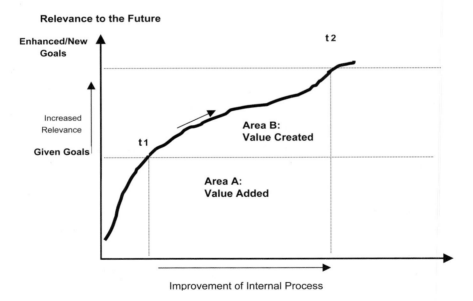

Figure 2. SBM for "value added" and "value created" in school effectiveness

We hope all SBM schools will become value-added and value-created schools in Israel or other parts of the world. Finally, I have a dream. In light of the great efforts to implement SBM in every school:

- All our students will become triplized MI students. They will fully enjoy life-long self-learning and actualization and become contextualized multiple intelligent citizens.

- All our teachers will become triplized MI teachers. They will share the joy of triplized learning and teaching with their students and pursue life-long learning and professional development.

- All our schools will become triplized MI SBM schools. All educators and teachers will be dedicated to making their contribution to triplization in learning, curriculum and pedagogy and to creating unlimited opportunities for life-long learning and development in the new century, for all of their pupils in different parts of the world.

REFERENCES

Albrow, M. (1990). Introducton. In M.Albrow & E. King (Eds.), *Globalization, knowledge and society.* London: Sage.

Alderfer, C. P. (1972). *Existence, relatedness, and growth*: Human needs in organizational settings. New York: Free Press.

Berman, S. (1995). *A multiple intelligences road to a quality classroom.* Palatine, IL: IRI/Skylight Training and Publishing.

Blackledge, D., & Hunt, B. (1985). *Sociological interpretations of education.* Sydney, Australia: Croom Helm.

Bolman, L. G., & Deal, T. E. (1997). *Reframing organizations: Artistry, choice, and leadership* (2nd ed.). San Francisco: Jossey-Bass.

Caldwell, B. J., & Spinks, J. M. (1992). *Leading a self-management school.* London: Falmer Press.

Caldwell, B. J., & Spinks, J. M. (1998). *Beyond the self managing school.* London: Falmer Press.

Cheng, Y. C. (1996). *School effectiveness and school-based management: A mechanism for development.* London: Falmer Press.

Cheng, Y. C. (1998). The knowledge base for re-engineering schools: Multiple functions and internal effectiveness. *International Journal of Educational Management, 12*(5), 203-224.

Cheng, Y. C. (1999, December). *Curriculum and pedagogy in the new century: Globalization, localization and individualization for multiple intelligences.* Keynote address at the 5th UNESCO-ACEID International Conference on Reforming Learning, Curriculum and Pedagogy: Innovative Visions for the New Century, Thailand.

Cheng, Y. C. (2000a). A CMI-triplization paradigm for reforming education in the new millennium. *International Journal of Educational Management, 14*(4), 156-174.

Cheng, Y. C. (2000b). New education and new teacher education: A paradigm shift for the future. *Asia-Pacific Journal of Teacher Education & Development, 3*(1), 1-34.

Cheng, Y. C. (2001a, February). *Towards the third wave of educational reforms in Hong Kong.* Keynote address at the International Forum on Educational Reforms in the Asia-Pacific Region, Hong Kong.

Cheng, Y. C. (2001b, January). *Educational relevance, quality and effectiveness: Paradigm shifts.* Invited keynote address at the International Congress for School Effectiveness and School Improvement on Equity, Globalization, and Change: Education for the 21st Century, Toronto, Canada.

Cheng, Y. C., & Chan, M. T. (2000). Implementation of school-based management: A multi-perspective analysis of the Hong Kong Case. *International Review of Education, 46*(3-4), 205-232 (Germany).

Cheng, Y. C., & Cheung, W. M. (1999). Towards school-based management: Uncertainty, meaning, opportunity and development. *International Journal of Educational Reform, 8*(1), 25-36 (USA).

Cheng, Y. C., & Ng, K. H. (1992). Economic considerations in educational policy analysis: A preliminary framework. *Primary Education, 3*(1), 55-64.

Cheng, Y. C., & Townsend, T. (2000). Educational change and development in the Asia-Pacific region: Trends and issues. In T. Townsend & Y. C. Cheng (Eds.), *Educational change and development in the Asia-Pacific region: Challenges for the future* (pp. 317-344). The Netherlands: Swets and Zeitlinger Publishers.

Daun, H. (1997). National forces, globalization and educational restructuring: Some European response patterns. *Comapre, 27*(1), 19-41.

Drucker, P. F. (1993). *Post-capitalist society.* New York: Harper Business.

Drucker, P. F. (1995). *Managing in a time of great change.* Oxford: Butterworth Heinerman.

Education Commission. (1999). *Review of education system: Framework for education reform – Learning for life.* Hong Kong: Government Printer.

Education and Manpower Bureau (1998, November). *Information technology for learning in a new era: Five-year strategy 1998/99 to 2002/03.* Hong Kong: Government Printer.

Gardner, H. (1993). *Multiple intelligences: The theory in practice.* New York: Basic Books.

Guild, P. B., & Chock-Eng, S. (1998). Multiple intelligence, learning styles, brain-based education: Where do the messages overlap? *Schools in the Middle, 7*(4), 38-40.

Guloff, K. (1996). *Multiple intelligences* (Teacher-to-Teacher Series). West Haven, CT: National Education Association of the United States.

Hargreaves, D. H., & Hopkins, D. (1991). *The empowered school: The management and practice of development planning.* London: Cassell.

Hinchcliffe, K. (1987). Education and the labor market. In G. Psacharopoulos (Ed.), *Economics of education: Research and studies* (pp. 315-323). Kidlington, UK: Pergamon Press.

Kim, Y. H. (1999). Recent changes and developments in Korean school education. In T. Townsend & Y. C. Cheng (Eds.), *Educational change and development in the Asia-Pacific region: Challenges for the future* (pp. 87-112). The Netherlands: Swets and Zeitlinger Publishers.

MacGilchrist, B., Mortimore, P., Savage, J., & Beresford, C. (1995). *Planning matters: The impact of development planning in primary schools.* London: Paul Chapman Publishing.

Manz, C. C. (1986). Self-leadership: Toward an expanded self-influence processes in organizations. *Academy of Management Review, 11,* 585–600.

Manz, C. C., & Sims, H. P. (1990). *Super leadership.* New York: Berkley Books.

Maslow, A. H. (1970). *Motivation and personality* (2nd ed.). New York: Harper & Row.

McMahon, W. W. (1987). Consumption and other benefits of education. In G. Psacharopoulos (Ed.), *Economics of education: Research and studies* (pp. 129-133). Kidlington, Oxford: Pergamon Press.

Mettetal, G., & Jordan, C. (1997). Attitudes toward a multiple intelligences curriculum. *Journal of Educational Research, 91*(2), 115-122.

Murphy, J., & Beck, L. G. (1995). *School-based management as school reform: Taking stock.* Thousand Oaks, CA: Corwin Press.

Naisbitt, J., & Aburdence, P. (1991). *Megatrends 2000.* New York: Avon.

Reynolds, D., & Cuttance, P. (1992). *School effectiveness: Research, policy, and practice.* London: Cassell.

Schein, E. H. (1980). *Organizational psychology* (3rd ed.). Englewood Cliffs, NJ: Prentice-Hall.

Stringfield, S., Ross, S., & Smith, L. (1997). *Bold plans for school restructuring: The new American schools designs.* Mahwah, NJ: Lawrence Erlbaum Associates.

Tam, W. M., Cheng, Y. C., & Cheung, W. M. (1997). A re-engineering framework for total home-school partnership. *International Journal of Educational Management, 11(6), 274-285 (UK).*

Teele, S. (1995). *The multiple intelligences school: A place for all students to succeed.* Redlands, CA: Citograph Printing.

Townsend, T., & Cheng, Y. C. (1999). *Educational change and development in the Asia-Pacific region: Challenges for the future.* The Netherlands: Swets and Zeitlinger Publishers.

Tsui, K. T., & Cheng, Y. C. (2000). Multi-dimensional teacher performance in the new century: Implications for school management. *Asia-Pacific Educational Researcher.*

Appendix
Contextualized Multiple Intelligences
adopted from Cheng (2000a)

In the light of the biological origins of each problem-solving skill, H. Gardner (1993) suggested that there are seven human intelligences, including musical intelligence, bodily-kinesthetic intelligence, logical-mathematical intelligence, linguistic intelligence, spatial intelligence, interpersonal intelligence, and intrapersonal intelligence. This biological perspective of multiple intelligences may be useful to understand an individual's cognitive competence in terms of a set of basic abilities or "intelligences" (Gardner, 1993). When we want to design a curriculum and pedagogic methods to develop students' related abilities and intelligences to survive a context of complicated technological, economic, social, political, and cultural environments, however, this perspective may be too "basic" and limited and does not have a strong and direct relevance to such a context in the new century. Comparatively, it is useful to design curriculum and pedagogy for early childhood education or lower primary education to develop their basic abilities, but it is not sophisticated enough for higher form education, which should be highly contextualized to the social, economic, political, cultural, and technological developments (Berman, 1995; Guild & Chock-Eng, 1998; Guloff, 1996; Mettetal & Jordan, 1997; Teele, 1995).

My previous research on school effectiveness (Cheng, 1996) has shown that there are five different types of school functions in the new century, including the economic/structural functions, social functions, political functions, cultural functions, and educational functions. All these functions represent the different contributions of education to development of individuals, the school as an institution, the community, the society, and the international community in these areas. To achieve these functions, education should develop students' intelligence in the areas of these five functions. Further, taking into consideration the traditional assumptions of human nature in social contexts (Bolman & Deal, 1997; Schein, 1980), as well as the importance of technology to development, we can assume that human nature can be represented by a typology, including technological person, economic person, social person, political person, cultural person, and learning person in a complicated context of the new century. Therefore, human intelligence should be contextualized: that is, in the context of the technological, economical, social, political, cultural and learning environments in the new millennium. As such, human intelligence can be categorized into the following six contextualized multiple intelligences (CMIs), including technological intelligence, economic intelligence, social intelligence, political intelligence, cultural intelligence, and learning intelligence (see end of Appendix for summary table).

Based on these contextualized multiple intelligences, a pentagon theory of CMIs development for reforming education, curriculum and pedagogy can be proposed to meet the developmental needs in the new millennium. It suggests that school education should be redesigned based on the premises of a new paradigm(see Figure A).

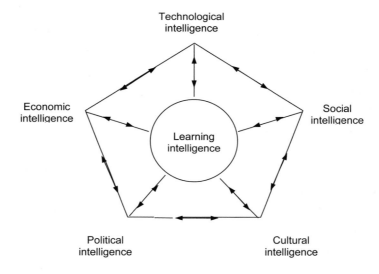

Figure A. Pentagon theory of CMI development for redesign of curriculum and pedagogy (with globalization, localization, and individualization)

1. *Relevant to the development of CMIs.* The development of students' contextualized multiple intelligences is the basic condition for the development of individuals, institutions, communities, societies, and international communities in the complex local and global contexts, particularly in the technological, economical, social, political, cultural and learning aspects. Therefore, the curriculum, pedagogy, and school education should be reformed with clear relevance and concrete linkages with the development of CMIs.

2. *Encouraging CMI interactions.* The relationships among these six CMIs are interactive and mutually reinforcing, with the learning intelligence at the center

as shown by a pentagon as in the Figure. The design of school education should encourage and facilitate such interactions and reinforcements among CMIs. This has strong implications for the needs of balanced curriculum and pedagogy not only in lower grades of primary and secondary education but also in tertiary education, if we want to have citizens with broad mind sets or multiple intelligences to deal with the diverse challenges in the new era.

3. *Facilitating intelligence transfer.* Intelligence transfer from one type to other types (e.g., from economic intelligence to political intelligence or social intelligence) should be encouraged and facilitated to achieve a higher level of intelligence or meta-thinking. The transfer itself can represent a type of intelligence creativity and generalization. It is hoped that inter-intelligence transfer can be transformed into a dynamic, ongoing and self-developing process not only at the individual level but also at the group, institutional, community, society, even international levels. This will be very important to the creation of a high level knowledge-based and thinking society or an intelligent global village.

4. *Placing learning intelligence at the center.* To accelerate the development of all other CMIs, the development of learning intelligence can play a central role. Instead of teaching and learning a huge volume of information and factual material, the content of curriculum and the process of pedagogy should put emphasis on developing students' ability to persistently learn how to learn systematically, creatively, and critically. This may partly reflect why the current educational reforms in different parts of the world emphasize the ability and attitude to life-long learning in curriculum and pedagogy (Education Commission, 1999; Townsend & Cheng, 1999).

5. *Developing CMI teachers and CMI schools.* The success of implementing CMI education for students depends heavily on the quality of teachers and the school. Whether teachers themselves can develop and possess a higher level of CMI, and whether the school can be a multiple intelligence organization and can provide a MI environment for teaching and learning, will affect the design and implementation of CMI education. Therefore, in the reform of school education, how to develop teachers as multiple intelligence teachers and schools as multiple intelligence schools through staff development and school development inevitably become an important agenda and necessary component.

6. *Globalization, localization, and individualization of education.* In order to maximize the opportunities for development of CMIs for students, teachers,

and the school, globalization, localization, and individualization in schooling, teaching, and learning are important and necessary to the reform of school education, curriculum, and pedagogy in the new era. The following paragraphs will highlight their conceptions and implications for development of CMIs.

	Contextualized Multiple Intelligences	Definition of the Contextualized Multiple Intelligences
Learning person	Learning intelligence	The ability to learn and think creatively and critically and to optimize the use of biological/physiological abilities
Technological person	Technological intelligence	The ability to think, act and manage technologically and maximize the benefits of various types of technology
Economic person	Economic intelligence	The ability to think, act and manage economically and to optimize the use of various resources
Social person	Social intelligence	The ability to think, act and manage socially and to effectively develop harmonious interpersonal relationships
Political person	Political intelligence	The ability to think, act and manage politically and to enhance win-win outcomes in situations of competing resources and interests
Cultural person	Cultural intelligence	the ability to think, act, and manage culturally, to optimize the use of multi-cultural assets and to create new values

THE SELF-MANAGED SCHOOL AS AN INTELLIGENT ORGANIZATION

Isaac A. Friedman

Researchers in the fields of education, economics, psychology and administration have dealt extensively with the role of the school and its ability to fulfill the tasks assigned to it. Over the last four decades, the literature has reflected a greater and more focused interest in this topic, with researchers concentrating on the degree to which the school is effective, both as an organization in general and as an educational organization in particular. Many studies have been conducted on this subject, and their findings have yielded important ideas capable of enhancing school performance and reinforcing the level of commitment and accountability of principals and school faculties. One of the important results of attempts to improve the performance of the school as an organizational unit, and that of its employees, is the concept of school-based management (or self-managed schools). This is a unique organizational culture characterized by feedback processes, shared decision-making, and a great deal of autonomy in the utilization of human and financial resources.

This article presents the processes and characteristics of schools in general, and self-managed schools in particular, from a different point of view, using the theory of human intelligence as the theoretical and conceptual framework. It proposes a definition of the concept of organizational intelligence, according to which the school is defined as an organization that functions on the basis of wisdom, knowledge and skill; in other words, an intelligent organization. The term "organizational intelligence" will serve as an analytical tool for understanding events that occur in both self-managed schools and schools that are not self-managing.

The goal of this article is to help researchers and practitioners understand the processes that take place in schools and to act in order to improve and enhance them. The intention is not to evaluate different types of schools, nor to recommend any one pattern of behavior. The chapter begins with a description of the key concepts of human intelligence, on the basis of which an organization's behavior patterns can be defined as organizational intelligence. A school's organizational intelligence is comprised of five major intelligences: reflective, strategic, contextual, collegial and ethical (which consists of three sub-intelligences). The practice and performance of a self-managed school is examined in light of these five types of intelligence.

Isaac A. Friedman

HUMAN INTELLIGENCE AND ITS DIMENSIONS

The concept of intelligence emerged from the examination of human functioning and was based in particular on observation of people as they confronted problem-solving and attempted to learn difficult and demanding subjects such as arithmetic, languages and history. While some people demonstrate no difficulty with study or problem solving, others do experience difficulty and there are those who fail utterly in their studies. This discrepancy in degrees of success indicates the differences in human abilities and the existence of interpersonal difference in the components that direct human intellectual activity. Efforts to identify these components and classify them can be found in the ancient philosophical thought of the Greeks. Plato clearly distinguished between three aspects of human knowledge and spirit, which he called intellect, emotion and desire. Plato compared intellect with a charioteer holding onto the reins, while emotion and desire were compared to the horses pulling the chariot. These images hint at a possible division of labor and the specific roles incumbent on the various aspects of human knowledge and spirit, and perhaps on the differential abilities of each. Aristotle simplified this triple classification by combining emotion and desire, making a single unit of them, and demonstrating the contrast between a person's cognitive or intellectual ability and his other abilities. Cicero, the Roman jurist, politician and orator, called the Platonic and Aristotelian concept that defines human cognitive or intellectual ability *intelligentia*, and the term we now use was thus coined (Eysenck, 1979).

Classic intelligence is defined as cognitive ability, but the precise and full meaning of this ability has never been wholly clarified, despite the many efforts that have been invested in this question (Colman, 2001). The systematic search for the meaning of human intelligence gained significant momentum during the early part of the last century. In a symposium published in 1921 in the American Journal of Educational Psychology, fourteen of the leading researchers at that time proposed their definitions of intelligence. These definitions included "the ability to perform abstract thinking" (Lewis Madison Terman); "the ability to react properly from the point of view of truth or facts" (Edward Lee Thorndike); and "the capacity for internalization, adaptation and instinctive adjustment, the ability to redefine an internalized adjustment in light of experience based on trial and error, and the ability to consciously realize the adjustments and changes to which the person is exposed in the form of observable behavior directed towards gaining advantages for the individual as a social animal"

(Louis Leon Thurstone). Simply put, the definition proposed by Thurstone describes an intelligent person as one who formulates certain thought patterns and behavioral modes, internalizes them, and is then capable of changing these patterns and methods at will in response to a changing reality and the messages that are transmitted to him from this reality. Such a person learns from his surroundings and from experience, draws conclusions from this learning and applies them in order to improve his position and well-being in the environment in which he functions. These definitions indicate the multiple abilities involved in intelligence, or intelligent behavior. They include the limitless ability to learn from mistakes – both those made by the person himself and those made by others, the ability to internalize these lessons, and the ability to change patterns of thought and behavior on the basis of lessons learned, information acquired and an understanding of the changed reality.

These definitions rest on the perception of man as a social animal, in other words a creature who exists in the society of other creatures, and who must be constantly alert in order to monitor the behavior of the others and adapt himself to changes in that behavior. The active nature of intelligence is reflected in the intelligent person's striving for achievements, perpetual exploration and searching, and choosing between multiple alternatives. Three typical patterns of intelligent behavior are: determined performance (the tendency to choose a defined direction for action and pursue it without being distracted or sidetracked from the original path); the ability to adapt means in order to achieve defined goals; and the capacity for self-criticism, which includes dissatisfaction with partial solutions that do not really solve the problems being confronted (Binet & Simon, 1909). Intelligence is, therefore, the general ability of the individual to function in a manner directed at achieving a goal, and to think rationally within his own environment (Wechsler, 1958). Towards the end of the twentieth century, papers appeared in the literature that proposed other types of intelligence, with emphasis on emotional and social aspects, and moral values, as complements to classic intelligence that focused on a person's cognitive abilities. These types of intelligence will be discussed in greater detail below.

The definition of the concept of intelligence is strongly related to its measurement. Several generations ago, first-year psychology students throughout the world learned to define intelligence as follows: "Intelligence is what intelligence tests measure" (Hilgard, 1962, p. 404). We no longer define human intelligence that way, but the strong connection between our definition of the concept and the methods used to measure it is still in place (Nevo, 1997). This strong connection is based on the idea that those human behaviors that can be observed and studied, measured and evaluated, must be distinguished from the hidden ability that underlies observed behavior, directing it and facilitating its existence. The existence of such a hidden ability is only indirectly evident, or can only be concluded with the help of the scientific rules of research procedure, which analyzes information obtained through observation and study. We can therefore only evaluate explicit behavior and observable performance, and draw conclusions as to a person's underlying abilities from the findings of our observations. Various tests investigate particular patterns of human behavior. If we find a strong degree of correlation that reflects a connection between these behavior patterns, then we may conclude that the different tests are measuring common latent characteristics that are hidden from the eye of the observer.

Early theoretical models of intelligence led practitioners and researchers to believe that intelligence is a single, one-dimensional conceptual unit. In other words, intelligence is in effect "a single entity" that has different aspects, and while each of those aspects can be measured separately, when taken together they measure a single attribute – which is intelligence. A person can therefore be defined as "very intelligent" or as "very unintelligent" (and of course as somewhere in between). This approach however, gave rise to many doubts among both the public and researchers. Practitioners and researchers both pointed out that people who had been perceived as "not intelligent" in academic studies and activities, were very successful in practical disciplines. These people were highly successful as musicians, athletes, and expert craftsmen (with "golden hands"), while their success on classical intelligence tests was very low. Doubts with respect to the single factor approach to intelligence are also evident in the work of Raymond Cattell (1966), who posited that intelligence has two factors rather than one. Cattell called the one factor fluid general intelligence and the second, crystallized intelligence. *Fluid intelligence* includes the capacity for creative thought, abstract thought, the ability to draw conclusions from data and to understand the essence of relationships and connections between different phenomena and people. *Crystallized intelligence* includes the things people learn from experience, and is thus strongly influenced by the environment.

With the development of cognitive psychology and the emphasis this scientific discipline placed on models of information processing, the way was paved for a new approach to the study of human intelligence. This approach is based on attempts to understand the cognitive processes that take place when we are involved in intellectual activities. Instead of trying to explain intelligence in terms of factors, this approach attempts to identify the intellectual processes underlying behavior. This approach assumes that differences in the performance of tasks is contingent upon the various cognitive processes people employ, and also on the speed and accuracy of those processes. This new approach engendered new theories of intelligence, three of which – the theories of Howard Gardner, Robert Sternberg, and Stephen Ceci – are particularly pertinent to our topic.

Gardner (1993) developed his theory of intelligence in direct response to the classical perception of intelligence as the ability to think rationally. He defined intelligence as "the ability to solve problems or generate results that are significant within a defined social context or community" (p. 15). He was influenced by the various roles adults fulfill in different cultures – the success with which they do so being contingent on a wide spectrum of skills and abilities. His observations led him to the belief that the assertion of a single intelligence is incorrect. Instead, people possess multiple intelligences that operate together and in concert. He proposed that there are seven distinct types of intelligence (linguistic, musical, logical-mathematical, spatial, bodily-kinesthetic, intrapersonal and interpersonal). Gardner stressed that each person has stronger and weaker intelligences, and this is what differentiates people from one another and explains their different behavior and abilities.

Sternberg's theory of intelligence (Sternberg, 1988), which is known as the *triarchic theory*, consists of three sub-theories: the componential sub-theory, regarding cognitive processes; the experiential sub-theory, also known as the two facet theory, concerning the effect of experience and learning on intelligence; and the contextual sub-theory, which takes into account the impact of the individual's environment and culture on shaping his intelligence. The most developed of the three sub-theories is the componential theory, which deals with the components of cognition. In this context Sternberg identified the following three components: *metacomponents,* used for planning, controlling and supervising, and for assessing the act of information processing during problem solving; *performance components,* used for implementation of the problem-solving strategies; *knowledge-acquisition components,* for screening information (and classifying it as more or less relevant), combining pieces of information into a whole, and making comparisons (between new information obtained and existing information). The second sub-theory relates to learning and experience. It claims that intelligence rests on two key tasks: coping with new situations (understanding the situation, identifying the main components needed for a solution, adding new information to existing information, and combining pieces of information into a comprehensive solution), and initiating a routine of cognitive processes so that they become almost automatic. The contextual sub-theory involves adapting to the environment, and there are three methods of coping with context-related problems: shaping the environment to suit one's needs; adapting to environmental conditions; and selecting a different environment.

Ceci (1990) bases himself on Sternberg's theory while emphasizing the context in which things happen and in which the individual's behavior and its impact on problem-solving are examined. Ceci also believes that there are multiple cognitive potentials rather than a single intelligence. From his point of view it is to a large extent context that determines intelligence. In other words, the degree to which a person is successful in solving problems and the way in which he confronts them are influenced by biological-personal background factors and contextual factors. These factors are the degree to which the person is familiar with the type of problem that he is facing, the degree to which the problem is tangible for that person, his degree of motivation to solve the problem, and the amount of relevant information he possesses in order to deal with the problem.

In summary it might be said that modern theories of human intelligence indicate that people have different abilities; that each of these abilities can have its own distinct force and space; and that they are readily distinguishable. In light of these theories, it is proper to examine human intelligence from different angles and define a person and his abilities differentially.

As recently as the second half of the 1990s, additional new directions became evident in research into intelligence. These were not attempts to refute existing theories of intelligence, but rather added other patterns of intelligence, such as emotional intelligence (Goleman, 1995) and spiritual intelligence (Zohar & Marshall, 1994), to them. Emotional intelligence is expressed in many ways, the fundamental one being the harnessing of emotions in order to enhance performance and learning. This does not only mean curbing our emotions or making them more effective, but also utilizing them in accordance with the task to be performed. Emotional intelligence is based on a high sense of self-awareness, which serves as the basis for many important behavior patterns, such as empathy. The more open we are to our own emotions, the better we are at reading our own feelings and those of others. The ability to know what others are feeling can be of use in a variety of areas in life: from sales and commerce to romantic relationships, from parenting and compassion to political activity. Emotional intelligence also encourages social intelligence. A person blessed with a superior sense of social intelligence is able to communicate well and easily with others, is keenly aware of their reactions and feelings, can lead and organize, and is capable of handling the controversies that often emerge in every human activity.

Another type of intelligence, which is perceived as complementary to emotional intelligence, is spiritual intelligence. Spiritual intelligence differs from emotional intelligence primarily in its power to change the shape of things. It facilitates asking whether a person wants to continue acting within the frameworks in which he lives, or whether he wants to change them or move on to other frameworks. Zohar and Marshall are credited with formulating this type of intelligence (Zohar & Marshall, 1994). Spiritual intelligence enables one to be creative, to change rules and alter conditions. It endows him with the capacity to notice, develops his moral sense, his ability to refine and moderate inflexible rules through understanding and compassion, while at the same time recognizing that such understanding and compassion have their own limits. Spiritual intelligence helps us deal with questions of good and evil, and to envision new, far-reaching possibilities.

ORGANIZATIONAL INTELLIGENCE AND THE INTELLIGENT ORGANIZATION

This paper proposes the idea of "organizational intelligence" – which expresses an organization's ability to achieve its goals – and uses it to coin a new concept: the intelligent organization. The notion of organizational intelligence is based on cognitive psychology and its emphasis on models of information processing, in the attempt to identify the mental processes that underlie behavior and assume that differences in the performance of tasks are contingent upon the different cognitive processes people use. This concept is also based on non-cognitive approaches in intelligence research, that is, emotional and spiritual intelligence. Organizational intelligence and the intelligent organization can be defined thus:

Organizational intelligence is an organization's collective ability directed towards achieving its goals. It is expressed through organizational processes and includes the combined abilities and experiences of its members. It constitutes a part of the organization's culture, which has been formulated during the course of its existence.

An intelligent organization is one that formulates its own cognitive patterns and clear behaviors, and employs them in order to achieve its goals, develop and flourish. Its members can accurately assess the present, draw conclusions from the past and from changes in the present, foresee the future and prepare for it. It is capable of changing these patterns and behaviors at will in response to a changing reality.

An administrative organization is "a network of roles and flow of activities aimed at achieving shared goals" (Robey, 1986, p. 16). "Network of roles" describes the organization's structure and "flow of activities" refers to organizational processes. Organizations are social tools planned by human beings, with that planning directed at the achievement of strategic goals. The strategy is defined as the determination of goals and objectives, and the allocation of the resources needed to attain them. Organizations function within an environment and not in a vacuum; as such they are context-dependent. The environment in which organizations function is comprised of numerous components and agents, the predominant ones being: consumers, suppliers, competitors, the work place, the scientific-technological community, and supervisory bodies. The environment constitutes a source of support as well as uncertainty, and also the resources required by the organization. Uncertainty is generated as a result of changes within the environment that occur unexpectedly. An organization must adapt itself to its environment and continue to adapt itself as necessary when changes take place in the environment or within itself. Organization managers may take a reactive approach, as well as a proactive approach, with a view to monitoring the sources of environmental uncertainty and those resources that are obtained from the environment as carefully as possible. Organizational strategy refers, inter alia – and perhaps chiefly – to the manner in which the organization chooses to manage its relationships with the environment. For example, the organization can adapt itself to demands dictated by the environment, but it can also proceed in directions that challenge environmental dictates. These adaptive behaviors, which are also considered adaptive organizational strategies, are designed to preserve the organization and ensure its continued existence and prosperity.

An organization contains processes directed at facilitating its existence and development. There are six such process that should be mentioned:

- *Planning.* The planning process includes decisions pertaining to the organization's goals and what members of the organization must do in order to achieve them. During the planning process, the organization's members ask themselves where they are at a given time, where they want to go, and how they should go about getting there.
- *Organization.* The organization process is the creation of a structure. This structure includes the work units and the people who staff them.

- *Motivation.* People in an organization need encouragement, support and direction in order to fulfill the jobs they are responsible for. The motivational process is meant to achieve this.
- *Feedback and control.* The feedback and control process is aimed at ensuring that the organization is indeed achieving its goals, and to what extent it is doing so.
- *Decision-making.* Decision-making processes are designed to help the organization choose a particular path of action, or a particular result, by making an informed choice.
- *Communications.* This process promotes the exchange of information between two or more people.

We can assess the intelligence of an organization by examining its organizational processes. The processes that reflect organizational intelligence will be those that permit the organization to formulate cognitive patterns and behaviors that will enable it to exist successfully within its commercial, organizational and social environment, and in particular – will enable it to change these patterns and behaviors at will, in response to a changing reality and the messages that are transmitted to it by this reality.

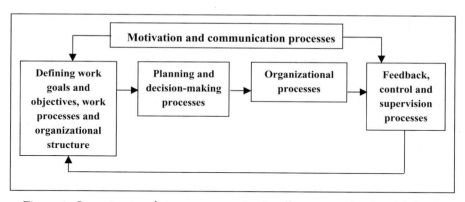

Figure 1. Organizational processes expressing intelligent organizational behavior

Figure 1 presents the continuum of an organization's major processes. From the point of view of organizational intelligence, the most important process is that of feedback, control and supervision. This process is designed to answer the key question of how and where the organization is progressing in its work and whether it is achieving its goals. Furthermore, this process answers other questions such as whether the organization's environment is changing in a way that is likely to have an impact on either its goals or the means for achieving them, and whether it is necessary to adjust the organization's behavior.

According to Sternberg's componential theory (Sternberg, 1988), the cognitive metacomponents include the processes of planning, control and supervision, which are also directed towards information processing and problem-solving. The performance components group involves the organization process. This includes, among other things, the creation of a structure, the ability to carry out the decisions that have been made, and the motivational process. The knowledge-acquisition components – which are used to screen information, classify it as more or less relevant, combine pieces of information into a whole, and compare new information obtained with existing information – include the communications processes and, to a large extent, the other organizational processes as well (see Figure 1).

All of the processes described above involve people who implement and influence the processes, and are influenced by them in return. These people act together, as a collective within the framework of an integrated social network, rather than as individuals. Each person brings his intellectual ability to the organization, that is, his personal intelligence. The combination of all these intelligences serves as the basis for the organization's collective intelligence. The organizational processes are therefore affected by the organization's collective intelligence.

An intelligent organization strives toward achievement and is perpetually exploring, searching and choosing actions from among the wide range of options available to it, on the basis of rational considerations. The organization chooses defined directions for action and resolutely pursues them, without swerving from its original path. It has self-critical facilities and is not satisfied with partial solutions that do not truly address the problems it faces. On the basis of the approach which holds that intelligence is a one-dimensional phenomenon, it might be argued that an organization can be either very intelligent or not all that intelligent (in which case it will be a failure). Conversely, on the basis of the approaches which hold that intelligence is a multi-faceted concept, we can try to characterize the organization according to a number of types of intelligence. Each type of intelligence can be related to as a potential, the existence of which affords the organization access to types of thinking and behavior that are suited to different subjects and actions. On the basis of Sternberg's triarchic theory (1988), the organization can be seen as even more complex. Ceci's theory (1990) emphasizes the context in which a person acts, and this corresponds to organizational culture and its role in assessing an organization's capability. The organization's culture relies most extensively on its history, the knowledge and experience it has accumulated, on its successes and failures. Organizational intelligence, according to this theory, depends on multi-cognitive potential, the expression of which is contingent upon the knowledge that the organization has acquired in its spheres of activity.

Of what benefit is the conceptualization of the organizational process as organizational intelligence, and how can it help us understand and improve the organization? This question can be answered on two levels. On one level – regarding the organization as an intelligent entity is an analytical tool that enables us to classify the organization and its abilities differentially, and thus analyze its ability to successfully fulfill its goals. Perceiving the organization as an intelligent entity can provide a cognitive basis upon which to work toward reinforcing certain types of intelligence within the organization in order to enhance the organization and increase its effectiveness. On the second level – conceptualization of the organizational processes as organizational intelligence generates an important link between two conceptual worlds: the world of human intelligence, with the tremendous knowledge and vast array of analytical tools it affords us, and the organizational world, which is an utterly applied and practical world.

We can also see organizational intelligence as a reflection of accountability. The behavior of an intelligent organization reflecting a high level of accountability. The concept of accountability in organization theory, which generally refers to the need to report the results of the organization's work and assume the consequences for these results, relies on administrative and economic theories pertaining to work incentives and control within the organization. Accountability reflects the relationship between those charged with operating organizations and institutions and those who have the power and ability to replace them. Accountability is the process in which those who are held accountable must explain, as rationally as possible, the results of their efforts to fulfill the goals and objectives associated with doing their jobs (Browder, 1975). Kirst (1990) claims that accountability can be expressed in six different ways: (1) Accountability through reporting on performance (performance reports include measurement and assessment using tests or indicators that demonstrate performance); (2) Accountability by meeting standards or regulations; (3) Accountability via incentive systems (reward for outcomes, with incentives that are aimed at encouraging the performance of specific actions; this approach ties performance to results); (4) Accountability through market reliance (market forces are likely to be the best assessment of an organization's functioning – a "good" organization will survive, a "bad" organization will not); (5) Accountability through changing the locus of control or authority within the organization (an organization that is functioning properly will be given more autonomy, an organization that is not functioning properly will be restricted through close supervision); (6) Accountability by means of position changes (internal evaluation versus external evaluation, with internal evaluation serving as a tool for accountability).

It can be demonstrated that intelligent organizational behavior reflects at least five of the six aspects described above. An intelligent organization maintains, above all, feedback and control processes, which also include performance reports (see Figure 1). The feedback and control relate to work goals and objectives defined by the organization (or for the organization by outside agencies authorized to do so), as well as all of the other processes and the standards that have been set for the organization's operations. Thus, the feedback and control processes reflect the first and second aspects of accountability (see above). Intelligent organizational behavior is directed toward ensuring that market forces do not cause the organization to disappear, and that it continues to exist and develop instead (reflecting the fourth aspect of accountability). An intelligent organization hence draws conclusions from the findings of its feedback, re-examines its goals, work process and other processes – including those concerned with motivation and communication. Changes are implemented as needed, as part of this intelligent behavior. Changes aimed at increasing motivation may reflect accountability through incentives (the third aspect). Changes regarding work methods and the organizational structure are likely to reflect accountability through changes in positions (fourth aspect).

THE GOALS OF THE SCHOOL AS AN ORGANIZATION

This chapter focuses on the administrative organization, the school. A school is also an "organization," something we tend to forget because of the focus on pupils, teachers, and the social and educational processes that take place within it. As an organization, the school directs its activities towards achieving the goals for which it exists. The question we must now try and answer is: what are the main goals or main tasks of the school as an organization, and which its collective intelligence is aimed at achieving? Many researchers have attempted to respond, only to find that the answer is not readily available. Attempts to assert the school's goals definitively have always engendered questions. Firstly, attempts to define the goals of the school have always been limited.

Every proposed definition was criticized on the grounds that the definition was either too narrow or too broad. Secondly, any definition of school goals was perceived as a "prescription" for success that did not take the possible diversity between schools into consideration. Thirdly, every proposed definition was based on values, or on certain value judgments, and could therefore not be adequate for different population groups.

In the most general sense it can be said that the school is designed to educate the pupils, to imbue them with knowledge and information, to train them for work, creativity, and a beneficial and satisfactory life within an advanced society (MacGilchrist, Myers, & Reed, 1997). Research during the second half of the twentieth century was not favorably disposed towards schools or teachers in terms of their contribution to pupils' education and their instruction. Since the early 1960s, studies – with extremely similar findings – have been published in several countries throughout the world, describing the minimal contribution of schools to their pupils' academic achievements. The research findings showed that pupils' scholastic achievement was linked to their family background, and to characteristics relating to their home and environment, rather than to what the school was doing for its pupils. For example, studies conducted in the late 1950s in England showed that only 5% of the pupils whose fathers had finished school at age 16 continued on to higher education, while 57% of the pupils whose fathers had finished school at age 18 and over continued on to higher education. These studies further showed that 45% of the pupils whose parents earned well (doctors, lawyers, senior-level clerks) continued on to higher education, while only 2% of those whose fathers worked in lower-paying or non-professional jobs continued on to higher education. These findings thus indicated that the achievements, academic level and future occupation of the pupil could be predicted on the basis of the socio-economic status of his parents, regardless of the quality of the teaching at his school (Beare, Caldwell, & Millikan, 1994).

The most cited documentation of the troubling link between a pupil's socio-economic background and his anticipated scholastic achievements was formulated in the early 1960s by an American team headed by James Coleman (Coleman et al., 1966). Coleman and his team conducted a very comprehensive study involving tens of thousands of pupils from all parts of the country, in an attempt to survey the achievements of the American school and to propose means of improving them. The primary finding that emerged from Coleman and his associates' research was that the likelihood of a pupil being prepared for employment in a prestigious profession, or being ready for academic studies after completing his high school studies, depended on the pupil's social background. A strong correlation was also found between the pupil's individual sense of ability, or his perceived ability to control his destiny, and his academic accomplishments. The pupil's individual sense of ability was found to be linked to his parent's level of education and professional occupation. Furthermore, studies performed by Coleman and his associates showed that the socio-economic status of the friends of a pupil from a weak background could predict his scholastic success better than the characteristics of this school and his teachers. Coleman's study further indicated that given the negligible influence of the school's characteristics, the teachers' characteristics (education, tenure) were more prominent contributors to predicting the pupils' scholastic successes, although in statistical terms this contribution was also minor.

The primary significance of the findings presented by Coleman and his colleagues is that the school is not "effective," in the sense that it does not succeed in leaving its mark upon the child. And the report's major recommendation can indeed be summarized as follows: Schools will be considered successful if they can reduce the degree to which a pupil's educational opportunities are contingent upon his social background. We can assume a series of contingent probabilities: among them the probability of a pupil's being prepared for work in a given profession or certain academic studies at the end of his high school education, which is contingent upon his background or social origin. The effectiveness of the school consists, in part, of making contingent probabilities less contingent, in other words, less dependent upon social background. Equal educational opportunity is directed not only at equality between schools, but at equalizing their effectiveness, so that their influence overcomes the disparity in starting points among pupils who come from different social groups (Coleman et al., 1966).

Studies similar to those carried out in England and the US were conducted in Australia and New Zealand during the 1960s and 1970s. These studies also tried to assess the degree to which schools successfully achieved their goals by examining their contribution to pupils' success in matriculation exams. These studies showed that if we could ascertain the parents' socio-economic level, their occupation and degree of satisfaction with the school, and if we could feed this data into a computer, we would be able to predict quite accurately what would happen with this young person, what his level of education, his achievements and his profession would be. The explanation offered by the researchers was that when attitudes towards education in the home conflict with the school's attitudes, the pupil tends to prefer the former and reject the latter. The dominant figures in such a possible conflict are the parents. They are the ones who convey the importance of schooling and education to their children, and they are the ones who urge the pupil towards higher academic achievements in school (Moore, 1974).

The findings of studies conducted in the 1960s and 1970s clearly indicate that although the school contributes to the pupil's education and success, its influence is far less significant than teachers or parents would expect. What the pupil brings to school from his home and family is much more important than what goes on in the classroom. The conclusion that was ruefully reached by education researchers in various countries was that under certain conditions the school does not have a significant impact on the achievements of the pupil and his success in later life. In light of these findings researchers and public officials averred that the school was not effective in determining the pupil's future. On the other hand, the more the school was able to increase the chances of pupils coming from socio-economically weak homes of succeeding academically and in life – the more effective the school was thought to be.

Educational researchers felt that schools should not continue to operate in their present format, because by so doing they were liable to perpetuate an undesirable social order. They also felt compelled to act in order to rehabilitate the injured pride of the school and restore it to its rightful and important standing. Klitgaard and Hall (1973) attempted to identify "unusually effective" schools after evidence had pointed to schools in socio-economically weaker regions that were producing particularly good pupils. These researchers, who were not educators, found that some of the schools they examined had particularly high levels of scholastic achievement, low drop out rates, and graduates who furthered their studies and became established adults. A movement of researchers and educators, sometimes known as the Effective Schools Movement, thus emerged. It worked to understand the factors underlying the school's effectiveness in order to reinforce them and enhance the level of school effectiveness. The Effective Schools Movement went beyond the social-academic aspect of school effectiveness and assigned additional tasks to the school. The school should also maintain proper decorum and discipline among its pupils, alongside their personal well-being; it should teach pupils professional abilities as well as daily life skills; and it should establish a harmonious relationship with the community.

The movement to restore the school's tarnished reputation gained momentum at the end of the 1970s (Reid, Hopkins, & Holly, 1988). One of the more important studies that outlined the unique characteristics of the effective school was conducted by Rutter and colleagues (Rutter, Maughan, Mortimore, & Ouston, 1979). The study, which encompassed twelve London schools and lasted for more than eight years, found that schools that succeeded in bringing the achievements of its weaker pupils to impressive levels possessed the following characteristics:

- Lessons were directed at the achievement of clear and predefined outcomes in the content areas being studied;

- Teachers planned their lessons and worked as a team, with older and more experienced teachers supervising the work of younger teachers who were just starting out;

- A system of incentives – both positive and negative – was in place, along with immediate feedback for pupils on their performance;

- Pupils were told that they were expected to take responsibility for their actions, their successes and failures, as well as their daily performance;

- Homework preparation was strictly monitored. The expectation that pupils would work hard and succeed was made unequivocally clear to both pupils and teachers;

- A positive and affirmative atmosphere and ethos prevailed.

Research on effective schools continued during the 1990s as well, and outlined strategies for augmenting the school's contribution towards the education of its pupils and the creation of a better future for them. Today it can be said that the contribution of the school that maintains a known set of conditions can exceed the contribution of the pupil's individual characteristics. Sammons (1999) summarizes the findings that were collected through the late 1990s, and lists eleven mechanisms of effectiveness that characterize effective schools (ibid., pp. 195-214). These are described briefly below.

1. *Professional leadership:* The leadership of the school principal was found to be the most prominent factor in studies on school effectiveness. The leadership of an effective principal is strong and directed at the accomplishment of clear goals. These principals tend to be proactive, regulating the external pressures exerted on the school and pushing for change and improvement. Such principals employ a cooperative and collegial management style by sharing leadership tasks with their

staff and delegating authority, but serving as the most senior professional within the school.

2. *Shared vision and goals:* The research indicated that schools are more effective when the staff agrees on the school's values and goals, and realizes those values and goals by means of collaborative work and decision making. Effective schools also display consistency in their work, which is reflected in the faculty members' agreement with regard to teaching processes and mutual assistance and support, both among themselves and between them and the pupils. A collegial and cooperative atmosphere was found to be a very important factor in increasing a school's effectiveness.

3. *Learning environment:* The school's ethos is partly determined by the vision, values and goals of the faculty and the manner in which they work together, as well as by the atmosphere in which the pupils operate; in other words, the learning environment. The learning environment must be orderly and attractive. An orderly learning environment not only requires order, quiet, and cleanliness in the building and its surroundings, but also that the pupils exercise self-control.

4. *Focus on teaching and learning:* The school's main goal relates to teaching and learning. The focus on teaching and learning is defined, *inter alia*, in terms of establishing quantifiable objectives, measuring outcomes and examining the processes leading to the achievement of these outcomes. Time spent in school must be devoted, as far as possible, to learning. This component of school effectiveness can be measured by several variables: (1) The amount of time during the day devoted to "scholastic" (academic) subjects, or the number of academic subjects taught in relation to the other subjects; (2) The amount of time the teachers spend on academic materials with the pupils; (3) The amount of attention teachers devote to academic objectives compared with the time spent nurturing interpersonal relations with the pupils; (4) The lesson plan; (5) The absence of external interruptions that can be a distraction to teaching and learning. This component places heavy emphasis on the academic learning and scholastic achievement demanded from the pupils.

5. *Task-oriented teaching:* Task-oriented teaching is based on the effective organization of lessons and the teacher's work, the clarity of the goals expressed by teachers, and lessons that are properly structured. Effective teachers address all the pupils in the classroom and speak clearly, are task-oriented, do not judge their pupils

during the lesson and manage a composed classroom. Effective teachers expect superior achievements from their pupils, and offer them encouragement and support.

6. *High expectations:* An effective school projects high expectations of teachers, pupils, and all those connected with the school's work. The faculty reflects these high expectations and does everything it can to pose intellectual challenges for both pupils and teachers.

7. *Positive reinforcement:* Reinforcement, whether in terms of discipline or pupil feedback, is an important component of effective learning. Reinforcement is expressed through understandable and fair rules of behavior, the giving of feedback, rewards and praise for all aspects of scholastic achievement and all aspects of the pupils' behavior in school.

8. *Monitoring and supervision of the pupils' progress:* Mechanisms based on supervision of the performance and progress of the pupils, the class, and the school as a unit, constitute an important aspect of school effectiveness. These mechanisms must monitor the performance of individual pupils, as well as the performance of the entire school. The combination of feedback with the supervision and information obtained from internal assessment during the school's decision-making processes, ensures that the information collected will be put to active use by the faculty and administration.

9. *Pupils' rights and obligations:* School effectiveness studies show that a pupil's self-respect and belief in his own ability are improved when they are given an active role to play in the school, and when they are afforded an opportunity to participate in shaping their learning processes.

10. *Partnership between the school, the home and the community:* Effectiveness studies have shown that a supportive and cooperative relationship between the school, the familial home and the community can have a positive effect. This is especially true when parents are involved in their children's studies.

11. *A learning organization:* Effective schools are learning organizations in which the teachers and principals learn continuously and stay up-to-date in their chosen disciplines in accordance with their individual needs and the needs of the school. School development generally takes place within the school itself, with the ongoing focus on helping to improve classroom teaching and the curriculum.

School effectiveness can be assessed from a dynamic point of view, and as such the changes taking place within organizations and their work environments must be taken into account. Public and private organizations have recently been undergoing rapid changes, primarily as a result of fast-paced technological changes having to do with the introduction of computers into many fields and advancements in communications. Added to these is the quality and quantity of information becoming available and accessible to everyone. Organizations therefore need to be able to adjust and adapt to changing environmental conditions. The structure of these organizations and their internal processes will change as their environments and the demands made upon them are transformed. High adaptive capacity is contingent on an especially high degree of flexibility, the commitment of responsible employees who are dedicated to the organization and its goals, the proper use of staff members to perform various tasks, and emphasis on basic professional skills. Now more than ever, organizations will have to define their vision and objectives clearly and openly. This will require the organization's personnel to clarify their goals for themselves; and determine and define the identity of their consumers and the recipients of their services, what their consumers want and what their service recipients value most. In order to operate more successfully, organizations will adopt democratic principles in the future. The practical implication of these principles is that organizations will share more with their workers and their environment, which will have a tremendous impact on both the employees and the organizational environment. The democratic principle in the organization's work will demand a greater personal contribution from employees and hence also give them a greater sense of responsibility and caring. Organizations will increasingly become "learning and modernizing organizations," because the knowledge needed to operate them will be updated more rapidly than we are accustomed to. The organization's employees will be able to become, and may have to become, more autonomous than before, by reinforcing their shared vision and goals and enhancing interpersonal and organizational unity.

Organizations will have to do more in future to find new channels of operation. The modernization approach must be instilled in all areas of the organization and its processes. It should guide the workers, engage teams in the planning of shared work, and become a natural and integral part of the organization's culture, work and thinking patterns. More and more, organizations will be required to direct their activities toward a more varied consumer market and provide for a broader range of service recipients. Finally, those who head the organizations will need, to a greater extent, to look beyond the boundaries of their organization and operate within a community framework that encompasses many people and organizations.

By the same token schools, as organizations, cannot remain in their present format and will have to undergo changes in their structure, processes, and the values upon which they are based. According to Leithwood (1999), schools in the near future will be based on the following three principal values: inclusiveness, efficient reliability and initiative. Inclusiveness means that schools will involve more agents in their decision-making processes and will cover more areas of activity in the pupils' education and development (such as social and emotional dimensions together with intellectual ones). Efficient reliability means that schools will have to fulfill the tasks with which they are charged more faithfully, doing so as efficiently as possible. Initiative implies that schools will have to be able to examine the systems in which they operate, to anticipate the changes they must make in order to continue operating successfully, and initiate the activities needed to achieve those changes. More than ever, the school will have to operate as an intelligent organization.

THE SCHOOL AS AN INTELLIGENT ORGANIZATION: THE FIVE SCHOOL INTELLIGENCES

The findings concerning the effective school and modern theories of human intelligence can serve as a foundation for formulating areas of activity in which the school can become an intelligent organization. Based on the concept of organizational intelligence, as defined above, we will now focus on the organizational intelligence of the school. Our discussion will be based on the assumption that in order for the school to succeed in fulfilling its goals, in order to ensure that its efforts and contribution towards the education of the younger generation are significant and meaningful, and in order to meet the challenges of the future and environmental pressures, it must be an "intelligent organization" with multiple intelligences.

Intelligent behavior on the part of the school can be expressed in three areas: the organizational, the pedagogic, and the values spheres. The organizational sphere refers to the school as an organization, and thus it does not distinguish between the school and any other administrative organization. The pedagogic sphere relates to the unique professional aspect of the school as an organization, while the values sphere particularizes the school and sets it apart from every other professional organization. This sphere can be considered the "keystone" of the school's intelligences. These intelligences are the driving force that pushes the school toward success in advancing its students to properly adapt to the environment and its rapidly-changing conditions, and to acquire work patterns that are appropriate for life in the 21st century.

The degree to which an organization succeeds in addressing its problems, and the ways in which the organization employs each of the five intelligences depends, according to Ceci (1990), on internal contextual factors: the extent to which the organization is familiar with the problems it must confront, the degree to which the problems are concrete issues for the organization, the organization's level of motivation to solve the problem and the amount of relevant information possessed by the person who must cope with the problem. The information the organization has accumulated during the course of its development is also very significant. Ceci's theory stresses that intelligence relies on high cognitive potential whose expression is contingent on the knowledge the individual has gained in a particular sphere. This theory emphasizes that organizational knowledge is essential for realizing intelligence.

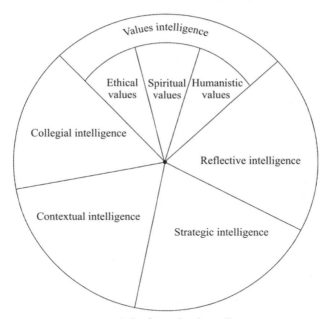

Figure 2. The five school intelligences

Figure 2 is a schematic representation of the school's five intelligences. We describe them below in greater detail and specify their different components.

Reflective intelligence

Reflective intelligence is *the ability to perform a critical, analytical assessment of processes and their outcomes, to draw conclusions, to find meaning and relationships between facts and the lessons learned from success and failure.*

The ability to learn from mistakes, both those made by the organization itself and those made by other organizations, and the capacity to internalize this learning, is what underlies the concept of intelligence. Therefore, this intelligence is "the mother of all intelligences" for a school and encompasses a group of capabilities. This intelligence expresses the active nature of intelligence, as perceived by Binet (Binet & Simon, 1909). The readiness to learn from mistakes, to be creative in finding solutions to the problems that led to errors or to the problems created as a result of the errors and, in particular, the ability to recognize the existence of errors – all these are based on spiritual intelligence (Zohar and Marshall, 1994).

A school's reflective intelligence is expressed in both the organizational and the pedagogic spheres and, naturally, in the values sphere. In the pedagogic sphere, this intelligence is teaching based on feedback-based teaching and includes the ability to assess pupils' progress in their studies by collecting quantifiable data, as well as information that is difficult to quantify but can be evaluated qualitatively. It is the ability to change and improve based on the information collected and the conclusions reached, and the ability to inculcate this intelligence as an educational heritage. In the pedagogic sphere, reflective intelligence encompasses the following three sub-components:

a. *Task-oriented:* Focusing on teaching and learning, which is expressed as setting quantifiable objectives, measuring outcomes and examining the processes leading to the achievement of these outcomes (how much time is spent on "academic" subjects compared with other subjects, such as discussing topics related to current events, social and public issues, etc.; the relative amount of time teachers spend discussing subject matter among themselves; the attention teachers devote to nurturing personal and interpersonal relationships with pupils), and a proactive approach.

b. *Professionalism:* Improving the teachers' professional knowledge in the subjects being taught and teaching methods; consistency in their work, effective organization of lessons and the teacher's activities; goals that are clearly defined by the teacher, and lessons that are properly structured.

c. *Innovation and improvement:* Searching for innovative methods and new subjects to teach, improving the level of teaching, improved feedback and, especially, implementing the feedback results in the school's work.

The school's reflective intelligence in the organizational sphere is feedback-based management. Feedback-based management constitutes ongoing and regular examination of the school's priorities by collecting data and information from within the school and the external environment. This intelligence is the ability to change and improve the school's functioning in light of the information collected.

Reflective intelligence is also found at the basis of a learning organization (Senge, 1990). Thus the school is seen as an organization that learns about itself and learns about learning. This intelligence ensures that learning and teaching are examined regularly and will be developed and improved, and it assumes that learning and teaching are subjects that can certainly be assessed and modified when necessary.

Strategic intelligence

Strategic intelligence is *the ability to establish goals and formulate objectives according to accepted rules and principles, to act with determination to achieve those goals, and to anticipate the effect the present will have upon the future. It enables the school to plan the activities needed to improve its performance, thereby realizing the school's vision.*

The school strives for achievement, does not stop searching and exploring, and chooses from among a variety of alternatives. Its activity consists of three components: the tendency to choose defined directions of activity and continue without deviating from them; the ability to adapt means in order to achieve defined goals; and the ability for self-criticism, an unwillingness to accept partial solutions that do not really solve the problem. Therefore, strategic intelligence expresses the dynamic aspect of intelligence, according to both Binet (Binet & Simon, 1909) and Wechsler (1958). It is also founded on spiritual intelligence, which allows one to see new, far-reaching possibilities (Zohar & Marshall, 1994).

This intelligence is comprised of the following three sub-components:

a. *Vision:* Formulating an organizational and pedagogical vision, based on the values and goals of both teachers and pupils.

b. *Objectives:* Defining operative objectives for the various components of the school's vision.

c. *Modes of implementation:* Defining methods of operation in order to attain the operative objectives defined.

The practical activities associated with strategic intelligence involve constant and regular examination of the school's priorities, and the ability to amend them in accordance with changes in the internal and external environments, objectives or new tasks. Strategic intelligence is reflected, in particular, in the organizational and pedagogic spheres. In the organizational sphere, this intelligence serves as the basis for defining the school's vision and the means for its realization (see the characteristic "common vision and shared goals" as described above in Effectiveness Studies), as well as the basis for developing the methods and means to improve the professional capabilities of those engaged in the educational process. Strategic intelligence is the foundation of the school's professional leadership, which is described in the Effectiveness Studies as the most prominent factor that can account for a school's success or failure. It isn't difficult to discern the connection, and perhaps even the dependence, between reflective intelligence and strategic intelligence, and for this reason they are depicted as being adjacent to each other in Figure 2.

Contextual intelligence

Contextual intelligence is *the school's capacity to integrate its social, professional and physical environment. It is expressed in the ability of the school's personnel to take a sober, informed and critical look at the environment and the community in which it functions and the world in which it lives, and to act in order to properly assimilate into this social space.* This intelligence is characterized by responsiveness and openness to new ideas and events in its immediate surroundings, and an ability to learn from the environment. It is also characterized by the ability to initiate internal changes necessary from exposure to outside ideas and events. This intelligence enables the existence of a supportive relationship between the school, the home and the community, which makes a significant contribution to the school's effectiveness. Included are the following three sub-components:

a. *Community-mindedness:* Familiarity with the community around the school, its desires, needs and problems, and the ability to understand the community's abilities and requirements.

b. *"Thinking big":* Being open to new ideas and events in the nearby surroundings, and the ability to learn from the environment.

c. *System-oriented perspective:* The ability to initiate the internal changes that derive from exposure to external ideas and events. The ability to see the impact of the school's decisions from a broader perspective.

Miles and Snow (1978) present four key strategies used by organizations to adapt to its environment, which are:

1. *Defensive strategy*: The organization does not change, in either its technology, structure or operating methods. Instead, the organization turns much of its attention toward improving existing operations and making them more effective.

2. *Investigative strategy*: The organization continually searches for new marketing opportunities and tries out new products. This strategy is fertile soil for generating changes and dealing with uncertainty.

3. *Analytical strategy*: Organizations that operate with two types of markets and sources of supply: one helps maintain stability, while the other generates change. With regard to stable markets these organizations employ formal, organized processes. In their less stable – or more stormy – markets, the organizations carefully survey their surroundings looking for new ideas, and quickly adopt those changes that offer the most promise.

4. *Reactive strategy:* According to this strategy, the organization reacts to its environment only when forced to do so.

Contextual intelligence, therefore, is strongly linked to strategic intelligence, and therefore they appear next to one another in Figure 2.

Collegial intelligence

Collegial intelligence is *the ability to benefit from working together through mutual support and cooperation in order to improve one's ability to function as an individual, and within society at large.* It includes the following three sub-components:

a. *Shared management within the school:* Defining procedures and processes so that teachers, and to a certain extent pupils as well, can share in defining the school's goals and objectives. Joint decision-making and sharing information from feedback. Dividing up tasks and delegating authority to the school staff.

b. *Involving parents and the community:* Defining procedures and processes that involve parents, and to a certain extent the community as well, in defining the school's goals and processes.

c. *Support, mutual assistance and "giving credit":* Agreement among staff members and mutual assistance. Cooperation and offering personal and professional support. Creating a work environment that is not merely order, quiet and cleanliness in the buildings and surroundings, but which also requires teachers to be self-critical.

Practical behaviors of this intelligence range from including teachers in the decision-making process, to teachers working together in teams, to involving pupils. Underlying collegial intelligence is a recognition of the power of synergy, that is, understanding that the shared efforts of the staff members to achieve organizational goals yield more than the sum of the efforts of each participant when working as an individual. This intelligence is an important factor in increasing the school's effectiveness. It also includes the ability to instill collegiality towards pupils as an educational heritage. This intelligence relates to intrapersonal intelligence and interpersonal intelligence, classifications proposed by Gardner (1993), and it draws heavily from spiritual intelligence (Zohar & Marshall, 1994) and emotional intelligence (Goleman, 1995).

Values intelligence: Humanistic, spiritual and ethical values

This intelligence is what differentiates the school from other organizations, and it serves as "the keystone" for the schools' other intelligences. It comprises three elements.

a. *Humanistic values:* Values intelligence in the sphere of humanistic values is the ability to enable the feelings of pupils and staff members to be expressed and recognized, through consideration and respect. The practical expression of this intelligence is an awareness of feelings, emotional management, the ability to understand what motivates other people and how to work together. This intelligence also includes attributes such as motivation, perseverance, controlling feelings and moods, and not allowing pressure to ruin the ability to think and act.

b. *Spiritual values:* Values intelligence in the sphere of spiritual values focuses on the ability to strive towards harmony, peace and spirituality. Spirituality is perceived as being the source of creativity. It sparks one's creative ability, enables consideration of people and events with empathy and encourages loyalty and caring, hope and compassion. Schools can define spirituality in various ways, but the basic idea underlying the different interpretations is that spirituality means recognizing the value of life and human beings, and recognizing the potential contribution of each person to others and to every member of the organization.

c. *Ethical values:* Values intelligence in the sphere of ethical values is the school's ability to define its ethical purpose and express this in practical terms as fairness, justice and equality. Ethical intelligence can find its practical expression within the curriculum, as well as through the proper distribution of resources within the school.

Values intelligence is based on emotional intelligence (Goleman, 1995) as well as spiritual intelligence (Zohar & Marshall, 1994). It requires a high level of self-awareness which, in turn, serves as a basis for empathy and a highly developed sense of social intelligence.

SCHOOL INTELLIGENCES IN RELATION TO INTELLIGENCE THEORIES

The combination of contextual intelligence and the intelligence of learning and experience allows one to choose the best strategy for adapting to the environment according to the classification of strategies proposed by Miles & Snow (1978 – see above for details). Reflective intelligence is closest in concept to learning and experience. Strategic intelligence can rely on Sternberg's componential sub-theory (Sternberg, 1988), which deals with mechanisms for processing information, performance components and knowledge acquisition components (sifting through the information that flows into the organization, dividing it into relevant and irrelevant information, comparing new knowledge with knowledge already in the organization's possession, and combining bits of information into a complete, coherent body of knowledge). Contextual intelligence, within the framework of the five intelligences, is very similar to – if not identical with – Sternberg's contextual sub-theory of intelligence. Collegial intelligence, is unique to the operation of an organization, where individuals join forces to work together. Ethical intelligence is unique, as emphasized above, to a school, although we may presume that other organizations also have distinct ethical values regarding which their members should display intelligent behavior.

The concept of school intelligence comprised of five intelligences is broader than Sternberg's triarchic theory of intelligence (Sternberg, 1988). According to Sternberg, an organization's processes and activities can be divided into the following three groups:

1. *Componential intelligence,* which includes three types of processes: (a) metacognitive processes: planning, supervision, control and decision-making; (b) performance processes: carrying out decision-making and problem-solving strategies; (c) knowledge-acquisition processes: processes for collecting information.

2. *Contextual intelligence*, which includes processes for studying the organizational environment, defining means for adapting to the environment using three strategies: adapting to the environment, shaping the environment to the organization's conditions, and selecting a different environment (by moving to a new geographic location or choosing a different sphere of occupation).

3. *Intelligence of learning and experience*, which includes processes of change and coping with new situations, identifying the key components needed to identify a solution, adding new information to existing information and combining bits of information to find a comprehensive solution. This type of intelligence also involves initiating a routine of cognitive process and allowing them to become automatic, such as work procedures, standards of work and a stable work environment.

The approach that the school's normative behavior directed towards maximum success in achieving its goals must be intelligent behavior comprised of five intelligences also corresponds with the findings obtained from the studies on effective schools. Below we see the connection between the different school intelligences and the eleven components that characterize effective schools (Sammons, 1999). Reflective intelligence includes both the components of the *learning organization* (no. 11) and *monitoring and supervision of the pupils' progress* (no. 8). Strategic intelligence includes *a common vision and shared goals* (no. 2), *a focus on teaching and learning* (no. 4), and *task-oriented teaching* (no. 5). Contextual intelligence includes *partnership between the school, the home and the community* (no. 10). This component is also a part of collegial intelligence, which includes the component of the school's *learning environment* (no. 3). Human intelligence includes *high expectations* from pupils and teachers (no. 6) as well as *positive reinforcement* (no. 7). Ethical intelligence includes the pupils' rights and obligations (no. 9). Thus, the findings of the school effectiveness studies provide an empirical basis for believing that the operation of a school based on the five intelligences will cause its level of effectiveness to be high. *Professional leadership* (no. 1) is the key to employing the school's processes of organizational intelligence, and without it the level of effectiveness will be lower.

THE SELF-MANAGED SCHOOL AS AN INTELLIGENT ORGANIZATION

The self-managed school is an organization whose decision-making core is internal. School-based management grew as an organizational-educational issue under the inspiration of the Effective School Movement, which established the goal of demonstrating that schools have the genuine capacity to have an impact on the education and development of their pupils. The effective school must be capable of overcoming the limitations and inadequacies found in the homes of pupils from lower socio-economic sectors of the population, and give them a better education than these homes can provide. The school's self-management is based on the fact that the school has significant autonomy in financial and administrative matters, and is subject to a minimum degree of supervision from the centralized authorities. In this way, the school's administrative goals can be defined according to the school's own characteristics and needs, while the teaching staff can (and must) be more responsible for how resources are used so they can address problems and engage in effective educational activities for the school's long-term development (David, 1989).

Beginning in the late 1970s, Israel became more aware of the need to increase the school's pedagogic and administrative independence. This concept, which was fundamentally different from the traditional idea of centralized administration, hoped to transfer the center of gravity from the Ministry of Education, the center, to the school. Attempts were made by the Education Ministry to increase school autonomy, aimed at expanding administrative decentralization, in order to achieve the following goals:

- Delegation of authority directly to the schools would enable them to concentrate on planning for education needs and budgeting them in the field;

- Authority and responsibility would be concentrated at the point closest to the pupil and his family;

- The school principal, staff and community would make effective use of existing resources based on the needs of the school and its pupils;

- Schools would be able to make real-time decisions better suited to addressing individual needs, because only the institution itself has the best vantage point for accurately assessing these needs;

- Fundamental and advanced conditions would be created to turn schools into "effective schools" characterized by clear institutional goals, staff satisfaction and high levels of achievement;

- An autonomous, enterprising management style would be ensured, one that seeks out resources rather than merely receiving them, adapts itself to the changing needs of the target population, the curriculum and the community at large, and helps relieve "bottlenecks" within a short period of time;

- A valid method would be developed for the assumption of responsibility, by combining responsibility with authority;
- A suitable, practical platform would be made available for involving parents and the community in education and developing the school's unique qualities as part of the greater community.

Before the 1996 academic year, the Ministry of Education decided to take things one step further in the decentralization of pedagogic and administrative authority, to turn schools into self-managed institutions. Self-managed schools were defined as institutions characterized by the following five points:

1. School-based definition of clear pedagogic goals for staff members;
2. Adaptation of the curriculum to the school's pedagogic goals;
3. School-based internal feedback for the purpose of advancing relevant pupil populations;
4. Expansion of the school's authority with regard to personnel matters;
5. Increased independence for the school in managing its budgets.

During the second half of the 1995 academic year, preparations began for implementation of the program as an experiment in nine schools. Two objectives were established for this experiment: (a) to provide relevant information in order to examine the model underlying the concept of school-based management; (b) to provide relevant information regarding the transition processes of traditional schools to school-based management. The experiment was introduced with the 1996 academic year, and was monitored by a follow-up study conducted by Friedman, Barma and Toren (1997). In this study, the researchers found that by the end of the first year of school-based management every school included in the experiment understood quite well the principles of self-management, its advantages and its limitations. The primary goals of the schools that had been part of the experiment on school-based management centered on the following three main issues:

1. Developing the pupils' individual capabilities (inculcating tools for acquiring knowledge, being able to choose subjects independently and to focus on them, etc.);
2. Developing civic abilities among the pupils (training the child to be a useful member of the community and society);
3. Developing an autonomous organization (this goal is centered on an organization comprised of teachers, pupils and parents who act autonomously).

Approximately one-half of the teachers (52%) indicated that the school goals had been defined by all of the teachers in the school, 42% of the teachers noted that the goals had been defined by the school staff, 5% stated that the goals had been defined by the principal himself, and 1% of the teachers indicated they didn't know who had defined the school's goals.

In a follow-up study conducted by the researchers (Friedman, Barma, & Toren, 2001), the self-managed school was defined this way:

> A self-managed school is an educational institution that defines for itself clear educational, social and administrative goals; in which the teachers, pupils, parents and the community share in decision-making; and whose principal and staff strive resolutely to achieve them. The pedagogy and administration in the school are flexible and change over time in accordance with the needs and desires of the various participants in the educational process. The school is largely independent in how it uses its personnel and financial resources, and resources are available to staff members, who are accorded flexibility in how they are used. The school's organizational climate is open and based on autonomy and trust. The school reports to the central authorities regarding the goals it has set, the manner in which it allocates its resources, the priorities it has defined, and its educational and social outcomes (ibid., p. 15).

Furthermore, the researchers found that self-managed schools, in accordance with the above definition, exhibit the following processes or phenomena:

1. *Feedback-based management:* The pedagogy and school organization are defined, and changed over time, through openness, sensitivity to what is happening "in the field," and awareness of the impact this effort and educational investment have on the service recipients and those involved in the education process. Teachers present their work to the parents, the school offers parents feedback on pupils' satisfaction with the programs it implements, parents are notified if their children stray from accepted performance levels.

2. *Goals:* The school has a clear vision that is known to everyone involved – teachers, parents and pupils – and the school's vision corresponds with its activities. The school establishes clear educational, social and administrative goals (as part of the school's philosophy and its vision), and the principal and staff work resolutely toward realizing them. The school's goals also reflect the desires of the pupils and the parents.

3. *Shared management:* Pupils, parents and community share in the processes and decisions under school-based management. Parents also participate in preparing (together with the teachers) social projects for the school; pupil representatives are included in making decisions in the school, and they are included on various committees and join in initiating or planning the school's social programs.

4. *Open organizational climate:* The school's curricula, as well as its organizational and educational frameworks, are flexible; authority is delegated to staff members, who are made to feel they are trusted.

5. *Autonomy in utilization of personnel and financial resources:* The school has a great deal of independence in deciding how to use its personnel and financial resources.

6. *Resources are available to the staff:* Resources are made available to members of the school staff (teachers and others), and they are entitled to use them with a great degree of freedom and flexibility.

The findings of the two follow-up studies (Friedman, Barma, & Toren, 1997, 2001) clearly indicate that the processes that characterize self-managed schools reflect a high level of several organizational intelligences:

a. *Feedback-based management.* This points to a high degree of reflective intelligence, in which the school's organization and pedagogy are defined and openly change over time, with sensitivity to what is happening "in the field" and awareness of the effect these efforts have on the educational activities. This reflection is also shared by parents and the community.

b. *Process of defining goals.* This indicates a high level of strategic intelligence, as it reflects efforts to formulate an organizational, pedagogic vision based on the values and goals of both staff and pupils. It also expresses the operative goals for the vision, as well as the means for carrying out and achieving the defined operative goals.

c. *Shared management.* This includes parents, teachers, pupils and the community, and indicates a high level of contextual intelligence, particularly regarding the community components and the system-oriented perspective of this intelligence.

d. *Open organizational climate.* This shows a high degree of *collegial intelligence*, especially regarding the components of support, mutual assistance and "giving credit" that are included in this intelligence.

e.   *The goals* specified in the research findings of Friedman, Barma and Toren (1997) point to a high level of *ethical intelligence*, and in particular, a high degree of humanistic intelligence (developing the pupil's individual capabilities, civil capabilities and autonomy).

The school's autonomy is related to its right to determine and define its own goals and values, which are linked to the general goals and values of the education system. In attempting to assess the goals related to the school's ethical intelligence, as seen in the studies of self-managed schools, we must remember that the schools included in the self-management program were not schools that had just been established. Rather these were schools that had been around for quite a while, schools possessing organizational and other values that had directed and guided their activities for many years. The study cannot offer findings regarding the changes that took place in these schools with the transition to self-management. Perhaps self-managed schools need to focus their attention on the issue of ethical intelligence in order to clarify their values, and ensure that these values are suited to those of society, and fit it with general policies around the country.

REFERENCES

Beare, H., Caldwell, B. J., & Millikan, R. H. (1994). *Creating an excellent school*. London: Routledge.

Binet, A. & Simon, T. (1909). New methods for the diagnosis of the intellectual level of subnormals. *Annals of Psychology, 11*, 191-205.

Browder, L. (1975). *Who's afraid of educational accountability?* Denver, CO: Cooperative Accountability Project.

Cattell, R. B. (1966). *The scientific analysis of personality*. Chicago: Aldine.

Ceci, S. J. (1990). *On intelligence…more or less: A bio-ecological treatise on intellectual development*. Englewood Cliffs, NJ: Prentice-Hall.

Coleman, J. S., Campbell, E. Q., Hobson, C. J., McPartland, J., Mood, A. M., Weinfeld, F. D., & York, R. L. (Eds.), (1966). *Equality of educational opportunity*. Washington, DC: US Government Printing Office.

Colman, A. M. (2001). *A dictionary of psychology*. Oxford: Oxford University Press.

David, J. L. (1989). Synthesis of research on school-based management. *Educational Leadership, 46*, 45-53.

Eysenck, H. J. (1979). *The structure and measurement of intelligence.* Berlin, Germany: Springer-Verlag.

Friedman, I., Barma, R., & Toren, S. (1997). *School-based management: Changing the school's management culture.* Jerusalem: Henrietta Szold Institute (in Hebrew).

Friedman, I., Barma, R., & Toren, S. (2001). *Self-management level in the school.* Jerusalem: Henrietta Szold Institute (in Hebrew).

Gardner, H. (1993). *Frames of mind: The theory of multiple intelligences.* New York: Basic Books.

Goleman, D. (1995). *Emotional intelligence.* New York: Bantam Books.

Hilgard, E. R. (1962). *Introduction to psychology* (3rd ed.). New York: Harcourt, Brace and World.

Kirst, M. (1990). *Accountability: Implications for state and local policy makers.* Washington, DC: Office of Educational Research and Improvement, Department of Education.

Klitgaard, R. E., & Hall, G. R. (1973). Are there unusually effective schools? *Journal of Human Resources, 10,* 35-47.

Leithwood, K. (1999). An organizational perspective on values for leaders of future schools. In P. T. Begley (Ed.), *Values and educational leadership* (pp. 25-50). New York: State University of New York Press.

MacGilchrist, B., Myers, K., & Reed, J. (1997). *The intelligent school.* London: Paul Chapman Publishing, Ltd.

Miles, R. E., & Snow, C. C. (1978). *Organizational structure and process.* New York: McGraw-Hill.

Moore, W. E. (1974). *In loco parentis: A research report from the generation study of secondary school students.* Sydney, NSW: NSW Education Department.

Nevo, B. (1997). *Human Intelligence.* Tel Aviv: The Open University (in Hebrew).

Reid, K., Hopkins, D., & Holly, P. (1988). *Towards the effective school.* Oxford: Blackwell.

Robey, D. (1986). *Designing organizations.* Homewood, IL: Irwin.

Rutter, M., Maughan, M., Mortimore, P., & Ouston, J. (1979). *Fifteen thousand hours: Secondary schools and their effect on children.* London: Basic Books.

Sammons, P. (1999). *School effectiveness.* Lisse, the Netherlands: Swets & Zeitlinger B.V.

Senge, P. (1990). *The fifth principle: The art and practice of the learning organization.* New York: Doubleday.

Sternberg, R. J. (1988). *The triarchic mind: A new theory of human intelligence.* New York: Viking.

Wechsler, D. (1958). *The measurement and appraisal of adult intelligence.* Baltimore: Williams.

Zohar, D., & Marshall, I. N. (1994). *The quantum society.* New York: Bloomsbury.

A THEORY OF LEARNING IN THE
SELF-MANAGING SCHOOL

Brian J. Caldwell

School-based management, also referred to as local management or self-management, is a feature of the school reform movement around the world. Caldwell and Spinks (1998) consider the building of systems of self-managing schools to be one of the three major "tracks" of change in education, the others being an unrelenting focus on learning outcomes and the creation of schools for the knowledge society. Once established, self-management appears irreversible. A noteworthy illustration is the support among the three major political parties in the British election in 1997, and its expansion under the Labor government to the extent that local education authorities are expected to decentralize a higher proportion of available funds than had been required under the Conservative government. It is not limited to the western or developed world, nor is it a policy thrust of a particular political ideology. A recent conference of UNESCO in Paris was concerned with implementation in developing nations. Most international aid agencies support major initiatives for the devolution of authority, responsibility and accountability to schools.

There is an increasing body of literature on developments in different nations. Each setting is unique and this is especially the case in Israel. Noteworthy is the account by Gibton, Sabar and Goldring (2000) of how principals of autonomous schools view implementation. Volansky (2001) provides a history of developments in Israel that is of great interest to researchers, policy-makers and practitioners in other nations, given its affirmation of issues arising elsewhere, but also its account of several distinctive features.

An important issue in every setting is the extent to which there is a theory of self-management that goes beyond descriptions of practice and statements of assumptions, beliefs and expectations. The purpose of this paper is to propose a theory of the self-managing school that is particularly concerned with the relationship between self-management and learning. Evidence is drawn from macro-research across national boundaries and micro-research that modeled the links to learning at the school and classroom levels.

Brian J. Caldwell

CONTEXT

While evidence will be drawn from different nations, particular attention will be given to research and development in Victoria, Australia. Australia is a federation of six states and two territories. Education is the constitutional responsibility of the states, although the national (commonwealth) government plays a major role because it provides much of the funds through general and special purpose grants. Approximately 70% of pupils attend schools owned and operated by the government and about 30% attend schools owned and operated by churches or other non-government organizations. There are roughly 1600 government schools in Victoria.

There has been a steady shift toward self-management in all Australian states over the last 30 years, but Victoria has gone further than any other in a nation of traditionally centralized school systems. It is now the largest system of public education anywhere to have decentralized as much as 90% of its state budget to schools for local decision-making, being 93.7% in 2001 (DEET, 2001). The comparable figure in Britain is 87% under the enhanced self-management policies of the Blair government.

There are four noteworthy features about the management of public schools in Victoria. First, is the decentralization of the budget. Second, is a curriculum and standards framework (CSF) in eight key learning areas that applies to all schools. Third, all except short-term staff members are employed by the state, even though they are selected at the school level. Fourth, is a framework of accountability that requires all schools to report to their communities and the school system on an annual and triennial basis regarding a range of indicators, with system-wide testing of pupils in several key learning areas at two points in primary education and one point in secondary. The integrating mechanism for this approach to school management is the school charter. All schools have a charter, which is a relatively short document that reflects an agreement between a school and its community on the one hand, and the school and the state education department on the other. It sets out the special nature of the school, priorities for planning and budgeting, and strategies for achieving those priorities. The charter has a three-year duration and is the focus of the triennial review. A school council, a majority of whose members are parents, makes policy and approves the budget of each school. The principal is the chief executive officer.

It is important to note that this approach to self-management has evolved over 30 years, with periodic major steps that raised the extent of local authority and responsibility to a new level. The last such step change followed the election of the

Kennett government in 1992 (see Caldwell & Hayward, 1998 for an account of the design and implementation of this reform). The Kennett government lost in 1999 and the new Bracks government commissioned an enquiry, which has recommended that the broad features of the 1992 reforms should be maintained, including self-managing schools.

THE CONCEPT OF THE SELF-MANAGING SCHOOL

The term "self-management" rather than "school-based management" is used in this paper. It is helpful to clarify the concept of the self-managing school, especially the roles of central authorities and schools.

Decisions with regard to resources are central to self-management, as illustrated in the definition of Caldwell and Spinks (1998) based on their earlier conceptualization (Caldwell & Spinks, 1988) and further refinement by Bullock and Thomas (1997):

> A self-managing school is a school in a system of education to which there has been decentralized a significant amount of authority and responsibility to make decisions about the allocation of resources within a centrally determined framework of goals, policies, standards and accountabilities. Resources are defined broadly to include knowledge, technology, power, materiel, people, time, assessment, information and finance (Caldwell & Spinks, 1998, pp. 4-5).

It is important to stress that "a self-managing school is not an autonomous school nor is it a self-governing school, for each of these kinds of schools involve a degree of independence that is not provided in a centrally determined framework" (Caldwell & Spinks, 1998, p. 5). The role of government in the "centrally determined framework" is noteworthy. A recent statement on self-managing schools in Victoria referred to

> an important caveat to the doctrine of self-management: Government clearly reserves the right to intervene where it believes it is necessary to ensure the appropriate levels of outcomes for all students. This caveat is part of an overall commitment to equity in education and training and is demonstrated in several initiatives (DEET, 2001, p. 1).

Operating in such a framework does not conflict with principals' preferences for self-management. It is noteworthy that principals in Britain value the central framework provided by their local education authorities. The results of a recent MORI poll of 1,000 principals included the following findings:

- 94% felt that local education authorities should stay;

- 78% stated that local education authorities are best placed to support and challenge schools that are causing concern;

- 93% believed their local education authorities had been helpful in the implementation of literacy and numeracy strategies.

Secretary of State David Blunkett stated that, "If Government reform is to be a success, central intervention must be balanced by autonomy for individuals, local communities, schools" (DfEE, 2001).

THREE GENERATIONS OF STUDIES ON THE IMPACT OF SELF-MANAGEMENT

After several decades of reform, it is fair to ask about the extent to which there has been any impact on scholastic outcomes for pupils. It is sobering to note the consistent finding in early research that there appear to be few, if any, direct links between local management, self-management or school-based management and learning outcomes (Malen, Ogawa, & Kranz, 1990; Summers & Johnson, 1996). Some researchers have noted that such gains are unlikely to be achieved in the absence of purposeful links between capacities associated with school reform – in this instance, local management – and what occurs in the classroom, in learning and teaching and the support of learning and teaching (see Bullock & Thomas, 1997; Cheng, 1996; Hanushek, 1996, 1997; Levačić, 1995; OECD, 1994; Smith, Scoll, & Link, 1996).

New ground is broken in this paper to the extent that research of the kind cited above can now be seen as constituting the first generation of studies of self-management, and that second and third generations of studies are now evident. It is in the third generation that the nature of the correlation between self-management and learning outcomes can be mapped in a manner that can be trustworthy in policy and practice.

The primary purpose of this paper is to report school-based evidence of links between self-management and learning outcomes for pupils in the third generation of studies. This evidence confirms the generally positive ratings of principals in second generation studies in public education systems where all elements of a comprehensive reform program have been in place for several years. Particular attention is given to findings from a five-year longitudinal project in Victoria. Links between self-management and learning outcomes are modeled and mapped. The paper concludes with implications for policy-makers and practitioners.

THE INCONCLUSIVE NATURE OF THE CORRELATION IN FIRST- AND SECOND-GENERATION STUDIES

The research that constitutes the main focus of attention in this paper is in fact from the third generation of studies on the broad phenomenon of self-management. Two earlier generations are discernible, the first of which was concerned with the impact of self-management, with most studies undertaken in the United States. The much-cited work of Malen, Ogawa and Kranz (1990) falls into this category, with Summers and Johnson (1996) providing a meta-analysis of the first generation. They located 70 studies that purported to be evaluations of self-management, but only 20 of these employed a systematic approach and only seven included a measure of pupil outcomes. They concluded that:

> There is little evidence to support the notion that self-management is effective in increasing student performance. There are very few quantitative studies, the studies are not statistically rigorous, and the evidence of positive results is either weak or non-existent (p.80).

Apart from the "overwhelming obstacles" in the means for assessing the impact of self-management, Summers and Johnson drew attention to the fact that few initiatives "identify student achievement as a major objective. The focus is on organizational processes, with virtually no attention to how process changes may affect student performance" (Summers & Johnson, 1996, pp. 92-93).

For Hanushek, the findings are not surprising because of the absence of a purposeful link between self-management and pupil performance. He noted the review of Summers and Johnson and observed that "decentralization of decision-making has little general appeal without such linkage and, indeed, could yield worse results with decentralized management pursuing its own objectives not necessarily related closely to student performance" (Hanushek, 1996, p. 45).

In a report on the effects of school resources on pupil achievement, Hanushek (1997, p. 156) drew attention to the finding "that simply decentralizing decision-making is unlikely to work effectively unless there exist clear objectives and unless there is direct accountability." It is the absence of this framework that characterizes the context for what are described herein as first generation studies. Self-management in the United States was and, for the most part, continues to be a modest initiative compared to local management in England and Wales, or the self-managing schools of Victoria. On the decentralization side, few resources were shifted to the school level for local decision-making. On the centralization side, curriculum and standards frameworks and requirements for accountability were rudimentary in most instances. Self-management was, for the most part, a well-intentioned effort to empower teachers and, to a limited extent, the community, and there was little correlation between expectation, process or outcome and pupil learning.

The second generation of studies accompanied the more far-reaching reforms in self-management, with most of the available budget in a school system decentralized to the local level within a comprehensive and centrally-determined curriculum, standards and accountability framework, as in Victoria. In general, the findings have been as inconclusive as the first generation. Levačić (1995, p. 190) found that, of four criteria associated with intentions for the local management of schools in Britain (effectiveness, efficiency, equity and choice), "cost-efficiency is the one for which there is most evidence that local management has achieved the aims set for it by government," especially through the opportunity it provides for schools to purchase at a lower cost for a given quality or quantity than in the past, and by allowing resource mixes that were not possible or readily attainable under previous, more centralized, arrangements. For effectiveness, she concluded that there is "little evidence from this [case study] sample of schools of local management stimulating any significant changes in the way schools operate with respect to their core technology of teaching and learning" (Levačić, 1995, p. 105).

In Britain, as elsewhere, there was no research that endeavored to map a cause-and-effect relationship between local management and discretionary use of resources on the one hand, and improved learning outcomes for pupils on the other hand, based on the findings of studies that yielded strong opinion-based evidence that gains had been made (for example, Bullock & Thomas, 1994). Drawing predominantly on evidence from Britain (England and Wales) but referring also to outcomes elsewhere, Bullock and Thomas concluded that:

> It may be that the most convincing evidence of the impact of local management is on the opportunities which it has provided for managing the environment and resources for learning, both factors that can act to support the quality of learning in schools. What remains elusive, however, is clear-cut evidence of these leading through to direct benefits on learning, an essential component if we are to conclude that it is contributing to higher levels of efficiency (Bullock & Thomas, 1997, p. 217).

Bullock and Thomas then went to the heart of the issue:

> If learning is at the heart of education, it must be central to our final

discussion of decentralization. It means asking whether, in their variety of guises, the changes characterized by decentralization have washed over and around children in classrooms, leaving their day-to-day experiences largely untouched. In asking this question, we must begin by recognizing that structural changes in governance, management and finance may leave largely untouched the daily interaction of pupils and teachers (Bullock & Thomas, 1997, p. 219).

A review of reform in Australia, Britain and New Zealand, Sweden and the United States led Whitty, Power and Halpin (1998, p. 111) to conclude that "there were insufficient grounds to claim that self-managing schools are currently enhancing student attainment." While these authors fail to cite findings from third-generation studies of the kind set out below, their conclusion is generally fair as far as findings in second-generation studies are concerned.

CLARIFYING THE LINKS IN THIRD GENERATION STUDIES

A third generation of studies emerged during the last two years of the 1990s. The policy context was the same as for the second generation, namely, local management in England and Wales and self-management in Victoria, with the emergence of more comprehensive and coherent systemic reform in the United States, such as in Chicago. There are, however, three important differences to mark this generation of study. First, by the late 1990s, a substantial set of data on pupil achievement had been established as a result of system-wide tests that enabled change at the local level to be tracked over several years. Schools were also able to draw on an increasingly extensive pool of other indicators. Second, the policy framework had become more explicit with respect to expectations for schools to make the link between elements in the school reform program and learning outcomes for pupils. This reflected changes on track 2 ("an unrelenting focus on learning outcomes") in the classification of Caldwell and Spinks (1998). Third, researchers were utilizing an increasingly sophisticated array of techniques for analyzing data, including structural equation modeling and data envelope analysis, along with more focused approaches to case study.

Macro-analysis of TIMSS data on pupil achievement

Support for policy settings that balance centralization and decentralization in a system of self-managing schools comes from recent analysis of pupil achievement in

39 nations. The Third International Mathematics and Science Study (TIMSS) was the largest international comparative study of pupil achievement ever undertaken. Information was gathered on a range of factors as part of the project, including pupil and family characteristics, resources and teacher characteristics, and institutional settings. Analysis of the performance of more than 260,000 pupils from 39 nations was undertaken at Kiel University in Germany and reported by Woessmann (2000). Regression analysis yielded interesting findings that confirm the efficacy of a balanced approach.

Woessmann (2000, p. 79) concluded that "the only policy that promises positive effects is to create an institutional system where all the people involved have an incentive to improve student performance." Among the policy settings that are favorable to pupil performance are the following:

- Centralized examinations;

- Centralized control mechanisms in curricular and budgetary affairs;

- School autonomy in process and personnel decisions;

- An intermediate level of administration performing administrative tasks and providing educational funding;

- Individual teachers having both incentives and powers to select appropriate teaching methods;

- Scrutiny of pupils' educational performance;

- Encouraging parents to take an interest in teaching matters.

It is important to note that "centralized control mechanisms in curricular and budgetary affairs" refers to centrally determined frameworks, not to the manner of implementation at the school level. In the case of budgets, this refers to the existence of a funding mechanism that specifies how funds shall be allocated to schools; schools then determine how these funds are deployed at the local level.

Comprehensive reform in Chicago

An increasing number of school districts in the United States are establishing local management on the scale now evident in England and Wales, but these are still a small minority among the 15,000 jurisdictions in that nation. The public school district in Chicago is one such system with a comprehensive and relatively coherent set of reforms dating from 1988. The stated goal of the Chicago School Reform Act was to raise the level of pupil achievement to match national norms. According to Hess (1999) the chief mechanism for achieving this goal is a system of school-based decision-making, with school councils and local responsibility for school improvement planning, budget allocation and selection of staff within a framework of system-wide standards and tests.

There is promising but contested evidence of the impact of school-based decision-making and learning outcomes in Chicago. As reported by Lawton (1997, p. 3), reading scores in 1990 were compared with those achieved in 1997. Nearly half of the schools included in the study posted impressive gains, with Donald R. Moore, Executive Director of Designs for Change that conducted the study reporting "'strong evidence that the schools that have taken the greatest advantage of that decision-making opportunity [under decentralization] are improving pupil achievement," with the most improved schools having higher ratings stemming from a school council focus on improvement, principals, teacher influence, teacher parent relationships, safety, cooperative teacher effort and learning. While the researchers included controls on pupil backgrounds in their analysis, other researchers not involved in the study questioned whether sufficient attention had been paid to changes in pupil demographics on a school-by-school basis.

The most powerful evidence of a correlation between self-management and learning outcomes in Chicago, arguably in any jurisdiction, has emerged in the longitudinal studies of the Consortium on Chicago School Research (Bryk, 1998; Bryk et al., 1998). Value-added measures of pupil achievement over a number of years were included in the design of an innovative productivity index. A model of direct and indirect effects, including a capacity for self-management, was derived. As with the earlier study cited above, this evidence is contested. Hess (1999) reported mixed experience in the analysis of longitudinal achievement data over a 10-year period and detailed case studies of experience in 14 schools. His conclusion on the importance of resources is striking:

> Budget analyses... and interview comments from principals show that discretionary funds were important to schools in their efforts to change. Principals said over and over that these funds were the engine that allowed them to make changes in their schools. We found, however, that their efforts were compromised to the extent that they were forced to siphon off resources to maintain programs cut by the board of education to balance the budget each year. Further, we have seen that some schools spent a lot of new discretionary money without much to show for those expenditures in terms of effective use of funds to foster improved student learning. More

money was crucial to improvement in the schools where improvement was taking place. But more money did not automatically translate into better student outcomes. How the money was used does appear to matter (Hess, 1999, p. 81).

Research in Victoria helps explain how money may be used in efforts to achieve improvements in learning outcomes for pupils.

Self-managing schools in Victoria

The objectives and purposes of the reforms in Victoria in the 1990s range from educational ("to enhance pupil learning outcomes," "to actively foster the attributes of good schools"); professional ("to recognize teachers as true professionals," "to allow principals to be true leaders"); community ("to determine the destiny of the school, its character and ethos") and accountability ("for the progress of the school and the achievement of its pupils").

Findings cited here are drawn from several research projects. The primary source is the Cooperative Research Project, a joint endeavor of the Education Department of Victoria (the state agency responsible for public education), the Victorian Association of State Secondary Principals, the Victorian Primary Principals Association, and the University of Melbourne. The project began in mid-1993 and concluded in mid-1998, completing on schedule a planned five-year longitudinal study of processes and outcomes. Seven statewide surveys of representative samples of principals were conducted and these covered virtually every aspect of the reform, including its impact on learning outcomes for pupils (Cooperative Research Project 1994, 1995a, 1995b, 1996, 1997, 1998). Seventeen investigations, including two reported here (Hillier, 1999; Wee, 1999a, 1999b) focused on discrete elements, including leadership, professional development, new workplace practices, resource allocation and school improvement.

More recent work, including the studies of Hillier and Wee, expanded upon the work of the Cooperative Research Project in an international collaborative effort, pooling research from Australia (University of Melbourne), Britain (Open University) and the United States (University of Wisconsin at Madison). There were two purposes for this larger effort, which was supported by the Australian Research Council: first, to develop models for funding that transcend national boundaries; and second, to investigate the impact of school-based decisions about resource allocation on learning outcomes for pupils.

Successive surveys of the Cooperative Research Project consistently found that principals believed there had been a moderate to high level of realization of the expected benefit in respect to improved learning outcomes for pupils. In the final survey in 1997, 84% gave a rating of 3 or more on the 5-point scale (where 1 is "low" and 5 is "high").

As in the second generation of studies, such findings do not shed any light on the extent to which the capacities fostered by the reform impact on learning outcomes. Structural equation modeling using LISREL 8 (Jöreskog & Sörbom, 1993) was employed in the analysis of data in the 1995, 1996 and 1997 survey. The model reported here derives from the 1997 survey (Cooperative Research Project, 1998).

The first step was to create seven clusters of related survey items and to treat these as constructs. These constructs were formed from 45 survey items concerned with attitudes to the reform (Confidence in the attainment of "schools of the future" [SOF] objectives), support (Curriculum and standards framework [CSF] curriculum support), and outcomes (Curriculum and learning benefits, Curriculum improvement due to the curriculum and standards framework, Planning and resource allocation benefits, School and community benefits, Personnel and professional benefits).

Figure 1 illustrates the explanatory regression model that depicts the interdependent effects among variables (in this instance, latent variables that represent the constructs) on the variable *Curriculum and learning benefits*, which is the object of interest in this section of the paper. Standardized path coefficients are shown, representing the direct effects (all paths are statistically significant beyond the $p < 0.05$ level by univariate two-tailed test). The fit between the data and model is very good indeed, with an "Adjusted goodness of fit index" of 0.969, indicating that almost all (96.9%) of the variances and co-variances in the data are accounted for by the model.

The path coefficients may be interpreted in this manner. The direct effect of *Personnel and professional benefits* on *Curriculum and learning benefits* is indicated by a path coefficient of 0.299. This indicates that an increase in the measure of *Personnel and professional benefits* of 1 standard deviation, as reflected in ratings of principals, produces an increase in the measure of *Curriculum and learning benefits* of 0.299 of a standard deviation.

The model shows that three variables have a direct effect on *Curriculum and learning benefits*, which includes improved learning outcomes for pupils. These are *Personnel and professional benefits* (which reflects ratings for realization of the expected benefits of better personnel management, enhanced professional development, shared decision-making, improved staff performance, more effective organization following restructure, increased staff satisfaction and an enhanced capacity to attract staff);

Curriculum improvement due to CSF (which reflects ratings for improved capacity for curricular planning, establishing levels and standards for pupils, moving to a curriculum based on learning outcomes and meeting the needs of pupils); and *Confidence in attainment of SOF objectives.*

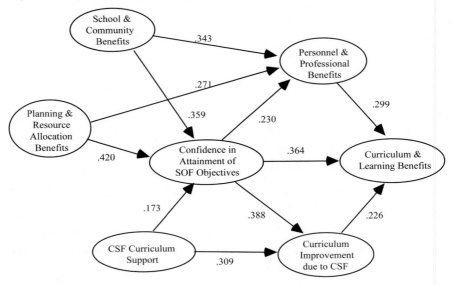

Note: SOF = Schools of the future (the reform initiative that included a higher level of self-management).

CSF = Curriculum and standards framework

Figure 1. Explanatory regression model showing interdependent effects among factors influencing percieved curriculum and learning benefits (Cooperative Research Project, 1998).

Noteworthy are the pathways of indirect effects, illustrated for *Planning and resource allocation benefits*, which is mediated in respect to its effect on *Curriculum and learning benefits* through *Personnel and professional benefits* and *Confidence in attainment of SOF objectives*. To put it another way, realizing the expected benefits of better resource management, clearer sense of direction, increased accountability and responsibility, greater financial and administrative flexibility, and improved long-term planning, will have no direct effect on *Curriculum and learning benefits* but will have an indirect effect to the extent they impact on *Personnel and professional benefits* which, in turn, have a direct effect on *Curriculum and learning benefits*.

Also noteworthy are the constructs that have direct effects on *Confidence in attainment of SOF objectives*. High ratings of confidence were associated with high ratings for the achievement of *Planning and resource allocation benefits, School and community benefits* and *CSF curriculum support*. The likely explanation is that unless principals experience benefits in these last three domains, they are unlikely to have confidence in the reform.

The findings in these surveys are limited to the extent that they are based on the perceptions of principals rather than measures of pupil achievement. This has been a concern in most efforts to determine the impact of reform in recent years. In the case of the Cooperative Research Project, there was no systemwide base-line data on pupil achievement when the reform was implemented, and efforts to compare achievement in schools in the pilot phase with that in schools that had not entered at the outset were thwarted by a union ban on the collection of data.

Principals were asked to indicate the basis for their rating of the extent to which the expected benefit of improved pupil learning had been realized. They rated the importance of certain achievement measures and indicators of attendance, time allocations in curriculum, participation rates, exit/destination data, parent opinion, staff opinion and level of professional development (23 indicators were provided). Most principals indicated moderate to high importance for these indicators in arriving at their ratings. In the absence of direct access to pupil achievement data that would put the matter beyond doubt, one way or the other, a high level of trustworthiness ought be attached to these findings, given consistency in ratings, the stability of the model over three years of surveys, and declarations by principals that they took account of a range of indicators in forming their judgments.

MAPPING THE LINKS

Two sets of case studies in Victoria (Hillier, 1999; Wee, 1999b) help illuminate the links illustrated in the model in Figure 1 under conditions where principals report improved learning outcomes. Are the correlations that were evident in the model confirmed in extensive on-site investigations in particular schools where improvement is claimed? The research design in both studies thus started with schools where principals made such a claim. The first task was to test the validity of these claims, drawing on evidence in the particular schools selected for study. The second task was to seek explanations for how such improvement occurred and then to match it against the correlations or pathways that are shown in the model in Figure 1.

A case study approach was adopted. The studies differed in one important respect. Hillier's was conducted in two stages, with one round of data collected in 1996, soon after each element of the reform was in place and the pool of indicators was in the early stages of implementation. The second stage took place in 1998, when Hillier returned to the three schools to assess progress since 1996.

Wee's study, as reported in detail here, was conducted in late 1997 when the pool of indicators was well developed and a substantial body of evidence was available to test claims of improved learning outcomes. A feature of her study was the relentless probing for evidence and an extended pursuit of explanations to account for improvement where this was found. The research was carried out in four primary schools in the Western Metropolitan Region in Melbourne. Eight primary schools that had expressed a willingness to participate in case studies following the survey of principals in 1996 were invited to name up to three areas of the curriculum where improvement in pupil learning had occurred and where they believed evidence was available to substantiate their claim. Four schools were selected, reflecting diversity in size, setting and curriculum area where evidence of improvement was claimed. A wide range of curriculum areas was covered.

Findings revealed that schools could cite evidence that their efforts have led to improved outcomes for pupils. They drew on many sources of data in recognizing improved pupil learning in their schools. This illustrated the capacity being developed in the system to gather information about the performance of schools. It was noted above, in connection with the findings in the final survey of principals in the Cooperative Research Project, that most respondents had been able to draw on up to 23 indicators in making their judgment of the extent to which there had been improvement in learning outcomes for pupils.

Maps of direct and indirect links were prepared by Wee for each school using the rigorous approach to data collection, data display and data reduction for qualitative research proposed by Miles and Huberman (1994). These maps show how school capacity associated with being a "school of the future" had led to improved outcomes for pupils. A synthesis of maps from the four schools is found in Figure 2.

Actions at the school level that have had a direct impact on pupil learning are in the spheres of professional development, implementation of the curriculum and standards framework and monitoring. The impact of resource allocation is indirect, mediated through curriculum, professional development, monitoring and staffing.

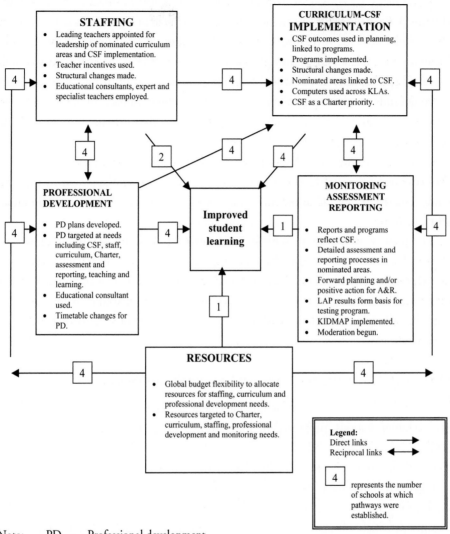

Note: PD = Professional development

CSF = Curriculum and standards framework

LAP = Learning assessment project (system-wide testing of pupil achievement in selected key learning areas)

KIDMAP = Computer-based management information system to support learning

Figure 2. Synthesis of maps from four schools showing direct and indirect
links between elements of self-managing schools and learning outcomes for pupils
(Wee, 1999b).

These maps are consistent with the explanatory model based on survey findings (Figure 1). Each of the direct and indirect links illustrated in Figure 2 is a manifestation of the links depicted in Figure 1, with the exception of the impact of monitoring, including assessment and reporting, which is not contained in the explanatory model. Developing a capacity at the school level for gathering and utilizing a wide range of techniques for monitoring pupil progress has had a direct impact on improvement in pupil learning and on the way staff have implemented the curriculum and standards framework.

Evidence from the four schools suggests that there have been important changes in the "core technology of teaching and learning" which was not apparent in the case study research of Levačić in the earlier days of local management in Britain (Levačić, 1995, p. 105).

The pool of indicators in schools in Victoria has now become quite extensive. Principals and their colleagues have an unprecedented amount of data to monitor developments in their schools, including levels of pupil achievement and other learning outcomes. Clearly, the next stage in this third generation of studies is to undertake more broadly-based research across a representative sample of schools that draws on these findings.

SELF-MANAGING SCHOOLS IN DEVELOPING NATIONS

The worldwide trend towards self-management is further illustrated by initiatives in developing nations, supported by international aid agencies, including the World Bank, UNESCO and UNICEF. UNESCO hosted a forum in Paris in February 2001 that provided an opportunity for the sharing of experiences in recent years.

It is likely that some of the best evidence regarding the impact of self-management on learning outcomes may come from these settings. An explanation lies in the manner in which self-management has been linked to learning. A published account is expected soon of experience in Indonesia where the author was invited to serve as international evaluator of a project supported by UNESCO and UNICEF under the title, "Creating Learning Communities for Children." Four initiatives were combined in a pilot project conducted in 79 schools in three provinces (Central Java, East Java and South Sulawesi), including the introduction of a limited form of self-management, with a small budget for each school; professional development for teachers; encouragement of parents and other members of the community to support their schools; and most important, changes to learning and teaching under the theme "active, joyful, effective learning." Improvement on key indicators such as pupil attendance and learning outcomes was documented for most schools.

IMPLICATIONS FOR POLICY-MAKERS AND PRACTITIONERS

The research suggests that structural rearrangements are but a precondition if there is to be any impact on learning outcomes. Whether there is impact depends on making links across several levels to reach the classroom and the pupil, so that "the changes characterized by decentralization have washed over and around children in classrooms" (Bullock & Thomas, 1997, p. 219).

The implications for policy-makers and practitioners are relatively clear. These may be expressed in the form of strategic intentions, along the lines proposed by Caldwell and Spinks (1998), who derived a set of 100 strategies from their review of developments on the three tracks for change around the world. The following reflect the findings reported in this paper. Each may be prefaced by an action statement for the system or school. For 1, this may be "In the metropolitan education authority, it is recognized that the primary purpose of self-management is ..." or "In the local secondary college, it is recognized that the primary purpose of self-management is ..." with the appropriate amendment in the subsequent text. Each such intention can form the basis of more detailed planning or the design and delivery of professional development programs.

1. The primary purpose of self-management is to make a contribution towards learning, so schools that aspire to succeed in this sphere will make an unrelenting effort to utilize all of the capacities that accrue with self-management to achieve that end.

2. There will be clear, explicit and planned links, either direct or indirect, between each of the capacities that come with self-management and activities in the school that relate to learning and teaching and the support of learning and teaching.

3. There is a strong association between the mix and capacities of staff and success in addressing needs and priorities in learning, so schools will develop a capacity to optimally select staff, taking account of these needs and priorities.

4. There is a strong association between the knowledge and skills of staff and learning outcomes for pupils, so schools will employ their capacity for self-management to design, select, implement or utilize professional development programs to help ensure these outcomes.

5. A feature of staff selection and professional development will be establishment of high performing teams whose work is needs-based and data-driven, supported by a culture that values quality, effectiveness, equity and efficiency.

6. Schools will have a capacity for 'backward mapping' in the design and implementation of programs for learning, starting with goals, objectives, needs and desired outcomes, and working backwards to determine courses of action that will achieve success, utilizing where possible and appropriate, the capacities that accrue with self-management.

7. A key task for principals and other school leaders is to help make effective the links between capacities for self-management and learning outcomes, and to ensure that support is available when these links break down or prove ineffective.

While there is much that is still uncertain about the nature and impact of school reform, it is evident that the means are at hand to create a system of public schools that will provide a high quality of education for all pupils and that will be professionally rewarding for teachers and other professionals. The challenge is how to put the pieces together. Ensuring an effective linkage between self-management and learning outcomes is a promising start. We are very close to a theory of learning in the self-managing school.

REFERENCES

Bryk, A. S.(1998, April). *Chicago school reform: Linkages between local control, educational supports and pupil achievement.* Paper presented with colleagues at the Consortium on Chicago School Research symposium at the annual meeting of the American Educational Research Association, San Diego, CA.

Bryk, A. S., Sebring, P. B., Kerbow, D., Rollow, S., & Easton, J. Q. (1998). *Charting Chicago school reform: Democratic localism as a lever for change.* Boulder, CO: Westview Press.

Bullock, A., & Thomas, H. (1994). *The Impact of local management in schools: Final report.* Birmingham: University of Birmingham and National Association of Head Teachers.

Bullock, A., & Thomas, H. (1997). *Schools at the center: A study of decentralization.* London: Routledge.

Caldwell, B. J., & Hayward, D. K. (1998). *The future of schools: Lessons from the reform of public education.* London: Falmer Press.

Caldwell, B. J., & Spinks, J. M. (1988). *The self-managing School.* London: Falmer Press.

Caldwell, B. J., & Spinks, J. M. (1998). *Beyond the self-managing school.* London: Falmer Press.

Cheng, Y. C. (1996). *School effectiveness and school-based management: A mechanism for development.* London: Falmer Press.

Cooperative Research Project (1994). *Base-line survey* (Report of the Cooperative Research Project on "Leading Victoria's Schools of the Future"). Directorate of School Education, Victorian Association of State Secondary Principals, Victorian Primary Principals Association, The University of Melbourne (Fay Thomas, chair) [available from Department of Education]

Cooperative Research Project (1995a). *One year later* (Report of the Cooperative Research Project on "Leading Victoria's Schools of the Future"). Directorate of School Education, Victorian Association of State Secondary Principals, Victorian Primary Principals Association, The University of Melbourne (Fay Thomas, chair) [available from Department of Education]

Cooperative Research Project (1995b). *Taking stock* (Report of the Cooperative Research Project on "Leading Victoria's Schools of the Future"). Directorate of School Education, Victorian Association of State Secondary Principals, Victorian Primary Principals Association, The University of Melbourne (Fay Thomas, chair) [available from Department of Education]

Cooperative Research Project (1996). *Three-year report card* (Report of the Cooperative Research Project on "Leading Victoria's Schools of the Future"). Directorate of School Education, Victorian Association of State Secondary Principals, Victorian Primary Principals Association, The University of Melbourne (Fay Thomas, chair) [available from Department of Education].

Cooperative Research Project (1997). *Still more work to be done, but... no turning back* (Report of the Cooperative Research Project on "Leading Victoria's Schools of the Future"). Department of School Education, Victorian Association of State Secondary Principals, Victorian Primary Principals Association, The University of Melbourne (Fay Thomas, chair) [available from Department of Education].

Cooperative Research Project (1998). *Assessing the outcomes* (Report of the Cooperative Research Project on "Leading Victoria's Schools of the Future"). Department of Education, Victorian Association of State Secondary Principals, Victorian Primary Principals Association, The University of Melbourne (Fay Thomas, Chair) [available from Department of Education].

Department for Education and Employment (2001, March 6). *'New heads' poll supports government's approach to education reform* (Press release). London: DfEE. Retrieved from http://www.dfee.gov.uk.

Department of Education, Employment and Training (2001). *An "actuals" school global budget: Steps towards enhanced self-management.* Melbourne, Australia.

Gibton, D., Sabar, N., & Goldring, E. B. (2000). How principals of autonomous schools in Israel view implementation of decentralization and restructuring policy: Risks, rights and wrongs. *Educational Evaluation and Policy Analysis, 22*(2), 193–210.

Hanushek, E. A. (1996). Outcomes, costs, and incentives in schools. In E. A. Hanushek & D. W. Jorgenson (Eds.), *Improving America's schools: The role of incentives* (paper 3, pp. 29-52). Washington, DC: National Academy Press.

Hanushek, E. A. (1997). Assessing the effects of school resources on pupil performance: An update. *Educational Evaluation and Policy Analysis, 19*(2), 141-164.

Hess, G. A. (1999). Understanding achievement (and other) changes under Chicago school reform. *Educational Evaluation and Policy Analysis, 21*(1), 67-83.

Hillier, N. (1999). *Educational reform and school improvement in Victorian primary schools, 1993-1999.* Unpublished doctoral dissertation, University of Melbourne, Melbourne, Australia.

Jöreskog, K. G., & Sörbom, D. (1993). *LISREL 8: User's reference guide.* Chicago: Scientific Software, Inc.

Lawton, M. (1997, November 5). Chicago study credits school-based reforms. *Education Week*, p. 3.

Levačić, R. (1995) *Local management of schools: Analysis and practice.* Buckingham: Open University Press.

Malen, B., Ogawa, R. T., & Kranz, J. (1990). What do we know about site-based management: A case study of the literature – A call for research. In W. Clune & J. Witte (Eds.), *Choice and control in American education: Vol. 2. The practice of choice, decentralization and school restructuring* (pp. 289-342). London: Falmer Press.

Miles, M. B., & Huberman, A. M. (1994). *Qualitative data analysis: An expanded sourcebook* (2nd ed.). Thousand Oaks, CA: Sage Publications.

OECD, Directorate of Education, Employment, Labor and Social Affairs, Education Committee (1994). *Effectiveness of schooling and of educational resource management: Synthesis of country studies* (points 22 and 23). Paris: OECD.

Smith, M. S., Scoll, B. W., & Link, J. (1996). Research-based school reform: The Clinton administration's agenda. In E. A. Hanushek & D. W. Jorgenson (Eds.), *Improving America's schools: The role of incentives* (pp. 9-27). Washington, DC: National Academy Press.

Summers, A. A., & Johnson, A. W. (1996). The effects of school-based management plans. In E. A. Hanushek & D. W. Jorgenson (Eds.), *Improving America's schools: The role of incentives* (pp. 75-96). Washington, DC: National Academy Press.

Volansky, A. (2001, April 2-3). *From experiment to educational policy: The transition in Israel schools to school-based management.* Paper presented at the First International Conference on School-Based Management, organized by the Israeli Ministry of Education, Kfar Maccabiah, Israel.

Wee, J. (1999a). *Improved pupil learning and leadership in self-managed schools.* Unpublished doctoral dissertation, University of Melbourne, Australia.

Wee, J. (1999b). *Making links in self-managed schools: Improved student learning and leadership.* Third in a series on excellence in education, School Effectiveness and Continuous Improvement Unit, Department of Education, Melbourne, Australia. (Available from the School Effectiveness and Continuous Improvement Unit, Department of Education, GPO Box 4367, Melbourne, 3000, Australia).

Whitty, G., Power, S., & Halpin, D. (1998). *Devolution and choice in education: The school, the state and the market.* Buckingham: Open University Press.

Woessmann, L. (2000). *School resources, educational institutions, and pupil performance: The international evidence.* Kiel Institute of World Economics, University of Kiel, Germany. Retrieved from http://www.uni-kiel.de/ifw/pub/kap/2000/kap983.htm.

Part II

Leadership

INNOVATIVE CONCEPTS FOR EFFECTIVE SCHOOL CULTURES: EARNED LEADERSHIP AND ELECTIVE CONTRIBUTORSHIP

Vivian Williams

INTRODUCTION

The cultures of all organizations respond to the influence of social and economic changes in their external environments. Additionally, cultural change produces both positive and negative effects through a conscious mutation of the internal organization, leading to the evolution of "new" cultures, which reflect the impact of differentiated processes of change (Kanter, 1989). In education, systemic reform introduces visible organizational changes such as those currently being implemented in several countries, e.g., decentralization of school governance and decision-making mechanisms. Subtle cultural changes that arise from ways in which schools are reorganized are greatly influenced by the demands of new decentralized systemic reform. For the specific purpose of this presentation, an examination of the effects of major changes in the education system of England and Wales might serve to illustrate the nature of cultural change in new opportunities for shared leadership within school systems.

CONTEXT: EDUCATIONAL REFORM IN ENGLAND AND WALES

Unprecedented legislative reforms in the education system introduced by successive Labor and Conservative governments, which have extended over a continuous period from the mid-1970s into the new millennium, have resulted in an unprecedented transformation in school organization and management of schools. Of many sweeping reforms, three have had profound effects on the organizational culture of schools.

First, the introduction of a prescribed national curriculum framework for teaching and learning involving a national system of performance-based testing of pupils followed by publication of test results on an individual school basis (Maclure, 1989). Second, a publicly demonstrable, nationally controlled, external inspection system of all schools on a four-year cycle was introduced in the early 1990s to provide a national database on individual school performance, with reports on every school published for the information of parents, teachers and local communities. Third, and within nationally prescribed parameters, the introduction of a universally devolved system of governance and control of schools, known as local management of schools (LMS) – similar to, but not identical with, other designated systems of school-based management (SBM). During the past two decades, key elements in the operation of LMS have been the devolution of financial and personnel control to the individual school level, within government prescribed criteria (Levačić, 1995). By the beginning of this century, the profound effects of these revolutionary changes in the governance and management of schools have completely altered the relationships among the "partners" or "stakeholders" in the education system (Williams, 1997).

In England and Wales, adaptation to unprecedented central government legislative reforms in the education system provides a continuous example of organizational change during the past 25 years. During that period a wholesale transformation of the governance, management and organization of schools and higher education has taken place. Briefly, the relative balance of power, authority and influence among traditional partners in education has shifted irrevocably, from control exercised by institutional "providers" to participatory "consumers" of education services – especially parents. Arising from more challenging and publicly accountable regulatory processes, central government control of educational policy has been explicitly strengthened. This centralized control has been achieved through rolling programs of parliamentary legislation and through an effusion of government appointed agencies, or quangos, since 1979. Formulation and control of policies formerly exercised by largely autonomous local education authorities (LEAs) have been dramatically reduced. The pendulum of power and influence has swung decisively towards central control resulting in secure public accountability processes through the exercise of constrained parental choice, removal of geographical zoning and circumscribed professional autonomy within schools (Williams, 1997).

Monitoring the operational application and outcomes of a broad and demanding range of national policies at the school level has become an explicit, and not always harmonious, partnership between providers and consumers. For most of the 20th century, and in an uncentralized education system, the conventional mechanism of accountability at the school level was a joint concern of the LEAs, which were elected district bodies in clearly demarcated geographical areas – rural counties, cities or towns. Within a broad national legislative framework, with many imprecise policy guidelines, each LEA possessed considerable autonomy over the formulation and development of educational policies within its boundaries (Williams, 1995).

CULTURAL CHANGE

One of the most significant outcomes of continuous government-led innovation has been the gradual acceleration of cultural change within schools. Changes have been notable in the broadening of authority structures, clearly visible in the distribution of organizational functions. During the 1960s, evolutionary change in the ways in which the majority of secondary schools were managed increased the number of tiered levels in hierarchically-organized schools – particularly at the secondary level. For example, increasingly specialized curricula, counseling functions and an upsurge in the number of pupils attending school underlined the necessity for, and introduction of, defined "middle-management" tiers in secondary schools. Similarly, a modest differentiation of roles through the appointment of "consultant" teachers with specific responsibilities for areas of the curriculum, e.g. literacy and mathematics, emerged in primary and, especially, in middle schools in response to the increasing organizational complexity.

In response to developments following major school reorganization during the 1960s and 1970s, in-service and professional training programs for teachers expanded rapidly. Many of these programs were focused on introductory training in the "management" of schools. During this period few school management studies or research projects existed in UK schools. Management programs for teachers relied almost exclusively on literature, models and techniques derived from industrial and commercial studies and practice. Accordingly, almost all education training programs provided by LEAs and universities were dependent upon theories and concepts based on the experience, research and practices developed in non-educational organizations. However, the work of such notable authors as Adair (1988), Bennis (1987), Blake and Mouton (1985), Burns (1978), Handy (1999), Hersey and Blanchard (1982), Kouzes and Posner (1987), and Likert (1967) have contributed to a better understanding by educators concerning the ways in which organizations function. All have clarified characteristics and patterns of human behavior within hierarchical organizations. The relevance and general applicability of more recent studies to relatively static hierarchical school organizations, together with "new" management thinking on the centrality of interpersonal relationships, has extended the range of options available to create more dynamic school cultures. Systemic reform characterized by the recent organizational swing towards self-governance of schools, in conjunction with a reduction in LEA control, and management training programs promoted by central government (such as the national qualification for head teachers and other teachers under the direction of the Teacher Training Agency [TTA]) are requiring teachers to "manage" and "lead" schools within school cultures that are fundamentally different from those of a decade earlier. However, many head teachers remain unconvinced that the prescribed training addresses the needs of the new school cultures because of its emphasis on the logistics of organizational site-management, rather than providing the leadership development perceived by teachers as being necessary to enhance their professional, rather than merely administrative, roles.

Fundamental changes in school cultures typically bring about serious problems, often arising from the pace of change and lack of preparatory understanding of the implications for organizational adaptation and professional relationships. The human condition has always demonstrated a tenacious capacity for resistance to change and teachers are not immune (Gross, Giacquinta, & Bernstein, 1971). Furthermore, and in the opinion of this author, a major problem for schools is directly attributable to the conventional dependence of in-service training programs on management studies and research derived from business and industrial settings. With few exceptions, during the past difficult decade schools have had to cope with unprecedented demands in ways that have won the admiration of parents and members of governing bodies. But this collective success has been achieved with a concomitant loss of some of the traditional strengths of the head teacher role. For many practitioners there has been a decline in the internationally admired role of the head teacher as the leading professional in schools through reduced class and pupil contact. The tradition of *primus inter pares*, much prized throughout the 20th century in the British system among parents and fellow teachers, is waning under pressure to assume LMS roles as business site-managers.

Apart from reservations over the pace of change, overseas educators also tend to be puzzled at the direction of cultural development. For example, many research studies and projects conducted in the USA over the past several years in the search for more effective schools have concluded that in the development of effective schools, the crucial role for principals is the acquisition of expertise in curricular and pedagogic domains. In effect, the more successful principals are those who function as instructional leaders. An unmistakable trend in the current "preparation for principalship" programs in the USA and associated advanced degree studies leading to principal certification is a clear emphasis on courses in curriculum development, learning theory and human resource development. Former emphases on post-experience programs on school law and financial management are in decline. It is not surprising, therefore, that major legislative reforms in England and Wales were not universally supported by head teachers, whose careers had been founded on success based on high quality teaching and interpersonal skills. The new requirements to develop expertise in personnel, accounting and public relations management supported by statutory ordinances continue to provide sources of regret and some resistance as "educationally focused" cultures in schools are perceived as being displaced by those more familiar to business management practitioners. For many practitioners, a paradox exists in that the literature on effective schools advocates the development of school cultures as "learning communities" (Sergiovanni, 1992) rather than business organizations. In addition, in the context of undertaking their professional roles in learning communities, characteristic school cultures have recognized teachers as "leaders" for their students, a perception endorsed by other teachers and many parents (Ball & Goodson, 1985; Nias, 1980).

With few exceptions, the literature directly relevant to educational organizations remains deficient in clarifying the ways in which more effective operation of professionally staffed public service organizations might be achieved. The continuing difficulty in adjusting to cultural change is the application of unmodified business principles and practice to schools. Management theories and practice are concerned "primarily with the organizing and controlling of workers rather than dealing with them as people. ....Their application to a person-centered enterprise such as education is deeply problematic" (Ball & Goodson, 1985).

For example, major social, educational and economic differences in relationships exist between "bosses" and "employees" in corporate organizations. However, in education it is usually accepted that a recognizable cultural homogeneity exists and this is evident through shared educational values and a professional commitment to the progressive development of students. Within an all-graduate occupation, many teachers have similar cultural, social and economic backgrounds and professional expectations. The existence of these similarities suggests that a boss-employee relationship is clearly inappropriate as an organizational framework for schools. In schools, it is customary for those holding senior positions to have managerial responsibility for some important organizational functions. However, in the presence of their colleagues few would claim that they possessed greater intelligence, wisdom, qualifications or even experience than colleagues with whom they shared duties. Even fewer would be able to demonstrate superior managerial abilities. The broad homogeneity of the culture of teachers as an occupational group, together with the professional commitment to educational processes rather than products suggest that the principles of leading, rather than conventional institutional management practices, are more appropriate for schools and colleges. Recent trends in the theory and practice of leadership in schools increasingly emphasize the benefits of cultures for collective educational purpose rather than ordered control through hierarchical management roles (Sergiovanni, 1990).

LEADERSHIP – ISSUES FOR INNOVATIVE CULTURES IN EFFECTIVE SCHOOLS

The social morphology of organizational culture has attracted much attention (Schein, 1985); others examine typologies of cultures (House, 1971). Deal and Kennedy (1982) believe that an effective culture comprises "a system of informal rules that spells out how people are to behave most of the time." More formally, Daft (1997) presents culture as "a set of key values, beliefs, understandings and norms that members of a society or organization share."

Following the introduction of various systems of semi-autonomous local management of schools, for example those characterized by LMS and SBM frameworks, a cultural change in "employees' values, norms, attitudes ...and behavior" has occurred. A sense of genuine collective educational purpose has become more apparent within schools. Many school functions are now undertaken through participatory and decision-making committees, permanent or temporary working groups and team organization (Sergiovanni, 1990; Torrington & Weightman, 1989; Williams, 1999). In 1988, a landmark school study published by Caldwell and Spinks was widely adopted in UK training programs for senior managers in schools. For education, it also underlined Drucker's (1980) key concepts about the central importance of individual effort in the success of organizations: "...the test of a healthy business is not the beauty, clarity or perfection of ...organizational structure. It is the performance of people."

An almost universal phenomenon during the past twenty years in most kinds of organizations has been the search for improved employee performance. Effective leadership, the elusive "Holy Grail" of organizational life, has been a constant preoccupation at all executive levels in corporate business, central and regional government agencies, regional and district offices and, more recently, in schools and universities. A substantial industry exists in training ambitious candidates for "leadership." The surplus of published texts on leadership have undoubtedly contributed to problems of deforestation. Although it is only the reckless who are prepared to generalize about the universality of theories of effective leadership in organizations, the majority of authors have personally preferred models based on many (and sometimes conflicting) concepts, usually within contexts of "learning organizations" (Senge, 1990).

In the author's educational experience the conventional emphasis in the business and industrial management literature is misplaced, in that success is not achieved predominantly through the performance of one person at the positional apex of the organization or team.

Various strategies are considered as highways to achieving corporate success through personal attributes, e.g., charismatic, visionary, philosopher, innovator, strategist, delegator, servant. The literature rarely provides detailed consideration of the contributory roles of the majority of members of any organization – those who do not hold the senior appointments and are perceived as "subordinates" or "followers". Even fewer writers and researchers have given careful consideration to ways in which the contributions of others are elicited, developed and enhanced. With some distinguished exceptions (Bennis, 1987; Burns, 1978; Covey, 1989; Handy, 1997; Sergiovanni, 1992; Williams, 1995) it appears the majority of authors perceive followers and subordinates as largely submissive, unthinking, powerless, lacking motivation and typically ovine. Nevertheless, during the past few decades biographies of political, military, corporate and public "great leaders" have invariably revealed a wide range of flawed personalities and invariable failures arising from the judgment and behavior of those who believed they were beyond human frailty.

For this author, an enduring problem with the conventional wisdom has been an explicit one, in that the literature and training are focused almost exclusively on attitudes and consequent behaviors of leaders in relation to methods for "controlling" the behavior of others – who are perceived as "followers." The literature rarely expresses these relationships in such candid terms. For most of the past century, when leadership theory developed to meet the increasingly complex requirements of collective working in modern organizations, most attention has been focused on ways in which leaders achieved levels of efficient task completion from employees holding subordinate positions. Little explicit attention has been given to ways in which followers are able and permitted to make valid contributions to the effectiveness and efficiency of organizations.

A relatively simple and very significant method of ascertaining evidence for the existence, or absence, of the recognition of the quality and importance of inter-relationships between those who hold senior status and other employees is to consult the index of any conventional text on leadership. Invariably, and appropriately, there are many references to "leaders" and "leadership". However, the term "follower" or "followership" rarely occurs. The inevitable conclusion is that the organic nature of these relationships is ignored or, worse, remains unrecognized. On other occasions where interdependence appears to be acknowledged, the relationship is defined or portrayed as one existing between senior and junior employees. Regrettably, the leader role is frequently conceived and developed as someone responsible for the performance of subordinates. Such attitudes have persisted for centuries and are enshrined in the structures and cultures of large bureaucratic and hierarchical organizations and "command" cultures.

Weber (1968) argues convincingly that "bureaucracy develops more perfectly the more it is 'dehumanized', the more completely it succeeds in eliminating from official business, love, hatred and all purely personal, irrational and emotional elements which escape calculation."

More recently, Handy (1999) believes that "…leadership has a dated air about it …it smacks of trench warfare ….raises specters of elites and privileged classes." Gradually and more recently, by recognizing the directly linked importance of differentiated contributions on a shared leadership basis, what emerges is that leaders cannot exist without followers (Williams, 1989). A better understanding of these crucial relationships arises from the increasing range and complexity of goals and outcomes that require expert knowledge and skills beyond the capability of any individual. This interdependent culture is most clearly recognized in organizations staffed by professional people. For example, schools are staffed by qualified teachers who have graduated from college or university. Through preparatory professional training programs, most share educational values and professional commitment to young people and recognize the value and essential integration of each other's contribution through collective achievement within chronological schooling processes.

These cultures of interdependence exist in many schools, and teachers who respect and admire their colleagues who hold senior staff appointments are sometimes bemused in their attempts to relate their experiences with the stereotypical bureaucratic models portrayed in many management texts. More authentic for them is the Peters and Waterman (1982) perception of leadership as "…being visible when things go awry and invisible when they are working well…. It's listening carefully much of the time, frequently speaking with encouragement, and reinforcing words with believable action

...a hundred things done a little better." This is a more realistic perception of schools with professional cultures, which are seen as more educationally effective.

AUTHENTIC LEADERSHIP FOR CONTEMPORARY PROFESSIONAL CULTURES

For many years a typical euphemism applied to leadership theory and biographical studies of leaders is that leadership is the most elusive and least understood of all human behaviors. Although the interpretive legacy of political and military history that "leaders are born and not made" has continued to permeate many business and government organizations during the past fifty or so years, modern organization theory and practice have promoted the importance of leadership training and development.

Generally, but not exclusively, and because it has only recently become a focus of intensive research effort in education, training perspectives for leaders in educational organizations such as schools have been acquired through a variety of strategies drawn from leadership studies in business organizations. Over several years, training programs derived from non-educational sources or research studies in the nature and practice of leadership in education have discomfited trainers and researchers – including this author. For example, early examples of "modern" perspectives offered by scholars such as Tannenbaum and Schmidt (1958) incorrectly refer to relationships between "leaders" and "subordinates." The application of business culture principles in professional organizations provides an immediate premise for unease and suspicion, not least arising from a failure to recognize that the terms "leadership" and "management" are fundamentally different concepts, and when applied in organizational practice stimulate entirely different perceptions and consequential behaviors (Williams, 1989).

These basic conceptual differences involve many more subtle processes than conveyed in the Bennis and Nanus aphorism (1985): "Managers do things right; leaders do the right thing." This simplistic distinction reduces concepts of leadership to a series of unexplained behaviors. It is a vague, misleading claim lacking understanding and awareness of the complex processes involved in the establishment, or dismantling, of interpersonal relationships which are influenced by context, content and pre-existing experience, all of which produce fluctuating responses visible, or sensed, evident in team activities and group exchanges. The cliché also ignores questions and processes involved in recognition, acknowledgement and acceptance. How is it known that managers are doing "things right?" Similarly, how do leaders convince others that they are doing the "right thing?" Do managers and leaders invariably know what is "right?" Are actions taken exclusively on the basis of individual decision or do they arise from contributions made by others following collaborative activity?

In pursuit of these and similar questions, this author conducted a series of exploratory seminars during the past two decades, initially with experienced teachers pursuing advanced degree studies in programs at the University of Oxford. The majority of these mature students held senior positions in schools in the UK and overseas. Without exception, they perceived themselves as positional "managers" or "leaders" by virtue of their appointments. Following an extended exploratory period, and based on the data derived from in-service seminars at Oxford and elsewhere, the author developed small-scale qualitative research studies in schools in a group of LEAs in England and Wales. In the early 1990s, preliminary conclusions arising from these extended studies were published (Williams, 1995).

Briefly, analysis of the data clearly suggested that the conventional wisdom concerning the nature and practice of being "led" or "managed" in schools was seriously flawed. Further, it was clearly apparent to a substantial majority of participants who had attended the author's seminars, and to respondents who provided data during the initial field research project, that their perception of leadership theory required serious revision because it was inadequate for defining its underlying nature, purpose and impact on others. In addition, most found it extremely difficult to clearly differentiate between "managing" and "leading" roles in schools. In effect, the main conclusions arising from the findings of the research study indicated unmistakably that serious deficiencies existed in the literature.

For the overwhelming majority of respondents the central focus of disquiet and criticism existed in the unreal embodiment of a school's success, achievement and vision in one person – the head teacher. Making a contribution throughout the entire teaching and learning processes was part of the normal purpose and function of all teachers. These in-school processes undertaken by professionally skilled and highly-trained practitioners were the raison d'étre of schools. Managing the associated complex processes was an organizationally essential task of senior colleagues, coordinated by the head teacher. Furthermore, all teachers were educational leaders. As teachers, being involved in organizational management was an important, but subordinate, role of teaching. In the experience of all teachers who participated in these studies, a professional equation existed that required a balance of priorities between leading and following colleagues and pupils. Recognition of these essential professional roles appeared to be largely overlooked or ignored in conventional literature on leadership concepts and, regrettably for some schools, in practice. A basic requirement for the existence of concepts of "followership" in education is both acknowledgement and attention, which are crucial for any detailed consideration and realistic understanding of contemporary leadership practices (Williams, 1995).

A preliminary examination of international texts on leadership reveal that usage of the term "follower" was extremely rare. Equally infrequent was the existence of any evidence of discussion, research or delineation of the nature, quality or significance of relationships between followers and leaders. Subsequent phases in the Oxford research studies initiated an unprecedented exploration of the significance of relationships between leaders and followers. It concluded that a complex set of reciprocal and inseparable relationships existed between leaders and followers (Williams & McCown, 1998).

On a broader theoretical canvas, the nature of these relationships is evident in the seminal work on transformational leadership by McGregor Burns (1978), who recognized the leadership role as being characterized and legitimized through complex sets of impermanent relationships with others. Nevertheless, for many self-styled leaders and appointed managers in education and other organizations, the truism that "leaders cannot exist without followers" (Williams, 1989) continues to elude many who hold appointments as positional leaders, who exercise authority only by virtue of the power conferred through holding specific appointments. In contrast, others intuitively realize the value of the participation of followers through collaborative activity. Interactive behavior leads to a more clear definition of mutually-agreed objectives, while recognizing the basic feelings of all who share in tasks and become involved in reaching mutually desired goals via means that satisfy individual commitment and effort and are personally rewarding (Goleman, 1996).

An understanding of the wants and needs of others arises through the processes of defining, and subsequently shaping, the collective purpose. This degree of sensitivity may be seen in the development of practices of participation and empowerment. It is a recognition that, "Leadership is not domination but the art of persuading people to work towards a common goal" (Goleman, 1996). However, until relatively recently, this kind of sensitivity has been submerged under the imperatives of the inevitably limited perspective of one individual – the positional leader or institutional manager. The final sections of this presentation will consider the Oxford research study, which explores concepts and relationships between leaders and followers in schools. The findings of these studies clearly advocate that contemporary concepts of professional leadership within innovative, effective school cultures require that leadership must be earned from colleagues who elect to follow.

INNOVATIVE CULTURAL CONCEPTS: EARNED LEADERSHIP AND ELECTIVE CONTRIBUTORSHIP

Briefly, the first phase of the research study undertaken by the author, revealed that collaborative and professionally-dependent relationships existed between leaders and followers in schools. It also demonstrated an inescapable requirement that within professionally-staffed organizations, leaders were expected to earn their status from colleagues who elected, or chose, to follow. Appointment to positional status roles, such as head teacher or principal, might ensure management control over colleagues but would not necessarily secure recognition or acceptance of their leadership status. Beyond the conventionally inadequate categorization of "follower," the research study refined and offered insight into the nature of followership in organizations. Analysis of empirical data during the first phase led to a useful preliminary categorization or typology of follower categories based on the type and quality of individual elective contributorship:

Positive contributors:	Intellectually independent; thoughtful, constructive, personal sense of ownership of both concepts and activities; especially valued and trusted by leaders.
Adversarial contributors:	Antipathetic, uncooperative, soured by earlier unpleasant experience, attributed to professional discourtesies in school; suspicious, resistant to change.
Compliant contributors:	Conscientious, conformist, trusting of decisions made by senior colleagues, accepting of conventional wisdom.
Minimalist contributors:	Sheep-like, unthinking, passive spectator of life and work of school, no holistic interest or understanding.
Self-serving contributors:	Egocentric, selfish, active in micro-political life in school, identified by others as being untrustworthy and manipulative.

(Williams, 1995).

For the author, recognition by teachers of the reality of the existence of these kinds of categories of identifiable relationships was gratifying. However, an acknowledged problem in the original research design was the static nature of the typology. Although identification of the five categories provided new and valuable categories – not least because it provided a valuable explanatory framework of reality and offered comprehensible insight into the ways in which teachers generally perceived their own roles and those of colleagues – the static nature of the categories lacked the realism of daily existence in school. Nevertheless, preliminary exploration of sources of elective contributorship offered opportunities for further studies. In the first study, the main priority had been to establish the extent to which hypotheses about concepts of followership could be pursued, explored for significance and possibly categorized. Upon providing overviews and feedback regarding the initial research to respondents in the original group of participating schools, and to other colleagues elsewhere, it was immediately apparent that the categories were recognizable and the relationships perceived as significant. Unequivocal support for a continuation of the research into unresolved issues in the existing group of schools was offered.

Through the generosity of the UK Leverhulme Trust, a further three-year research study was undertaken. The main purpose of the second phase was the exploration of concepts in connection with the dynamic relationships between earned leadership and elective contributorship. This phase of the research produced an extended and more subtle conceptualization of the term "follower." Although broadly identified in the initial study, the research more fully developed concepts regarding the dynamic function of individuals who chose a variety of means and reasons for contributing within specific contexts, existing relationships and organizational time frames. Thus, although the original typology was confirmed, the flexibility of responses became more clearly delineated and led to a new phase, in the sense that the term "follower" was replaced with a more accurate and professionally satisfying term, "contributor" (Williams & McCown, 1998). Accordingly, the typology and individual categorization was redesignated as elective contributorship. Subsequent research has emphasized and endorsed with greater clarity and realism the nature of the dynamic relationships between leaders and colleagues in contemporary school cultures.

The most recent and current application of the ground-breaking concepts associated with elective contributorship suggest that improved understanding of earned leadership within the schools, which Weick (1976) designates as "loosely coupled organizations," is both appropriate and convincing to practitioners. It provides insight and the necessary flexibility in conveying an understanding of the essential realism that must exist between leaders and followers, and clarifies their relationships within the professional cultures of schools. Even within familiar organizational structures it is apparent that teachers are strongly influenced through experiencing differences in values, norms and patterns of behavior derived from specific histories and unique traditions in schools.

One significant response has been that concepts of contributorship offer a new perspective on the fluctuating roles, both positive and negative, adopted by leaders and followers in their relationships. Elective contributorship provides the "buckle" that secures interdependent relationships between leaders and followers in the achievement of mutually-desired educational, organizational and social goals for pupils and communities. The concepts rest entirely on a realization that leadership has to be earned from followers who elect to contribute in a collective process. For most respondents who participated in all phases of the study these concepts have also clarified and extended other accepted theories that leaders cannot exist without followers and have displaced earlier notions that leaders have subordinates.

LEADER–CONTRIBUTOR CULTURES IN SCHOOLS: A REVIEW OF PROFESSIONAL REALITIES

Historically, and contemporaneously, the literature reflects four main groups of leadership theories: trait, style, contingency and best-fit. While none wholly ignores relationships between leaders and followers, the latter have been, or are, regarded, *inter alia*, as docile, submissive, subordinate, unthinking and/or intellectually inferior. In effect, until very recently the main corpus of literature on leadership had presented a unilateral perspective. The Oxford studies sought to provide a bilateral view of leader-follower relationships through a new perspective on cultures of earned leadership and elective contributorship in schools.

Regular reporting of the key research findings over the past few years at various conferences and publication of the studies' main assertion has attracted considerable attention. It appears to reveal an existing awareness which, anecdotally, appeared to have been submerged in "control" cultures inherent in positional status hierarchies. Quite simply, the key finding for most teachers who have been involved in these research studies is: Leaders earn their status from others who elect to follow.

While the central preoccupation of existing literature was almost exclusively on the role of the leader, it was evident that a major lacuna existed over the identity and motivation of followers. For several years, unease over, and questioning of, the conventional wisdom in the literature was endorsed during weekly seminars at Oxford by the experience of many mature, advanced-degree students, most of whom held senior appointments in UK and overseas schools. Their reported experience rarely corresponded positively with the claims advanced in the literature on leadership. A general perception that theories and accounts concerning the nature of leadership were extraordinarily skewed provided the momentum for the development of a leader–follower research project proposal in 1992.

THE SCHOOLS LEADERSHIP RESEARCH PROJECT: AN INITIAL TYPOLOGY OF CONTRIBUTORS

As mentioned earlier, the central theme of the initial investigation focused on teachers' perceptions of themselves as either leaders or followers within school contexts, and the ways in which they responded to other colleagues. During the mid-1990s the author reported on conclusions drawn from the initial project at international conferences held in the UK, Israel and the USA.

Crucially, earned leadership is an accorded status and not an appointed one. An immediate implication of earned leadership is that the status must be renewed and exercised with vigilance in order to maintain the support and acquiescence of elective followers through the consideration of their attitudes, values and comprehension. For example, some 74% of respondents indicated significant distrust (and probable rejection) of leaders who required acceptance of their individual "visions." However, a leader's vision which was subsequently modified through valued contributions from followers and which then become an accepted collective vision invariably attracted an elective followership. Similarly, more than 85% of teachers were suspicious of the intentions, integrity and consistency of charismatic leaders and did not elect to follow. However, leaders who were consistent, clear, dependable and trustworthy invariably attracted an elective followership. Analysis of empirical data in these early phases led to a useful development in the categorization of followers based on the type and quality of contributorship made by individuals.

These studies indicated that although the initial typology was a static one that had not incorporated the dynamism of leader-follower relationships in the cultures of self-governing schools, it provided a model that was useful in clarifying initial thinking among respondents. Quite simply, it was an unprecedented study for schools to consider the identification and motivation of followers and to explore individual attitudes and associated behavioral activity.

THE SCHOOLS LEADERSHIP RESEARCH PROJECT: CULTURES OF CONTRIBUTORSHIP

One critical refinement of the original typology of followership occurred through further development of the ground-breaking concept of contributorship. It provided insight and the necessary flexibility to reflect the practical realism that exists between leaders and followers. It exposed means by which relationships within the uniquely different cultures of schools could be understood, explored and developed. Even within immediately familiar organizational structures teachers are influenced by experiencing differences in values, norms and patterns of behavior derived from earlier histories and traditions in every school.

Theoretically, in an "ideal" school culture, both leadership and contributorship would be logically and appropriately distributed according to expertise, ability and elective behavior. All contributions would be "positive," rendering most of the initial typology of followers redundant. As with many other spheres of human activity, the reality of organizational life is rarely as problem-free as theoretical models suggest. Nevertheless, this research project led to a confident assertion supported by the data that in the practical realization of earned leadership/elective contributor concepts in professional practice, individuals should have a certain degree of control over the way in which they elect to contribute to the life and work of organizations, specifically within the context of schools. Anecdotal evidence from other professional occupational groups acquainted with the main findings of this research project suggests that the concepts of elective contributorship are powerful factors in the quality of individual and team interaction.

As leadership is an accorded status earned from followers it was essential to explore the rationale for accepting offers of leadership. All respondents were skeptical of the historic notion of one "great person" as the leader of a school. The concept of one person with mastery of all school functions – curriculum, finance, personnel, assessment, external relations and site management – with a detailed knowledge of statutory requirements, is demonstrably obsolete. Equally, most respondents (in excess of 90%) distrusted charismatic leaders simply because the "vision" offered by most was a unilateral one. In the increasingly complex environment typical of contemporary education systems, respondents wished to participate in shaping school development and prioritizing goals and achievement. Respondents were explicit regarding the importance of participating in the formation of school cultures, not least because of the ways in which their own lives and well-being were influenced – positively or negatively – through organizational frameworks, and reflected by the directions in which the culture developed.

Within this generalized encapsulation of internal school culture, personal decisions concerning elective behavior were made. It appeared that most choices were made on a considered basis, usually in connection with career planning, job expectations or satisfaction. Invariably, teachers were either dissatisfied or pleased over ways in which their tasks in schools offered or denied opportunities, experience, ownership, empowerment or participation in the shaping of improvement policies or effective practices. On the other hand, for a minority of teachers, personal lives outside of school were considered central to providing a unique identity of self. Life beyond school was perceived as the main source of personal satisfaction and fulfillment, as well as resolving problems of economic self-sufficiency. For these individuals teaching was the main salaried employment, school tasks were completed adequately but without commitment, and collaboration with others was seen essentially as a stratagem of least resistance in school. Several years preceding the Oxford studies, Ball and Goodson (1985) examined the subjective experiences of teachers in relation to their careers in teaching. Interestingly, the more recent studies undertaken by the author, and in schools with markedly different cultures, unearthed similar polarized motivational choices. However, in these studies a greater emphasis on the self-perceived importance of seeking fulfillment beyond a school-based career path was evident. Recent foci revolved around the importance of enjoying a personally satisfying life compatible with individual predilection and measured through the degree of being at ease with oneself in a society beyond the pressures of occupational and career achievement.

It appeared that decisions over choosing to follow were not necessarily linked with feelings of presumed inadequacy or personal modesty but arose through deliberate and considered decisions of personal preference and degrees of commitment to the school, speciality, colleagues or students. Parenthetically, it should be noted that for leaders to earn their status, the value and significance of contributions offered by very positive followers should not mask that others have made different personal choices; everyone contributes: positively, adversarially, weightily or marginally. Although the language is somewhat dated, Mintzberg's assertion (1979) that "the effectiveness of a manager is dependent on the degree of personal insight into the requirements of the role" is equally applicable to an understanding of the impermanent authority of earned leadership and the differentiated existence of elective contributorship.

The final phase of the project sought to establish the criteria conducive to existing, or desired, effective school cultures within which teachers, as leaders and contributors, would be motivated to contribute positively in the formulation and pursuit of collective goals. Furthermore, data was sought about ways in which the existence of earned leadership/elective contributorship school cultures might be identified. In this phase the perspective moved from positive or negative concerns of individuals to the identification of broader organizational foci for effective schools.

This phase of the study explored personal perceptions of ways in which elective contributions were influenced by organizational frameworks – formally structured responsibility "trees" with positive or negative effects on opportunities for personal contributorship. A second, and closely related, theme explored perceptions of ways in which elective contributions were accepted or rejected by others, and the influence of contributory activity on others at individual, team and faculty levels. An important consideration within these thematic concerns was an attempt to examine whether an organizational perspective would lead to significant modification of the original follower typology. With the focus shifting from identification of follower types to the flexibility of contributorship under differing organizational circumstances and within fluctuating sets of relationships, careful consideration was required of a possible contributorship continuum, extending from unequivocally positive to perennially negative with intermediate positions corresponding to the original five main categories.

During 1999, from the original group of schools, a representative profile across three career stages provided the data needed through extensive discussion of perceptions, beliefs and experience. The sample consisted of a further 105 respondents – classroom teachers who reflected a three-stage career or experiential pattern: those with five or fewer years of teaching experience (28%); mid-career departmental team leaders; and curriculum chairpersons (42%) and senior management administrators (30%).

Following collection and analysis of the data, feedback sessions were arranged at participating schools. Opportunities were provided for the researchers to report on their findings and tentative conclusions. Concurrently, respondents were able to raise matters of personal interest and provide additional commentary about ways in which contributors elected to participate and the positive and negative effects of holistic school cultures on both individual and group activities. Interestingly, respondents expressed pleasure with the foci of the study, primarily because none had ever been invited to consider or provide serious, reflective perceptions on "how" and "what" they felt as teachers who expressed support for or withheld support from other colleagues in school, and ways in which they were influenced by the school culture or had helped to shape its values and conventions.

The research study also provided opportunities for extended discussion with respondents and others who attended a variety of seminars. Invariably, these sessions produced a wide range of expectations among practitioners at all status levels in schools. It was unanimously acknowledged that although no schools had identical cultures, there were educational and personal values and principles that were likely to encourage the development of leader-contributor cultures within every school. To encourage leaders and contributors to recognize and value their differentiated roles and subscribe to concepts of earning status, an ethical basis of mutual trust, honesty, confidence, consideration of individual needs, and creation of shared value systems were essential to genuinely effective schools.

Throughout the final phase of research the values and behaviors described below were seen as characteristic and consistent elements of collaborative activity and mutually supportive relationships. Although implicit, rather than explicit, in schools perceived as effective, these values were consistently mentioned by a clear majority of respondents as crucial to the development of innovative school cultures. Although this phase was essentially a preliminary exploration, leaders who were acknowledged as individuals who continuously earned their status, and followers who chose to make positive contributions, would be successful and effective in cultures in which shared trust and mutual respect were central to all interpersonal behavior and where principles were embedded in organizational frameworks. In effect, these were school cultures where the following principles were practiced routinely, not merely espoused, through professional and collegial values:

Mutual trust	Recognition of personal contribution
Praise culture	Celebration of collective achievement
Respect for others	Acceptance of different perspectives
Team membership	Confidence in self and others
Professional growth	Job satisfaction
Job security	Quality of personal lives
Comfortable work environment	Salary linked to professional, peer evaluation

Ways in which these values might be further developed and sustained within collaborative leader-contributor cultures during the early years of this new century offer significant opportunities for further study in self-governing schools. However, it is becoming evident that innovative concepts are based on a more balanced appreciation and understanding of the organic, umbilical and nurturing relationships between leaders and followers released from the negative constraints of authority derived from positional, hierarchical power.

CONTRIBUTOR CULTURES IN SCHOOLS: THE PROFESSIONAL FUTURE?

It is worth recalling that the origins of this study arose from expressed practitioner concerns that leadership as an accepted construct in the literature and practiced in schools was indistinguishable from positional management. An enduring confusion over the use of the term "leadership" has existed for many years beyond educational organizations and, undeniably, has been a disservice to the professional status of educators. The complex qualitative, and surprisingly unpublished, nature of interpersonal relationships between leaders and followers stimulated further study and research. Although largely ignored in conventional management literature, through their inherent ability to offer or withhold support on a basis of personal choice, it became clear during the early phase of the research that the power of followers was a highly significant determinant in the existence of genuine leadership – which has to be earned from others. With these insights, earlier perceptions found in the literature on leadership describing followers as powerless, unthinking, sheep-like conformists appeared to be entirely misconceived.

Although conceptually innovative and experientially interesting, the original work by the author raised other important issues. One issue was to establish reasons why some individuals were intermittent or, contrastingly, habitual followers. Equally, it appeared essential to explore reasons why others cast themselves as leaders without exercising any of the appropriate behavior and whose claims rested entirely on formally appointed positional status and organizational authority to manage and control others. Among many holders of positional status appointments, an enduring, pervasive assumption persists that others are merely subordinates who undertake tasks through supervised activity and within prescribed bureaucratic procedures. A surprising but gratifying by-product of the original study was to learn that respondents had greatly enjoyed a unique dialogue about earned leader/elective contributor concepts. For more than 95% of respondents, it was an unprecedented experience to be involved in any research seminar or study on the nature, practice or styles of leadership, followership or contributorship.

A further conclusion from these research studies suggests that a continuum of school cultures exists within two polarized models of organization. First, and less effective, is the conventional extreme of a control culture where leadership is inaccurately conceived as a control process exercised by those who hold hierarchical positional status by virtue of differentiated formal appointments. At interpersonal levels, and however benignly practiced, relationships are essentially between managers and subordinates within frameworks controlled by rules and procedures. At the other end of the continuum is an innovative contributorship culture where leadership is earned from others who choose to contribute on a personal basis through positive purpose, expertise and experience. Such cultures are characterized by recognition of mutual interdependence, shared esteem and reciprocal collaboration.

In summary, these research studies demonstrate that older, more traditional organizational models for the effective working of schools are neither appropriate nor fully capable of engaging the talents, abilities and experience of graduate and skilled professionals who work in schools, not least because they are unenthusiastic about positively contributing as subordinates. Within external cultures of national and local expectations and public accountability, all practitioners should be encouraged to recognize the value of their contribution to both the life and work of schools. Additionally, as schools are increasingly becoming ethically, academically and socially complex organizations, an explicit expectation is that all who work within them will make an active contribution to the development of effective schools through high quality professional practice. From these studies there is persuasive evidence that the majority of teachers in our schools would always choose to contribute fully to the development of more effective schools within cultures of collective purpose that valued them and the quality of their contributions. That elective contributors should be led by those who earn leadership roles through mutual trust and recognition of professional commitment to education is no less than they deserve.

REFERENCES

Adair, J. (1988). *Developing Leaders*. Guildford: Talbot Adair Press.

Ball, S. J., & Goodson, I. F. (Eds.). (1985). *Teachers' lives and careers*. London: The Falmer Press.

Bennis, W. (1987). *Why leaders can't lead*. San Francisco: Jossey Bass.

Bennis, W., & Nanus, B. (1985). *Leaders: The strategies for taking charge*. New York: Harper and Row.

Blake, R. R., & Mouton, J. S. (1985). *The managerial grid* III. Houston, TX: Gulf Publishing Company.

Burns, J. M. (1978). *Leadership*. New York: Harper and Row.

Caldwell, B. J., & Spinks, J. M. (1988). *The self-managing school*. London: The Falmer Press.

Covey, S. R. (1989). *The seven habits of highly effective people*. New York: Simon & Schuster.

Daft, R. L. (1997). *Management*. New York: The Dryden Press.

Deal, T., & Kennedy, T. (1982). *Corporate Cultures*. Reading: Addison-Wesley.

Drucker, P. (1980). *Management*. London: Pan Books.

Goleman, D. (1996). *Emotional intelligence*. London: Bloomsbury

Gross, N., Giacquinta, J., & Bernstein, M. (1971). *Implementing organizational innovations: A sociological analysis of planned educational change*. New York: Basic Books.

Handy, C. B. (1997). *The hungry spirit*. London: Hutchinson.

Handy, C. B. (1999). *Understanding organizations*. Harmondsworth: Penguin Books, Ltd.

Hersey, P., & Blanchard, K. H. (1982). *Management of organizational behavior: Utilizing human resources*. Englewood Cliffs, NJ: Prentice-Hall.

House, R. J. (1971). A path-goal theory of leader effectiveness. *Administrative Science Quarterly, 16*.

Kanter, R. M. (1989). *When giants learn to dance*. London: Simon & Schuster.

Kouzes, J. M., & Posner, B. Z. (1987). *The leadership challenge: How to get extraordinary things done in organizations*. San Francisco: Jossey-Bass

Levačić, R. (1995). *Local management of schools*. Buckingham: Open University Press.

Likert, R. G. (1967). *The human organization: Its management and value*. New York: McGraw-Hill.

Maclure, J. S. (1989). *Education reformed*. London: Hodder & Stoughton.

Mintzberg, H. (1979). *The structure of organizations.* New York: Wiley.

Nias, J.(1980). Leadership styles and job-satisfaction in primary schools. In T. Bush et al., (Eds.), *Approaches to school management.* London: Harper & Row.

Peters, T. J. & Waterman, R. H. (1982). *In search of excellence.* New York: Harper Collins.

Schein, E. H. (1985). *Organizational culture and leadership.* San Francisco: Jossey-Bass.

Senge, P. M. (1990). *The fifth discipline.* New York: Doubleday.

Sergiovanni, T. J. (1990). *Value-added leadership.* San Diego: Harcourt Brace Jovanovich.

Sergiovanni, T. J. (1992). *Moral leadership: Getting to the heart of school improvement.* San Francisco: Jossey-Bass.

Tannenbaum, R., & Schmidt, W. (1958). How to choose a leadership pattern. *Harvard Business Review, 36*(2).

Torrington, D., & Weightman, J. (1989). *The reality of school management.* Oxford: Basil Blackwell.

Weber, M. (1968). *Economy and society.* London: Bedminster.

Weick, K. E. (1976). Educational organizations as loosely-coupled systems. *Administrative Science Quarterly, 21.*

Williams, V. (1989). Schools and their communities: Issues in external relations. In J. Sayer & V. Williams (Eds.), *Schools and external relations*: *Managing the new partnerships.* London: Cassell.

Williams, V. (1995). Towards 2000 – Organization and relationships. In V. Williams (Ed.), *Towards self-managing schools.* London: Cassell.

Williams, V. (1997). School autonomy and parental choice: Circumscribed realities of reform. In R. Shapira & P. Cookson (Eds.), *Autonomy and choice in context*: *An international perspective.* New York: Elsevier Science.

Williams, V. (1999). Leadership in schools: New expectations. In D. Bar-Elli (Ed.), *Towards a new perspective of school leadership.* Jerusalem: Ministry of Education, Culture and Sport (published in English and Hebrew).

Williams, V., & McCown, R. R. (1998). *A new typology of contributors to reciprocal leadership functions in British secondary and American high schools.* Paper presented at the annual meeting of the American Educational Research Association, San Diego, CA.

ORGANIZATIONAL VISION IN SELF-MANAGING SCHOOLS: WALKING ON THIN ICE

Adam E. Nir and Ronit Bogler

There is no more powerful engine driving an organization toward excellence and long-range success than an attractive, worthwhile and achievable vision of the future, widely shared. (Nanus, 1992)

INTRODUCTION

Vision is one of the key elements for effective leadership in organizational settings. The lack of a clear vision is among the major causes of the declining effectiveness of many organizations in recent years (Bennis & Nanus, 1985). This assertion is shared by many scholars (e.g., Peters & Waterman, 1982; Terry, 1993) who have argued for the importance of organizational vision and, as such, for the need to update visions periodically because of ongoing changes that are taking place in an ever-evolving environment. An organization should follow the direction expressed in the vision, and because the vision serves as a compass for the organization's members, it must not only be defined in general terms and be inspirational, it should also constitute an accurate reflection of the organization's internal qualities and its interactions with the environment.

This last statement must be taken into account by schools in general, and by self-managing schools in particular, in considering their increased authority and flexibility, which enables them to express their vision in accordance with their professional values and local needs and expectations. However, it is important to note that an organizational vision is directed not only inward, to be used by school personnel as a compass but also outward, towards people within the school's local community and district, and that this duality may produce a conflict of interests under certain circumstances.

How this conflict is resolved and what qualities are eventually chosen to characterize their vision has a tremendous impact on the organizational behavior and effectiveness of self-managing schools.

DECENTRALIZATION AND SCHOOL-BASED MANAGEMENT

In recent years, decentralization has become an international trend (Sleegers & Wesselingh, 1995; Wohlstetter & McCurdy, 1991). This movement is supported by arguments claiming that the monitoring of school performance has failed under centralized structures (Gaziel & Romm, 1988), and arguments that focus on the potential of decentralized structures to increase the effectiveness of the education system and the schools.

Decentralization, which refers to transferring the locus of decision-making control from the center to the periphery (Lauglo, 1995), is favored for a number of reasons: it is assumed to promote the participation of school-level educators and increase the chances of plans being implemented (Bray, 1985). It enhances the flexibility of schools and encourages educators to be more sensitive to local needs (Benson, 1978). Decentralized structures are assumed to increase the accountability and responsibility of educators at the school site (Brown, 1991) and enable schools to operate more efficiently and rapidly in comparison with the commonly described slow and cumbersome centralized structures (Hanson, 1984). Hence, decentralization has a potential to promote school productivity and effectiveness.

One manifestation of decentralization is school-based management (SBM), which has recently become the centerpiece of the current wave of reforms (Sackney & Dibski, 1994). Simply stated, SBM is a proposal to decentralize school control (Guthrie, 1986) and increase authority at the school site (Clune & White, 1988). SBM emphasizes maximum delegation of decision-making to the operational level within a centrally-coordinated framework (Boyd, 1990). It is based on the assumption that decisions made closer to the client level are better than those made by central government officials who lack precise knowledge regarding specific local needs (Conley, 1991; David, 1989).

In essence, by empowering schools, SBM is assumed to impact the coordination between the school's environment, its organizational processes, and the aspirations, qualifications and values of school level educators. SBM provides a mechanism that enables schools to tighten their fragmented and loosely-coupled components (Weick, 1976) based on what they consider to be beneficial for pupils and other community members, as well as for the school enterprise. It is believed that under SBM, professional responsibility replaces bureaucratic regulation, and school staff accountability for children's achievements increases (Brown, 1990; Cohen, 1988;

Garms, Guthrie, & Pierce, 1978; Sergiovanni, 1990). Moreover, SBM is assumed to enhance managerial efficiency (Johnes, 1995) since management at the school level can meet local needs better and more quickly than can centralized organization. These arguments have led to the belief that SBM is an important means for improving school effectiveness and student performance (Purkey & Smith, 1985).

Consequently, SBM enhances the impact of school-level educators on the educational and managerial processes they conduct. In addition, it grants schools the authority and ability to increase their influence over their modes of operation and organizational culture. However, at the same time, SBM raises high expectations by community members, as well as by district personnel and high-ranking officials, regarding school effectiveness, responsiveness and school staff accountability. Educators in SBM schools are expected to prove more than ever before that the increased authority delegated to their schools contributes to their ability to respond to the needs of their clientele (Sackney & Dibski, 1994) and promote the pupils' achievements and satisfaction (Conley, 1991).

As noted earlier, the articulation of an organizational vision is vital for the effectiveness of self-managing schools. Sergiovanni (1990) indicates that "vision gets the most attention in the leadership literature" (p. 57) because it has been credited for the success of organizational leadership on the one hand, and blamed for organizational failure, on the other. Organizational vision is highly valued because it enables teachers and principals in SBM schools to incorporate their educational beliefs, values and professional preferences with the particular needs and characteristics of pupils and the school environment. An effective vision reflects a blend that best integrates these qualities. Thus, it provides a managerial tool that enables the school leadership to concentrate the organizational energy and direct it in accordance with the unique attributes characterizing each particular school.

CONCEPTUALIZING AND CONSTRUCTING A VISION FOR SBM SCHOOLS

A vision has been conceived variously as "just a vague dream, and at other times ...as concrete as a written mission statement" (Yukl, 1994, p. 363); "a thing of imagination" (Bell & Harrison, 1995, p. 2), or as a "mental image" (Holmes, 1993, p. 16). These notions portray a somewhat unrealistic and intangible view of the concept. Practically speaking, a vision in organizational settings is a concrete idea that describes what needs to be achieved by the organization's members and how this should be done (Creemers, 1997). A vision that mainly reflects "vague dreams" or "thing(s) of imagination" may be detached from reality. A vision cannot be mystical or mysterious. It must be expressed in simple terms that enable everyone related to the organization to understand the challenges it entails, and at the same time, inspire the members to achieve them. Thus, it is essential that the vision be articulated explicitly and that it generate enthusiasm. In Yukl's words, "The genius of the leader is to articulate a vision simple enough to be understood, appealing enough to evoke commitment, and credible enough to be accepted as realistic and attainable" (1994, p. 364).

Though a shared vision is meant to encompass everyone related to the organization, the task of putting it together is expected to remain in the hands of the leader and not be delegated (Bennis & Nanus, 1985). An effective leader is one who is aware of the needs, qualifications and expectations of the people involved, both within and outside of the organization. Such a leader actually embodies the beliefs, philosophy, and goals that are crucial to the organization's survival and success. Therefore, we claim, formulating a vision is a very complex venture, especially if its architect – in this case the school principal – intends to improve the effectiveness of the school.

What, then, do leaders of SBM schools need to consider when articulating a vision for their school?

To achieve a vision that is a "mental image" representing a desirable future position, school leaders must use identifiable metaphors and concepts that unveil the direction for the future and articulate defined mission statements, along with the possibly vague ideas. Rather than constituting a detailed blueprint for action, a mission statement is a general picture that reflects the vision's major themes and values (Yukl, 1994). The mission statement should incorporate the philosophy and ideology of the school in such a way that it will direct the teachers toward accomplishing the goals stated therein.

Moreover, to promote school effectiveness, the vision should represent the expectations and the interests of the followers as well as the leader. It has to create a "sense of commonality" and reflect "a common caring" among all the school personnel (Terry, 1993, p. 158). This last argument may be better understood if we keep in mind that most definitions refer to leadership as a social interaction in which one person (the leader) influences the activities of other people (the followers) within a given frame of circumstances (the organizational environment), toward achieving a shared mission statement – the vision. Vision is at the heart of leadership, and since leadership denotes the interaction between these components, we believe that a leader who articulates a vision must take them into account.

Finally, a vision has to be realistic and credible, and should project a future attractive enough to convince teachers to invest their efforts in pursuing it, rather than simply continuing with the status quo.

As we stated elsewhere (Bogler & Nir, 2001), there are three essentials that school leaders need to consider when articulating a vision:

Firstly, school leaders have to make sure that the articulated vision corresponds with their personal interests and professional style and capabilities; if it does not, it may not be realized. Therefore, it is important that the articulated vision corresponds with the leader's orientation (people-oriented vs. task-oriented; Likert, 1961, 1967), with his/her leadership style (democratic, authoritative or laissez-faire; White & Lippit, 1960) and with the type of person the leader is (transformational or transactional; Bass, 1985; Burns, 1978). Secondly, the characteristics of the followers must also be carefully assessed and taken into consideration to ensure feasibility of the vision. By this we mean the teachers' level of psychological maturity (i.e., their ability and willingness to confront obstacles and complexities), their job maturity (i.e., ability or competence to perform any kind of professional activity demanded by the job; Hersey & Blanchard, 1972) and their level of motivation (Hoy & Miskel, 1991). It is important for leaders to consider these qualities when articulating a vision because followers characterized by different attributes are likely to differ in their ability to confront ambiguity, postpone gratification, deal with long-term commitments and cope with multiple goals.

Finally, school leaders need to carefully analyze the qualities of the environment and their potential influences on their schools. This assertion is relevant for schools in general but for SBM schools in particular, which are expected to better meet and correspond with the demands and expectations of people of their local community.

A school's organizational environment can be viewed as either homogeneous or heterogeneous, stable or changing (Thompson, 1967) [the latter is sometimes referred to as "dynamic" (Daft & Steers, 1986, p. 299), "diverse" (Bolman & Deal, 1991, p. 71) or "turbulent" (Emery & Trist, 1965)]. Understanding the qualities of a school's environment is important because different levels of heterogeneity lead to different rates of change, as well as a sense of uncertainty that may be felt by the organization's members with regard to its future (Scott, 1981). These, in turn, affect the organization's functioning and the leader's ability to plan ahead and define relatively ambiguous and long-range mission statements.

In essence, leaders involved in the process of communicating a vision need to consider these three vital leadership components and determine how to combine them so that the vision will best serve their schools. Because of the complexity involved in characterizing each of these components, school leaders may misjudge or miscalculate various aspects related to their followers' characteristics or the nature of the organizational environment, or fail to be fully aware of their own personal motivations and drives. Consequently, the multiple facets that potentially characterize each of these components make this task extremely complicated for leaders wishing to define a vision that will become a point of reference and agreement for people within the self-managing school – as well as for outsiders.

Analytically, school visions may be grouped into two types, reflecting two combinations of these three essential leadership components:

1. A pure type of vision, which implies that the articulated vision exhibits sufficient congruence between the characteristics of the leader (leadership style and orientation), the situation (followers' maturity and nature of environment) and those of the vision in terms of time span, number of tasks and mission clarity. The articulation of a pure type of vision and its realization presents a relatively less complicated challenge for school leaders because of the similar implications that these three leadership components produce in terms of the school's mission statement and organizational behavior.

2. A mixed type of vision presents a totally different challenge for school leaders. It reflects a contradiction between two or more of the essential vision components that leaders need to consider. Inevitably, the articulation and fulfillment of mixed type visions produce tension for leaders. Their decision as to how to resolve these contradictions and reduce the tension will be affected by their personality type, orientation and motivation.

It is important to note however, that in reality, congruence between these vision components is less prevalent and leaders of SBM schools are more likely to encounter conflicting circumstances while articulating their school's vision.

WALKING ON THIN ICE

Educational leaders need to consider the three essential components of leadership when articulating a vision for their schools. Failure to do so, by disregarding one or more of these components, is likely to have a negative impact on the organizational performance of a school. In SBM schools, this lack of congruence may prevent educators from maximizing the autonomy delegated to the school site.

Nevertheless, leaders articulating a vision for SBM schools are expected to address the particular needs and aspirations of the people within the community the school serves, even when these expectations are not in line with the school's internal qualities. Thus, the inclination of school leaders to be attentive to parents and district-level expectations may lead to the articulation of a populist vision. Such a vision conforms to these community expectations even if it has little bearing upon the teachers' attributes, their professional preferences and qualifications, and the actual educational needs of the children in that school. In such a case, leaders may be motivated to intentionally articulate a vision that will imbue their followers with "a sense of challenge and a motivating force for change" (Conger & Kanungo, 1989, p. 85) on the one hand, and one that will satisfy parents' expectations, on the other hand. In other words, since organizational vision is a powerful managerial tool, leaders in SBM schools may want to use it in a manipulative manner, to achieve what they consider to be better results for their schools in terms of increased member involvement and dedication and greater satisfaction of parents. Although they may be fully aware of their own characteristics, the specific attributes of their followers, and the nature of the organizational environment, school leaders may still choose to articulate a vision that intentionally disregards some of these characteristics. They may be tempted to do so under the assumption, or conviction, that this strategy will best serve the school's purposes. However, in doing so, leaders promote a vision that has relatively little relationship to reality. This approach actually exploits the discrepancy between the given circumstances and the vision as a strategy to induce followers to apply themselves to achieve a mission statement that serves mostly populist purposes rather than educational goals.

Assuming that leaders are cognizant of, and take into consideration, their personal motives for work and their leadership styles, there are still several choices they can make in reference to the other two situational conditions: the followers' attributes and the nature of the environment (see Table 1).

A leader who intentionally ignores the actual qualities of the followers and the environment is a *detached* leader. Following such a strategy is likely to produce a mission statement that has little relevance for the actual life of the organization. Consequently, the vision becomes an illusion: it creates the impression that the organization is functioning according to the plan delineated in the vision's mission statement. Yet, in reality, that vision has little bearing on the professional aspirations and qualification of teachers, nor does it address the particular educational needs of children and parents within the community. Therefore, such a vision is detached from reality and cannot serve as an effective compass and rallying point for people inside and outside the school. The greater the discrepancy between the school's vision and the reality, the greater the illusion. A vision that has transformed into an illusion ceases to function as a realistic objective that can drive the organization's members to aspire towards achieving the organization's goals and mission. Rather, such an unrealistic vision constitutes a stumbling block and is detrimental to the effective operation of the school.

Table 1

Typology of leader's orientations

Leader's orientation	Followers' characteristics	Environment
Detached	-	-
Inward	+	-
Outward	-	+
Attentive	+	+

The "+" sign implies that the condition is being considered.

The "-" sign implies that the condition is being neglected.

An *inward-oriented* leader is one who is biased towards attending to the interests of his followers. Such a leader puts much emphasis on maintaining good and close relationships with teachers and other people involved in the organization's activities when articulating a vision. In a school setting, this would mean, for example, fulfilling the staff members' demands at the expense of the students' or parents' needs and expectations. However, leaders of SBM schools are less likely to employ such a manipulative strategy. SBM grants schools their authority and autonomy on the assumption that these will be used to increase the schools' internal congruence as well as their inclination to deal with and address expectations directed toward the school environment. In any case, articulating a vision while overlooking local as well as global environmental trends may produce a dysfunctional vision and such a school may eventually lose its relevance.

The leader who is oriented *outward* is concerned solely with the characteristics of the environment and tends to put less emphasis on the followers. This type of leader is concerned mainly with satisfying the demands and expectations that are directed towards the school from the outside rather than responding to its followers' professional abilities and personal aspirations. A principal who strives to implement new ideas and projects that are praised by parents or by district members, but does so without taking into consideration the limitations of the school staff, may encourage a vision that is likely to fail in expressing substantial educational processes in the school. The outward orientation is tempting for leaders of SBM schools since it enables them to gain, rather quickly, greater support from people within the school's surroundings and to encourage central authority officials to further decentralize the education system and increase the authority being delegated to schools.

Finally, there is the *attentive* leader who takes into consideration the characteristics of both the followers and the environment. Such an orientation increases the probability that the articulated vision will correspond to the needs, attributes and expectations of the followers, and to the circumstances of the organizational environment. A vision that incorporates these important conditions is the optimal one, since it increases the probability that the vision and its mission statement will correspond and provide the finest possible answer for the three leadership components: the leader, the followers and the environment. However, employing such a strategy requires greater personal and professional maturity from school leaders, which is essential for maintaining the delicate balance between the particular characteristics of a school and its tendency to satisfy parents' as well as district-officials' expectations.

A leader who deliberately manipulates the information regarding the followers and the environment in the belief that this will yield more benefits than drawbacks to the organization may eventually lead his school to the very opposite of the desired results, namely, loss of interest, loss of spirit and, ultimately, poor organizational performance.

Whatever the reason for incongruity between the articulated vision and the reality, the contention of this paper is that too great a discrepancy between the vision and the organizational reality is liable to yield a counterproductive mission statement for the organization.

THE ATTENTIVE VISION: A ZERO-SUM GAME

A major principle of SBM is that it increases the school's flexibility and ability to cope with and address the needs and expectations of the local community, and this in turn promotes the relevance of the education it provides. However, the tendency of leaders in self-managing schools to respond to local expectations may have a negative impact on the performance of schools, especially when such expectations lead to the articulation of a populist-type of vision which is actually an illusionary vision.

A school's vision should be conceived as a blend between the qualities of the school's environment and its internal attributes. In an attentive type of vision, a balance is achieved between internal and external forces so that the vision can address, as fully as possible, the expectations of people within the school's community, and the professional needs and interests of school members, as illustrated in Figure 1.

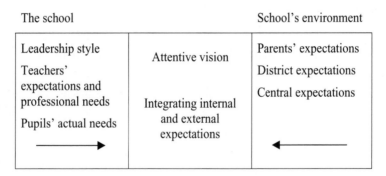

Figure 1. School factors vs. expectations from the school's environment

However, leaders in self-managing schools may confront varying degrees of complexity when articulating a vision, depending on the discrepancy that exits between a school's internal qualities and the expectations directed towards the school from external sources.

The relations between the internal and external expectations of school may be grouped into three categories: correspondence, resemblance, and incongruity.

When the internal and external expectations correspond, the task of articulating an attentive vision is rather simple. People within the school's environment expect the school to define a mission statement with certain qualities, which correspond with the professional judgement and aspirations of both the teachers and the principal. In reality, however, such a correspondence is rare, primarily because parents and district-level politicians lack the relevant professional knowledge for planning and conducting meaningful educational processes. Moreover, professional educators ascribe longer time frames and place greater emphasis on educational processes in comparison to nonprofessionals, who focus mainly on short-term and concrete outcomes.

Resemblance is a second type of discrepancy, referring to circumstances in which a school's internal and external expectations have a relatively significant common denominator. Articulating an attentive vision under such circumstances is a rather complicated task. It requires careful identification and synthesis of the mutual interests of the school and the environment, in order to enable people from within as well as those from outside school to identify with the articulated vision.

Finally, educational leaders may encounter circumstances characterized by incongruity between internal and external expectations regarding school performance. When people in the school's environment expect the school to implement educational processes that teachers are unable and/or unwilling to conduct, the school leader is likely to be faced with the problem of deciding between articulating an inward-oriented vision while failing to meet the expectations of parents and district officials, and articulating an outward-oriented vision, while failing to meet the professional qualifications and educational values of teachers. Articulating a vision under such circumstances presents leaders with a highly complicated task. Attentive leaders of self-managing schools, in particular, are likely to encounter conflict in considering their inclination to define a vision that may be used as a reference point for all. Therefore, a significant discrepancy between a school's internal qualities and the external expectations directed towards the school is more likely to promote the articulation of an illusionary vision. This may happen, not because of a leader's deliberate attempt to manipulate but rather, because of the objective difficulty in finding a common denominator that may equally address the expectations of people within school as well as those from the outside.

Hence, although the assumptions inherent to SBM emphasize the school's increased ability and need to address and be responsive to local expectations, we believe this assertion needs to be moderated. We further contend that school responsiveness to local needs should be treated as a multi-dimensional concept, and that referring to "different degrees of responsiveness" is more appropriate when addressing the many possible interactions between schools and their environments.

Responsiveness is a means and not a goal in itself. It is a tool to be used by self-managing schools to improve their effectiveness and relevance by creating a better fit between the educational services they provide and the needs and expectations of community members. However, expecting schools to fully meet local expectations may encourage educators to abandon professional educational considerations and may eventually undermine schools' effectiveness. Therefore, an SBM policy should emphasize the school's obligation to address local needs. Yet, at the same time, it should provide school leaders with sufficient legitimacy to articulate a vision that will enable schools to conduct meaningful educational processes based on the better judgment and professional skills of school-level educators. If SBM fails to do so, it may sow the seeds of its own failure.

REFERENCES

Bass, B. M. (1985). *Leadership and performance beyond expectations.* New York: Free Press.

Bell, J., & Harrison, B. T. (Eds.). (1995). *Vision and values in managing education: Successful leadership principles and practice.* London: David Fulton.

Bennis, W., & Nanus, B. (1985). *Leaders: The strategies for taking charge.* New York: Harper and Row.

Benson, C. S. (1978). *The economics of public education* (3rd ed.). Boston: Houghton Mifflin.

Bogler, R., & Nir, A. E. (2001). Organizational vision: The other side of the coin. *The Journal of Leadership Studies, 8* (2), 135-144.

Bolman, L. G., & Deal, T. E. (1991). *Reframing organizations: Artistry, choice and leadership.* San Francisco: Jossey-Bass.

Boyd, W. L. (1990). Balancing control and autonomy in school reform: The politics of Perestroika. In J. Murphy (Ed.), *The educational reform movement of the 1980s.* Berkeley, CA: McCutchan Publishing.

Bray, M. (1985). Education and decentralization in less-developed countries: A comment on general trends, issues and problems, with particular reference to Papua New Guinea. *Comparative Education, 21* (2), 183-195.

Brown, D. J. (1990). *Decentralization and school-based management.* New York: The Falmer Press.

Brown, D. J. (1991). *Decentralization.* California: Corwin Press.

Burns, J. M. (1978). *Leadership.* New York: Harper & Row.

Clune, W. H., & White, P. A. (1988). *School based management: Institutional variation, implementation and issues for further research.* New Brunswick, NJ: Center for Policy Research in Education, Rutgers University.

Cohen, M. (1988) *Restructuring the education system: Agenda for the 1990s.* Washington DC: National Governors Association.

Conger, J. A., & Kanungo, R. B. (Eds.). (1989). *Charismatic leadership*: *The elusive factor in organizational effectiveness.* San Francisco: Jossey-Bass.

Conley, S. (1991). Review of research on teacher participation in school decision-making. *Review of Research in Education, 17,* 225-226.

Creemers, B. P. M. (1997). *Vision that works.* Paper prepared for the American Educational Research Association. Chicago.

Daft, R. L., & Steers, R. M. (1986). *Organizations: A micro/macro approach.* Glenview, IL: Scott, Foresman, & Co.

David, J. L. (1989). Synthesis of research on school-based management. *Educational Leadership, 46*(8), 45-53.

Emery, F. E., & Trist, E. L. (1965). The causal texture of organizational environments. *Human Relations, 18,* 21-32.

Garms, W. I., Guthrie, J. W., & Pierce, L. C. (1978). *School finance: The economics and politics of public education.* Englewood Cliffs, NJ: Prentice Hall.

Gaziel, H. H., & Romm, T. (1988). From centralization to decentralization: The case of Israel as a unique pattern of control in education. *European Journal of Education, 23*(4), 345-352.

Guthrie, J. W. (1986). School-based management: The next needed educational reform. *Phi Delta Kappan, 68,* 305-309.

Hanson, E. M. (1984). Administrative reform in the Venezuelan Ministry of Education: A case analysis of the 1970s. *International Review of Education, 30*(2), 119-141.

Hersey, P., & Blanchard, K. H. (1972). *Management of organizational behavior* (2nd ed.). Englewood Cliffs, NJ: Prentice-Hall.

Holmes, G. (1993). *Essential school leadership. Developing vision and purpose in management.* London: Kogan Page.

Hoy, W. K., & Miskel, C. G. (1991). *Educational administration – Theory, research, practice* (4th ed.). New York: McGraw-Hill.

Johnes, G. (1995). School management: How much local autonomy should there be? *Educational Management and Administration, 23*(3), 162-167.

Lauglo, J. (1995). Forms of decentralization and their implications for education. *Comparative Education, 31*(1), 5-29.

Likert, R. (1961). *New patterns of management.* New York: McGraw-Hill.

Likert, R. (1967). *The human organization: Its management and value.* New York: McGraw-Hill.

Nanus, B. (1992). *Visionary leadership. Creating a compelling sense of direction for your organization.* San Francisco: Jossey Bass.

Peters, T. J., & Waterman, R. H. (1982). *In search of excellence: Lessons from America's best-run companies.* New York: Harper Collins.

Purkey, S. C., & Smith, M. S. (1985). School reform: The district policy implications of the effective schools literature. *Elementary School Journal, 85*(3), 353-389.

Sackney, L. E., & Dibski, D. J. (1994). School-based management: A critical perspective. *Educational Management and Administration, 22*(2), 104-112.

Scott, R. W. (1981). *Organizations: Rational, natural, and open systems.* New York: Prentice-Hall.

Sergiovanni, T. J. (1990). *Value-added leadership: How to get extraordinary performance in schools.* San Diego, CA: Harcourt Brace Jovanovich.

Sleegers, P., & Wesselingh, A. (1995). Dutch dilemmas: Decentralization, school autonomy and professionalization of teachers. *Educational Review, 47*(2), 199-207.

Terry, R. W. (1993). *Authentic leadership: Courage in action.* San Francisco: Jossey-Bass.

Thompson, J. D. (1967). *Organizations in action.* New York: McGraw-Hill.

Weick, K. E. (1976). Educational organizations as loosely coupled systems. *Administrative Science Quarterly, 21*, 1-19.

White, R., & Lippit, R. (1960). Leader behavior and member reactions in three social climates. In D. Cartwright & A. Zander (Eds.), *Group dynamics.* New York: Harper and Row.

Wohlstetter, P., & McCurdy, K. (1991). The link between school decentralization and school politics. *Urban Education, 25*(4), 391-414.

Yukl, G. (1994). *Leadership in organizations* (3rd ed.) Englewood Cliffs, NJ: Prentice Hall.

Part III

The Dynamics of

School-Based Management

THE DEVELOPMENT OF SELF-MANAGED SCHOOLS IN ENGLAND: COMBINING LOCAL CHOICE WITH CENTRAL REGULATION

Rosalind Levačić

INTRODUCTION: WHAT IS SCHOOL-BASED MANAGEMENT?

The objective of the conference in Israel was to share ideas, experience and research findings on school-based management (SBM) as it has been implemented in different countries. It is well known that great care is needed in applying lessons from one country's system to another because of political, social and organizational differences. School-based management is itself an imprecise term because the areas over which schools have management discretion can vary quite considerably, as can the stakeholders who have managerial power. These two domains of school-based management (what is managed at school level and by whom) are reflected in the different emphasis given in the two major definitions of school-based management which can be found in the literature. Good examples of these two definitions of SBM are:

1. Decentralization to the school level of responsibility for decision-making in a number of domains (e.g. curriculum, method of teaching, resources, people, selection of pupils) (Caldwell, 1990);

2. The sharing of decision-making power among the key stakeholders at the school level – head teachers, teachers, parents, students, other community members (David, 1989).

Similarly, the related concept of school autonomy is also often, as Berka (2000) comments, "an ambiguous and ambivalent notion." Berka considers that the autonomy of an entity must be defined in relation to other sources of power and influence. Hence autonomy for schools should be defined in relation to the state. He distinguishes three levels of autonomy:

1. External autonomy of the school in relation to state organizations.

2. External autonomy of individual professionals in relation to the state.

3. Internal autonomy of groups and individuals within the school.

Thus, the first and second forms of autonomy correspond with the first definition of school-based management and the second and third, to the second (SBM definition).

Different reasons for advocating and introducing school-based management reflect the different emphases stated in the two definitions of school-based management. In England, the main driving force behind school-based management was, and remains, improving efficiency and raising educational standards (DFE, 1992, 1994). A further reason is the political appeal of giving parents wider scope in expressing a choice of school.

It is very important to appreciate that the development of school-based management in England has been accompanied by considerable extension of central government power over schools and a diminution in the powers of local education authorities (LEAs)[1]. These are the education departments of multi-service local government units which, prior to 1988, managed the local school system with little interference from central government. Decision-making power, particularly with respect to resources and personnel, has been decentralized from LEAs to head teachers (school principals) and school governing bodies. It must be borne in mind that local government in Britain depends entirely upon legislation passed by Parliament, which is supreme, for its powers and duties. There are no constitutional guarantees of educational rights for individuals or communities.

Thus, English school decentralization is of an entirely different type than that undertaken, for example, in the transition economies of central Europe, which have re-established independent local government units and decentralized the responsibility for managing schools. Yet another form of SBM is the "high involvement" model emphasizing teacher empowerment, school restructuring and teaching innovation (Wohlstetter, Van Kirk, Robertson, & Mohrman, 1997). This has featured much less, and some would say not at all, in the English form of SBM.

In order to share ideas and experiences from the English example of school-based management this paper aims to:

---

1   The 149 Local Education Authorities in England are part of local government units that operate a whole range of local services. Eighty percent of local government expenditure is funded by central government through a block grant to local authorities and only 20% raised by local property tax.

- Examine English school-based management as a key component of a particular set of governance arrangements, which I call regulated school-based management.

- Provide a general framework for analyzing the governance of schools from an economics perspective, which asks, "What institutional arrangements will best promote efficiency and equity" (noting that equity is subjectively defined as one's preferred distributional outcomes for society).

- Consider some particular aspects of SBM in England and Wales concerning the allocation of resources to schools and their management within schools.

- Present a brief overview of available evidence on the implications of SBM in England for school management, the efficiency of the school system and – to a more limited extent – on equity in educational opportunities.

SCHOOL-BASED MANAGEMENT IN ENGLAND: THE CURRENT DIVISION OF RESPONSIBILITIES

The English school system educates 7.6 million pupils in approximately 8,000 primary schools and 3,600 secondary schools (DfEE, 1998c), all of which have extensive autonomy in resource management. We may begin with a look at the present status in the development of SBM. Experience illustrates that governments do not conceive of a complete governance model for schools and then implement it; rather, the model evolves over time. The growing desire of central government, under both of the major political parties, to become more involved in school education can be traced to the mid-1970s. However, the watershed legislation did not appear until the 1988 Education Reform Act was passed This introduced local management of schools (LMS) and other key features, such as:

- formula funding of schools;

- a national curriculum and new national tests at ages 7, 11 and 14;

- measures to enable schools to opt out of local government control and become grant maintained via direct central government funding.

Subsequent legislation has amended some of these features (grant maintained schools were abolished in 1998) or introduced new ones, in particular, extensive monitoring and regulation of school performance undertaken by central government and its agencies. Both the Conservative and Labor governments have developed the regulated model of school-based management in broadly the same direction[2] as shown by comparing key documents of both governments (DFE, 1992; DfEE, 1997).

The net result is that we now have a model of school governance, which conforms to the M-form model of an industrial firm, a concept attributed to Alfred Sloan of General Motors in the 1920s (Chandler, 1966; Levačić, 1993; Williamson, 1975). In the M-form – or multi-divisional – model of a firm, the headquarters management (viz. the Department for Education and Employment) determines the company's strategy and manages the performance of its subunits (LEAs and schools) by establishing performance targets, monitoring them against these targets and applying sanctions and rewards accordingly. The subunits are given managerial discretion over how to utilize the resources allocated to them by headquarters. Thus HQ managers are freed from detailed daily supervision of inputs and are able to concentrate on strategy and performance management. Subunit managers are given the incentives (rewards and sanctions for meeting performance targets) and the means (management discretion over how to use resources to satisfy customers).

The superior efficiency of this organizational form (in contrast to a unitary firm, in which the inputs of each branch are managed by a central functional department) depends on appropriate information communicated to the right people who are then motivated to perform well by the incentives the system signals to them (Williamson, 1975).

The domains of managerial responsibility

To outline how the M-form model operates in the English school system, it is useful to consider how responsibility for decisions concerning key management domains are now distributed among central government, local government and schools.

The major domains of management responsibility are listed in the left-hand column of Table 1 below, which summarizes how decision-making power is distributed between the three levels of central and local government and the school.

---

2   Major differences were the Labor government's abolition of grant-maintained schools, although these were able to retain a considerable degree of autonomy within the LEA, and ending of the assisted places scheme, which subsidized places in private schools for able children from low-income families.

Table 1

Distribution of management decision-making power between central and local government and school levels in England and Wales

Domain	Central government	Local government	School: Governing body and head teacher
Curriculum	National curriculum National literacy and numeracy strategies	Must implement national literacy and numeracy strategy training	Time allocations, text books, schemes of work
Assessment	Standard assessment tests at age 7, 11, 14, and national exams at 16 and 18.		Some choice of syllabus at secondary level.
Performance management: Setting and monitoring objectives	Requires LEAs to have an approved *educational development plan* and schools to set targets for test results. OFSTED inspects schools, reports are published. Failed schools put into *special measures*.	Coordinates targets with schools. Responsible for school improvement and standards. LEAs inspected by OFSTED and Audit Commission.	Sets legally required and other targets. Expected to have a school development plan. Governors must set head teacher performance targets and review these for pay award. Head teachers monitor teachers' performance.
Provision of places and pupil admissions	Legislative framework and appeals process for admissions and exclusions.	Responsible for providing sufficient places. Coordinates admissions policy with community schools. Cannot allocate individual pupils to schools. Organizes appeals panels. Responsible for education of excluded pupils.	Foundation and denominational schools set own admissions policies. All schools determine which pupils to admit in accordance with admissions policy. May exclude pupils under certain conditions.
Financial resources	Largely determines level of general funding. Sets rules for LEAs to distribute global budgets to schools.	Determine budget allocation to schools within legally prescribed rules. These now include a devolved capital budget for building work. Can withdraw budget delegation if school is mismanaged.	Determines how to spend the delegated budget for purposes of the school. Some constraints on what certain moneys can be spent on, including projects funded from devolved capital budget. Preschool: 30 class size limit.

Table 1 (continued)

Domain	Central government	Local government	School: Governing body and head teacher
Personnel	Employment legislation. Nationally agreed terms and conditions for teachers.	Community schools: LEA is employer of staff; sets terms and conditions for non-teaching staff.	Determines staff complement. Appoints head teacher and other staff members
Capital assets: buildings	Requires LEAs to submit Asset Management Plans and allocates capital grants and permission to borrow to LEAs.	Prepare Asset Management Plan: includes survey of all schools. Determines which major school projects to invest in. Manages supply of school places.	Makes case to LEA for major capital works that cannot be funded from devolved capital budget.

At the school level, managerial responsibility is shared between the governing body and the head teacher, with the former being held responsible for the strategic level of decision making. The governing body of a school consists of about 14-20 persons, about a third of whom are elected parents; there are also 1-2 elected teachers, one non-teaching staff member, LEA-nominated governors in community schools or foundation governors in foundation and denominational schools; the final category is governors co-opted from the local community. A governing body is a legal entity and is responsible for promoting high educational standards and for the general conduct of the school. It manages the school budget, ensures the curriculum meets legal requirements, determines the staff complement and oversees policies for managing staff (DfEE, 2000a). In practice, as head teachers have greater knowledge and time than part-time lay governors, much of the strategic level decision-making is undertaken by heads and senior management teams, the latter existing in larger schools (Levačić, 1995b).

Curriculum

In 1988, the government introduced a national curriculum. This was a major reduction in the decision-making powers of schools, which had previously been largely left to determine what they taught, although they were constrained by the syllabus requirements of external examining bodies for the national school examinations first taken at age 16 (after 11 years of compulsory schooling) and also at age 18 or later.

Assessment

A key element in the introduction of a more rigorous system of performance management for schools has been institution of national tests for all pupils at ages 7, 11 and 14 in English, math and science, and the publication of these results and the national examination results for every school. This has provided information for performance management, and for parents, to enable an informed choice regarding schools.

Performance management

From 1993 onward, legislation required all schools to be inspected on a four-year cycle by a new non-departmental government agency, the Office for Standards in Education (OFSTED). These inspections have become crucial for schools. They are performed against a published set of standards, though applied by different inspection teams. Reports are published on the Internet and schools are judged in their local communities on the basis of the inspection findings. If a school fails its inspection it is put through a process of special measures designed to improve educational standards, and is often closed if no improvement occurs.

Further performance management arrangements appeared from 1998 onwards. Schools are now legally required to set targets for the national tests given at age 11 and 16, and are encouraged to do so for the other tests. The Labor government's School Standards and Framework Act of 1998 tightened performance management further. Each LEA has to draw up a government approved educational development plan, showing how it will raise educational standards. As part of this, the LEA has to coordinate targets with schools. LEAs are inspected by OFSTED and the Audit Commission and the reports are published. Poorly performing LEAs are required to have some or all their services for schools contracted out to other providers, usually from the private sector.

The Labor government has also instituted performance management for head teachers and teachers (DfEE, 2000b, 2000c). Beginning in autumn 2000, governing bodies have been required to set performance targets for the head teacher, related to school targets and other objectives. Given the apparent lack of success with earlier attempts to get governing bodies to review head teachers' pay against performance targets, the government insisted that head teacher targets be set utilizing the services of an external consultant. Table 2 shows an example taken from a primary school where I was involved in this process as a governor. The head teacher's performance is reviewed annually against the performance targets set by governors, as part of the head teacher's salary review. Teachers are also assessed by the head teacher against performance criteria and awarded additional points on the pay scale (known as "passing the threshold").

Table 2

Example of head teacher performance targets set at Blunkett First School, 2000-2001

Objective	Success criteria
1. Improved standards: in literacy	70% of pupils to achieve Key Stage 1 reading at level 2 or above; 45% KS1 reading at level 2b or above.
2. Improved standards: in numeracy	97% of pupils to achieve Key Stage 1 math at level 2 or above; 74%: KS1 math at level 2b or above.
3. Management: All class teachers to set targets for individual pupil performance in literacy and numeracy based on an understanding of the relationship between tests of prior attainment and predicted levels of future attainment.	Targets will be set for all classes at the end of the summer term for the next school year, 2000/01. The literacy and numeracy coordinators will be involved in the target-setting process.
4. Community: Successful establishment of the Out of School Club. This opened in November 2000, with funding obtained from National Opportunity Fund grant.	Parental satisfaction as shown by a questionnaire. Covers costs.

The performance management system is a key feature of regulated school-based management. Considerable responsibilities are placed on governing bodies and head teachers in determining and achieving their own targets but within a tight procedural framework. A particular managerial model is imposed on schools and reinforced through new head teacher training. Clearly there is room for head teachers and governing bodies to manage according to their own styles within the constraints of the policy, and considerable leeway for interpretation at the local level.

School places and admissions

Another key aspect of the degree of school autonomy is determining the number of school places and the admission of pupils. In England, each school has a defined full capacity number of pupils. If the school falls below this number, it must admit any pupil who meets its admissions criteria. Some schools select on religious grounds, and some secondary schools have admissions policies that enable them to select on the basis of ability or aptitude. A governing body can admit pupils over the school's capacity and there are no legal restrictions on class size except for preschool classes (ages 5-7) where the limit is now 30. There is a system of parental appeals. Prior to the Education Reform Act 1988, LEAs could manage school rolls by limiting the entry of pupils to more popular schools and directing them towards less popular ones. Increased parental choice meant that parents could not be refused admission to a school with spare places, provided their child meets the school's admissions criteria, of which residing in the school's reserved area is the still the predominant criterion for most schools.

However, popular schools are restricted in their ability to expand by not being able to enlarge buildings and facilities without LEA permission and approval of the capital expenditure. LEAs still retain responsibility for planning the provision of school places and hence for starting new schools, major expansion of existing schools and school closures, all of which require DfEE agreement.

Resource management and delegated budgeting

It is in the domain of resource management that schools have acquired extensive autonomy, and this is the aspect of school-based management on which I wish to concentrate for the remainder of this paper. Local management of schools was brought in by the 1988 Education Reform Act and implemented from 1990 to 1994. Prior to this two LEAs – Cambridgeshire and Solihull – had introduced their own, less radical versions of local financial management. Local management of schools consists of three key features.

1. Each school is allocated a delegated annual budget from the local authority to cover the majority of its needs. The governing body and head teacher determine how to spend the budget for the purposes of the school and can carry forward a deficit or surplus into the next financial year.

2. The budget sum each school receives is determined by a transparent and objective formula, whereby at least 80% of the amount delegated must be allocated according to the number and ages of the pupils.

3. Along with pupil-driven funding, parents were given greater choice of school.

There have been two subsequent developments concerning resource allocation under the Labor government (i.e., since 1997).

*   Fair Funding – The revised financial regime under which an increasing proportion of school resources is allocated to schools via their delegated budget and hence, must be purchased by school. As of 2001 capital funding is also devolved to all the schools, even the smallest.

*   Standards Funding – In direct antithesis to the subsidiarity principle underpinning delegated budgeting, the Labor government has increased the amount of central government funding it allocates directly to schools via a set of grants, many of which relate to particular categories while others are non-specific. The Department for Education and Employment has become highly interventionist in its desire to promote specific school improvement programs, such as the national literacy and numeracy strategies and projects to assist socially disadvantaged schools and pupils. Central funding of schools has risen from only £200 million in 1995/96 to £1,500 million in 2001/02 or about 10% of school funding[3].

Personnel

From the introduction of local management, schools have been able to determine their own staffing complement and to appoint and dismiss teachers, even though the LEA remained the employer of staff members in LEA maintained schools – now community schools. Previously, LEAs had managed teachers on a LEA-wide basis; teachers in schools with declining rolls were often redeployed to other schools.

Now, this can only occur if schools agree. Schools with budget deficits are forced to declare staff redundant in order to correct the deficit and this has clearly decreased

---

3   Another reason for the growth of central funding is that the DfEE cannot authorize LEAs to spend any specific amount of central government grants they receive on education, since they are non-specified grants. Local authorities only finance 20% of their spending from their single tax on residential property. Hence additional amounts in the national budget intended for schools have been directly allocated to schools via standards funding.

job security for teachers. However, with certain exceptions, schools must adhere to national pay and employment terms agreements.

There are few countries that have introduced SBM with this degree of discretion for schools to determine staffing establishments, appoint their own teachers and dismiss teachers on grounds of redundancy. In countries with strong teacher unions this aspect of SBM is naturally difficult, if not impossible, to introduce. The ability of a school to appoint its own teaching staff, rather than have teachers allocated to it, is important for creating staff teams who share the particular ethos and values of the individual school (Hill, Pierce, & Guthrie, 1997). However, it does make it more difficult for schools with a disproportionate number of difficult-to-teach pupils to attract teaching faculty, unless they can offer additional financial inducements, as were recently introduced in England.

Capital assets and buildings

The buildings and other assets of community schools are owned by the LEA, but clearly expenditure on maintenance and repairs is important in maintaining the capital value of buildings. Detailed regulations were drawn up to distinguish between the parts of the building that are the responsibility of the school and those of the LEA. The new arrangements under so-called fair funding have now allocated schools devolved capital budgets of £4000 per school plus £10-15 per pupil for small capital works. For major capital works, schools still need to make a case to the LEA which in turn applies for capital approvals from the DfEE. LEAs have been required to survey schools and draw up asset management plans (AMPs) based on three categories or reasons for capital investment: condition, suitability and sufficiency. The asset management plans are submitted to the DfEE for approval and the allocation of grants and permission to borrow funds is based on the AMPs. This is certainly a more rational method of allocating capital expenditure to LEAs and schools than the previous system.

The model of regulated school-based management we now have in place has evolved over the last twelve years. Key aspects of this evolution have been:

- Increasing the proportion of school resources that are delegated to schools.
- Increasing the extent of performance regulation, first through national inspection and then through a hierarchical system of target-setting – from national to LEA to school level targets – accompanied by performance management for head teachers and teachers.

- Increasing central government intervention in the delivery of education at the school level, linked to the growth of specified central government grants.

MIXING THE PUBLIC AND THE PRIVATE

One of the significant impacts of school-based resource management has been the extension of private sector provision of services to schools, as schools were able to seek alternative suppliers to the LEA, with a commensurate decline in LEA provision. Table 3 shows an example from the Blunkett Primary School. The list of goods and services, which even a small, 135-pupil primary school has to purchase for itself is indicative of the extent of budget delegation. The private sector accounts for 78% of the purchases in this example.

The example presented illustrates the two forms of productive activity which take place within schools:

1. Final production: The production of educational outcomes, i.e. the skills, attitudes and knowledge acquired by pupils as a consequence of the learning provided.

2. Intermediate production: The creation of the learning environment by providing the physical environment and staff resources needed to create learning (i.e. produce the final product).

The example also illustrates how intermediate production can occur in the private sector while final production of educational outcomes remains within the public sector. A major aspect of SBM in England has involved moving intermediate production of activities that support educational production from the LEA bureaucracy to private sector firms, while the school itself has remained within the public sector.

Market and organization as coordination mechanisms

There are two major forms of economic organization that can undertake both types of production described above: public and private sector organizations, where the latter includes non-profit organizations.

Finally, we can distinguish two major types of coordination mechanism for determining what is produced, how it is produced and for whom: the market and the organization. The distinguishing feature of the market is that the participants coordinate their activities by engaging in exchange of goods and services at a price. Activities that are coordinated within an organization, which can be either in the

Table 3

Blunkett Primary School: Private and public sector sources of goods and support services

Resource	Annual planned expenditure 2001/02	Private sector	LEA
Supply teachers	2,000	Yes	
Cleaners	2,880	Yes	
Repairs & maintenance	7,500	Yes (4000)	Yes
Repairs & advice	385		Yes
Grounds maintenance	1,350	Yes	
Energy	2,310	Yes	
Energy management	56		Yes
Cleaning materials	1,030	Yes	
Water	700	Yes	
Books, materials, stationery	7,000	Yes	
Equipment, furniture, materials	7,000	Yes	
Health, safety and security	1,500	Yes	
Office costs	2,000	Yes	
Financial administration	2,220	Yes	
Creditors' payments	500		Yes
Payroll	745	Yes	
Personnel advice	555	Yes	
Governors' support and training	1,000		Yes
Pupil performance data analysis	263	Yes	
Insurance	996	Yes	
Purchasing advice	109		Yes
IT services	1,635		Yes
School secretary meetings	60		Yes
School library service	1,330		Yes
Caretaking training	50		Yes
Ethnic minority support service	1,710		Yes
TOTAL	46,884	36,529	10,335

private or public sector, have different mechanisms of coordination. In a bureaucratic organization coordination occurs through a hierarchical chain of authority, by which superiors pass on orders to subordinates and grant subordinates the resources needed to implement the orders. Another method of coordination used in organizations is mutual adjustment or networking, whereby participants engage in informal exchanges of services, including information exchange. Mutual adjustment can occur both within the organization and between organizations. Thus, there are three major forms of coordination through which goods and services are provided (Douma & Schreuder, 1998; Thompson, Mitchell, Levačić, & Frances, 1991; Williamson, 1975):

- market

- hierarchy (bureaucracy)

- networking or mutual adjustment.

The fundamental issue for the efficient allocation of resources is whether organizing production using market or hierarchical coordination mechanisms will result in more efficient production. In other words, what institutional arrangements will result in the most efficient production of output in a particular sector? We can pose the same question for equity, but here the emphasis will be on mechanisms to distribute goods and services to individuals with differing needs.

Efficiency consists of two elements (Levin, 1990, 1997). The first is productive efficiency, which is the relationship between the amount of output produced and the cost of inputs used to produce that output. A cost-efficient method of production produces a given set of outputs at least cost. The second aspect of efficiency is known as allocative efficiency. A system is allocatively efficient if, with a given amount and distribution of resources, it produces a combination of the goods and services that consumers value most[4].

Adapted to schools, allocative efficiency is about giving parents greater diversity in the educational provision (e.g., in school curriculum and ethos) from which they can choose. Productive efficiency is concerned with schools producing the maximum possible educational output (e.g., as defined by examination results from a standard national curriculum) from a given quantity of resources.

When considering the best institutional arrangements for providing a particular commodity or service, an important consideration is the extent to which the benefits and costs are private or public. In the case of education, it is a complex commodity in that it yields both private and public benefits. Private benefits are those that only the individual can enjoy and which, when consumed by that individual, leave nothing

---

4   Economists often use the Pareto definition of efficiency: An allocation of resources is efficient if there exists no change from the current situation which can increase the welfare of at least one individual without making another worse off. An alternative definition is to define a social welfare function for society as a whole (which involves making interpersonal value judgements). An efficient allocation then, is one which maximizes social welfare (see Stevens, 1993, ch. 1).

over for the benefit of others, such as the income earned and retained by the individual as a consequence of their education. In contrast, a public benefit is one which yields benefits to all in society and from which no one can be excluded. The commonly cited public benefits of education are social cohesion, pro-social behavior and the contribution of more productive individuals to economic growth. Left to market allocation, insufficient quantities of a public benefit will be produced because the price cannot signal to producers the value of the public (i.e., external) benefits to society. Hence, social efficiency is improved if the government acquires the production of public goods. Equity provides a further argument for state intervention in the provision of education in order to ensure equality of educational opportunity.

However state intervention in education need not imply state provision. The private or public source of funding of a commodity can be separated from whether it was provided (i.e., produced) in the public or private sector. Public sector funding of education can ensure access to education for all children at a zero price of schooling to parents, whether or not schools are in the public or private sector.

Thus there are four possible combinations of public and private funding and provision as shown in Figure 1, in which intermediate and final production of education are distinguished.

PROVISION

FUNDING	Public		Private	
	School inputs	*School ownership*	*School inputs*	*School ownership*
Public	Traditional welfare state: bureaucratic provision		State-subsidized private sector educational provision	
Public		Quasi-markets: mixed economy of bureaucratic and market provision		
Private	User charges and sponsorship		Pure market provision of education	

Figure 1. Combinations of public and private funding and provision of schooling

The traditional welfare state model is the public provision and funding of schools, where the bulk of intermediate production is done within the public sector. The coordination mechanism used is hierarchy within a bureaucracy. The main economic arguments against this model, which are now long-standing and well-rehearsed, are that it is inefficient because of:

- A lack of incentives for public sector employees to be both productively and allocatively efficient and produce the kinds of outputs valued by consumers, and to do so at least cost. The inefficiency is due to the absence of links between the rewards which public sector employees receive and what is valued by the consumers of public services.

- An absence of information about consumer tastes and production costs that is signalled in a market system through prices.

These arguments are persuasive but they are not theoretically or empirically proven. However, their power is evident in the dissatisfaction expressed in many countries with the traditional welfare state model and developments of alternatives, in education and other social service sectors.

SCHOOL-BASED MANAGEMENT AND ALTERNATIVES TO THE TRADITIONAL WELFARE STATE MODEL

At one extreme is the abandonment of public funding and provision of education, leaving it entirely to market forces, with voluntary action as the only means of addressing the public good and equity reasons for non-market provision. Very few advocates have gone this far. This leaves three possible models:

Model 1: State funding and provision with quasi-market arrangements;

Model 2: State funding and private sector provision;

Model 3: Private sector funding and state provision.

Model 1: State funding and provision with quasi-market arrangements

The key feature of a quasi-market is that it uses the market coordination mechanism within the state sector by creating an internal market (Le Grand, 1990; Levačić, 1992, 1995a). The essential feature of this is the separation of purchaser and provider functions. In the English model the LEA becomes the purchaser of final educational output on behalf of parents, who can exercise some choice of school, and schools act as providers. The legislation sets the terms of the contract between the purchaser and provider. LEAs must fund schools by a formula and schools must provide education of sufficient quality. If they do not, parents will choose alternative schools, if they are able to do so, and ultimately OFSTED, the LEA and the DfEE will intervene. LEAs are also providers of services to schools, which are free to purchase a wide range of goods and services required for their intermediate production from providers other than the LEA. Under the School Standards and Framework Act the LEA has four major functions:

- strategic management;

- improving standards in schools;

- providing sufficient school places and access to them;

- ensuring the provision of special educational needs, including certain SEN services, such as educational psychology.

In Model 1, core educational provision remains with public sector schools despite the development of quasi-markets, and private sector organizations that compete with those in the public sector in supplying intermediate services to schools. The extension of budget delegation under the revision of local management of schools by the Labor government, called Fair Funding, which took place between 1999 and 2001, has now enlarged the schools services market to a potential £2.5 billion (Mansell, 2000). It is reported (Mansell, 2000) that an index of the financial performance of 40 education and training companies quoted on the stock exchange more than trebled in value from 1996-2000. The value of the education market is estimated to grow to £5 to £8 billion within the next three years (Targett, 1999) and is proving an attractive opening to both specialist and non-specialist education companies.

Model 2: State funding and private sector provision of core educational services

One example of this is the now-abolished assisted places scheme, whereby able children from lower income families were provided subsidized places in selective private schools. This was discontinued in 1997 by the new Labor government.

However, the outsourcing of core educational services to the private sector has been further developed under Labor as part of its "Third Way" policies, when state sector management has been deemed inadequate. Two forms of private sector provision of core services have been developing.

1. The first is the four sets of functions listed above, which have been retained by LEAs under the Fair Funding regime. However, if an LEA's services are deemed inadequate by an OFSTED-Audit Commission inspection, all or some of them may be privatized. So far, 20 LEAs out of 123 inspected have "failed" their inspections. Three LEAs in London have had their all their services contracted out to private sector companies. The DfEE is promoting the development of the market by taking active steps to widen the pool of approved private sector providers of services to LEAs (Kelly, 1999).

2. The second is the contracting of school management to private sector organizations, while the funding remains almost totally within the public sector. Two secondary schools in Surrey, which had experienced long term difficulties in recruiting pupils were contracted by the LEA, through a process of competitive tendering, to be managed by a non-profit-making private sector company, 3Es. The non-profit company is now a federation of three schools, including the original one, a city technology college in Birmingham. The company is managed by an ex-education director and head teacher and so provides an interesting example of alternative institutional arrangements other than the public sector for certain personnel.

Model 3: State provision and private sector funding

Delegated budgeting gives schools further incentives to raise money on their own accord, either through "voluntary" parental contributions, fundraising activities, including school business projects, and sponsorship by private sector companies. However, local income (fundraising, fees and charges, and sponsorship) are estimated at £230 million which is less than 1 per cent of £17.9 billion from formula funding plus £1.5 billion from standards funding (Audit Commission & OFSTED, 2000c). Schools in England (unlike those in Australia and New Zealand) usually do not charge parents "voluntary contributions" for general education services, as opposed to specific school trips and events.

Larger scale examples of private funding involve the private sponsorship of complete schools. An early example is the 15 city technology colleges (CTCs) introduced in 1986. Private sector sponsors were invited to fund and establish trusts to create new schools, with a technology specialty, serving inner-city communities. The government contributed considerable additional funding as the sponsors provided £37 million out of the £150 million initial capital expenditure, and the government continues to provide the bulk of recurrent expenditure (West, Noden, Kleinman, & Whithead, 2000). The CTCs select pupils across the ability range but are allowed to interview as part of the selection process. These schools operate outside the LEA-maintained sector as charitable trusts, and thus are really an example of Models 2 and 3 combined. The Labor government is now attempting to establish city academies, sponsored by churches and other organizations as an alternative to LEA schools, which have been deemed "failing" over several years. Such long-term failing schools are concentrated in socially-deprived areas (DfEE, 2001b).

Both Conservative and Labor governments have encouraged private sector sponsorship of secondary schools via the establishment of specialty schools, which remain within the state sector. These schools have to make a successful application to the DfEE to develop a specialty in sports, languages, arts or technology and to have secured at least £100,000[5] in private sector sponsorship. The schools then receive an additional capital grant of £100,000 and recurrent expenditure grants of £100 per pupil to develop and maintain their specialty and improve standards. Since 1998 specialty schools have also been required to share facilities and expertise with neighboring schools. In January 1998 there were 290 specialty schools (out of 3,500 in England). By 2001 there were nearly 600 specialty schools, which the government intends to increase to 1000 by 2003 (DfEE, 2001b).

A further example of government promotion of private sector involvement and sponsorship is education action zones (EAZs). The first wave of 25 EAZs has now been operating for just over two years (1999-2001). A further 48 EAZs were started in late 1999 and 2000. Each zone is being funded by the DfEE to the tune of £750,000 over 3 years[6] with an additional £250,000 to be raised from the private sector (DfEE, 1998a).

They have the following features:

- consist of 2-3 secondary schools and special schools, with 15-25 associated (feeder) primary schools;

---

5   Reduced to £50,000 in 1999.

6   It may be continued for a further two years.

- located in socially disadvantaged areas with low educational achievement, geographically dispersed across England, mainly in urban areas;
- a partnership between the LEA, business interests (essential) and local public sector and quasi-governmental organizations;
- initiatives for raising achievement, reducing social exclusion, and supporting families and pupils;
- teachers' national pay and conditions and the National Curriculum can be disapplied;
- each EAZ has a Forum, which includes DfEE appointees and representatives from governing bodies. The Forum oversees the management of the EAZ and is accountable for its funding.

Most EAZs are led by the LEA; in a few cases, a private sector organization is the lead partner (e.g., Shell International in Lambeth and Comcast in Middlesborough). Press reports suggest that private sector involvement has taken some effort to drum up and that much business support is in terms of personnel time rather than hard cash. An OFSTED inspection of six zones found that two had not succeeded in raising the £250,000 a year in cash or kind from private sector sponsors.

Public-private partnerships cover all kinds of commercial relationships in which a private sector contractor finances and provides a school or LEA with a facility and takes on its long-term operation. The school or LEA pays for its utilization of the facility out of its recurrent revenues. According to the DfEE, the purpose of PPP is to provide more cost-effective public services and to transfer risk to the private sector (DfEE, 2001a). These arrangements also satisfy the Treasury's desire to reduce the proportion of borrowing that is classified as public sector debt. Examples include long-term LEA contracts to replace whole school buildings, modernize heating systems, and provide ICT hardware, software and training. Governing bodies can enter into PPP contracts but only with the agreement of the LEA or school trustees. Examples of joint ventures with individual schools are an ICT company investing in a computer suite used by the school and for company training, and a franchise music school setting up in secondary school premises, where the school can use the equipment during school hours.

Mixed models

Thus, in England, we have elements of all three models being attempted, but the main emphasis is on retaining core educational production within the state sector.

176

In the US, for example, there is more emphasis than in England on Model 2, with the introduction of voucher schemes that enable children from low-income families to attend private sector schools, and the development of charter schools run by non-profit-organizations. In addition, whether a school is classified as being in the private or public sector depends on the national legal framework. In Britain, denominational (church) schools were incorporated into the state school sector under the 1944 Education Act[7], whereas in other countries (e.g., Netherlands, France, Australia) they are regarded as being within the private sector even though they receive extensive state funding.

THE POLICY RATIONALE FOR MODEL CHOICE

The extent to which it is deemed suitable to use Model 2 (private provision and state funding) rather than Model 1 or 3 (state provision of final educational output with public or private funding) depends on the extent to which policy-makers perceive education as a public good. If education is seen primarily as a private good, which as a merit good should be available to all regardless of income, then state funding with private sector provision will be deemed the best solution.

Private schools are more likely to ensure diversity of provision and thus satisfy a wide range of parental preferences, which would be a more allocatively efficient arrangement than the greater uniformity of public sector provision. The only concern would be on equity grounds, that parents who are "inert" choosers (Willms, Nash, & Stern, 1997) will disadvantage their children by letting them attend poor schools, where socially-disadvantaged children will be concentrated.

However, if policy-makers view school education as having a high element of public good, then they will be more concerned with productive efficiency than with allocative efficiency. In fact, satisfying a diverse range of parental preferences reduces the public benefits of education in the form of social cohesion (achieved by all schools

---

7   Denominational schools, until very recently, were almost exclusively Church of England and Roman Catholic, with a few Jewish schools. The LEA funds all of their recurrent costs and 85% of their capital costs, if voluntarily aided. The church can nominate some of their own governors (foundation governors). Under the School Standards and Framework Act, denominational schools are foundation schools and thus are the employers of staff and own the school assets in trust.

subscribing to a common set of civic values and drawing from a cross-section of the population) and ensures the mutual curriculum content and standards of achievement deemed necessary to produce future workers with the requisite labor market skills (Levin, 1991). Given that the traditional welfare model is rejected on efficiency grounds, then the degree to which a country's education policy favors Models 1, 2 or 3 will depend on the extent to which schooling is viewed as a public or private good. This correspondence between institutional models and the relative emphasis given to the private or public aspects of schooling is indicated in Figure 2.

Model 1: Public provision and funding within a quasi-market	**Model 2: Private provision and public funding**
Schooling: a high **public good** element	Schooling primarily a **private good**
Emphasis:	Emphasis:
productive efficiency and	**allocative efficiency** and
equity	**equity**
Model 3: Public provision and private funding (from companies)	**Model 4: Private provision and private funding**
Schooling: a high **public good** element mainly from contribution to productivity	Schooling primarily a **private good**
Emphasis:	Emphasis:
productive efficiency and	**allocative efficiency**
equity	

Figure 2. Correspondence between institutional arrangements and the private/public good emphasis given to schooling

In Britain, the national emphasis on improving educational standards is extensively justified in economic terms, for increasing national competitiveness in the global economy and for reducing the extent of social exclusion (DfEE, 1997). Schools are social agencies, which are seen to be more susceptible to state influence than the family. Hence, in Britain, increased central regulation of school performance, accompanied by school-based management of resources, can be explained in terms of its being perceived as the most effective institutional arrangement for achieving productive efficiency for the public good aspects of schooling.

At the same time, the government is promoting diversity in secondary education, within the constraints of national standards and performance monitoring, by recommending the extension of Model 3 (private sponsorship and fund raising for state schools) (DfEE, 2001b). However, the argument put forward, with limited empirical evidence, is that such diversity promotes a distinctive school vision, which creates a more educationally effective school. In other words, underpinning the promotion of diversity is the productive efficiency rationale.

In countries with a different national agenda, for example Israel, where satisfying the diverse preferences of parents from a wide range of social and religious backgrounds may be more important than insisting on a state imposition of a defined standard of education, the English model of regulated school-based management may not be appropriate. However, there are elements of it, such as the successful implementation of school-level resource management, an examination of which may prove to be useful.

ISSUES IN THE IMPLEMENTATION OF SCHOOL-BASED RESOURCE MANAGEMENT

The impacts of local management on efficiency and equity

There is widespread agreement that local management of schools in England was a successfully implemented policy that has been largely favored by head teachers, as it gives them greater control to secure efficiency in the running of their school (Association of Metropolitan Authorities, 1994; Audit Commission, 1993; Audit Commission & OFSTED, 2000c; Bullock & Thomas, 1994, 1997; Levačić, 1995a, 1998; Maychell, 1994). These studies broadly concluded, from qualitative evidence on resource allocation decisions by schools, that local management enables schools to improve their cost-efficiency. Schools took advantage of the increased flexibility and speed of decision-making to improve the school's physical environment, change staffing patterns (in particular, to employ more support staff, especially primary classroom assistants) and to secure better value for money by using alternative suppliers to the LEA's direct labor force. While schools put any money saved through better value purchasing into learning resources, there was no evidence in the early years of LMS that direct increases in educational outcomes occurred as a result. The government's relentless pressure on schools to raise standards became apparent from the mid-1990s and relied on performance management rather than SBM alone. In fact, the Labor government, in its national literacy and numeracy strategies, has centralized further by directing schools to use specific teaching approaches.

Concerns about the impact of local management relate to equity rather than efficiency. Anxiety has been expressed about the greater incentive schools have to exclude difficult pupils, whose behavior disrupts the learning of other pupils and damages the school's marketing image, and who lower the school's examination results. The numbers of excluded pupils rose from the early to mid-1990s (Parsons, 1996), causing the DfEE to express concern and institute targets for LEAs and schools to reduce exclusions. These have now fallen back to 0.14% of the school population[8].

The other issue is whether schools catering disproportionately to socially-disadvantaged pupils have suffered from the competition that is an essential ingredient of the quasi-market system. There is conflicting evidence as to whether schools have become more socially segregated or not, depending on the time period and measures used (e.g., Gorard & Fitz, 1998, 1999a, 1999b; Noden, 2000). Levačić and Hardman (1998) found that socially-disadvantaged schools, while funded more generously per pupil, tended to experience declining total revenues over time due to a decline in the school roll. On the other hand, much more action than in the past has been taken to raise educational standards for the least able students and for those in schools with the poorest academic records. However, this has been activated through performance management policies, in particular, special measures for schools failing OFSTED inspections (Gray, 2000; OFSTED, 2000b) and a program of central government intervention for inner-city schools called "Excellence in Cities," rather than through SBM.

Three key factors in the successful implementation of school-based resource management have been:

- Strong pressure to force LEAs to devolve a substantial proportion of resources to schools;
- Funding formulae based on objective criteria;
- Development of increasing expertise in financial and resource management in schools.

---

8   For education statistics on permanent exclusions, see www.dfee.gov.uk/statistics

Enforcing financial devolution by LEAs

When initially implementing LMS, the Department for Education insisted that only certain resources could be retained by the LEA: some *had to be* retained by the LEA (at that time capital expenditure, home-to-school transport), while other items *could be* retained (structural repairs and maintenance, insurance, special staff costs, special needs support). Money for all other items had to be delegated. LEAs were required to delegate at least 85% of the maximum that could be delegated to schools. Grant-maintained schools, which between 1988 and 1997 could opt out of LEA control, then had 100% devolution.

When reintegrating GM schools into the LEA maintained sector, the Schools Standard and Framework Act brought in a common funding regime for both foundation schools (a category for ex-GM schools and others applying for this status) and community schools. In so doing, the government chose to extend the degree of devolution to community schools. By 2001 all schools will have budget devolution almost as extensive as that experienced by GM schools[9].

The Schools Standards and Framework Act (1998) establishes the manner in which the total amount of recurrent revenue the LEA delegates to its schools must be determined. This is shown in Figure 3. The local authority first determines how much its total LEA revenue budget will be for the coming financial year. From this it subtracts non-school expenditures and then certain school-related expenditure items that should not be financed by the individual schools. The remaining amount is the local school budget (LSB). From this the LEA can deduct expenditures for its key functions. What remains is called the individual school budget (ISB), which must be allocated in its entirety to schools via the LEA's funding formula.

Over the years the DfEE[10], under both governments, has argued that some LEAs delegate an insufficient proportion of their local school budgets (DfEE, 1998b). LEAs are required to submit an annual statement of their expenditure allocations. From these, performance indicators of the proportion of the LSB delegated are published by the Audit Commission (see figure 4). The government has determined that LEAs must delegate 85% of the local school budget by 2001/02, and 90% by 2002/03.

---

9   Foundation schools differ from community schools in being the employer of their staff and owning their assets in trust.

10 Prior to 1997 the DfEE was the Department for Education (DFE). It was then combined with the Department for Employment.

TOTAL LEA REVENUE BUDGET

subtract:

non-school expenditure

subtract:

on-going school-related commitments:

debt-servicing

early-retirement and redundancy costs (before April 1999)

recruitment and retention schemes

equals:

LOCAL SCHOOL BUDGET   (LSB)

subtract LEA expenditure for:

strategic management

access (infrastructure, admissions, attendance)

support for school improvement

special education

special cases (music service, school insurance)

equals:

INDIVIDUAL SCHOOL BUDGET

100 per cent delegated to schools by the LEA funding formula.

In addition schools may receive earmarked sums for SEN statemented pupils, which are put directly into the school budget.

Figure 3. The determination of the individual school budget

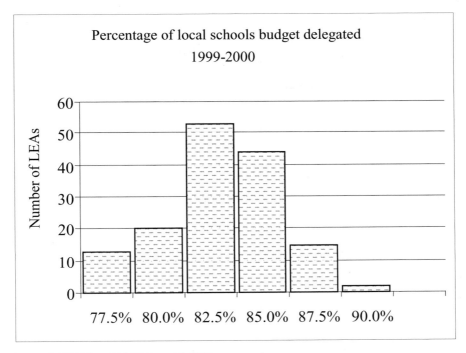

Source: DfEE News 288/99 June 24, 1999.

Figure 4. Percentage of LSB delegated by LEAs

School funding formulae

Each LEA is required to allocate a budget share to each school by distributing the individual school budget using a formula (Levačić, 1999). Separate formulae are developed for primary, secondary and special schools – the latter can be funded on a per-place, as well as a per-pupil, basis. The DFE (1994, p. 7) stated that:

> The purpose of formula funding is to bring about an equitable allocation of resources between schools, based on objectively measured needs rather than historical patterns. Within each LEA, schools with the same characteristics and the same number of students should receive the same level of resources.

There are a number of desirable objectives a funding formula should serve (Levačić & Ross, 1999):

•   To promote effectiveness and efficiency in the use of resources by schools;

- To be equitable between schools according to their different needs;
- To promote accountability by being transparent and simple;
- To economize on administrative costs;
- To be sensitive to local conditions and reflect local preferences.

Not all the objectives are mutually consistent. For example, fine-tuning formulae to reflect differences in schools' educational needs and cost structures tends to make formulae more complex and less transparent.

LEAs are free to devise their own formulae but within the parameters set down by the DfEE. LEA funding schemes must be submitted for DfEE approval and must be developed via a process of consultation with the LEA's schools. An important constraint is that 80% of the individual school budget must be allocated according to the number and ages of pupils. The remaining 20% must be allocated by objective factors, not officer discretion. LEAs use the remaining 20% to allocate additional funds for:

1. Special educational needs which can be assessed in a number of ways, such as the percentage of pupils eligible for free school meals and/or tests of educational attainment or cognitive ability;

2. Compensating small schools for additional costs due to lack of economies of scale;

3. Differences in premises costs which depend on:
   - size of school premises
   - split sites
   - condition of premises
   - facilities, such as swimming pools.

Table 4 shows an example of a school funding formula for Devon LEA. This is a large rural authority with quite a complex formula.

Resource management in schools

The success of school-based resource management is clearly dependent on the quality of decision-making and financial administration at school level, and on the quality of support given to schools by the LEA. The latter is important because delegated budgeting does not necessarily imply that schools are actually allocated money to place in a bank account. When LMS was first introduced, the bulk of the school's budget

Table 4

Example of a school funding formula

Formula element	Cash allocation, in £ per unit
Age-weighted funding	
Primary sector:	
Part-time reception class (aged 4)	1,533.94
Full-time reception class (age 4)	1,190.49
Statutory age reception (age 5)	1,476.39
Years 1 & 2 (age 5 & 6)	1,260.59
Years 3 to 6 (ages 7 to 10)	1,168.11
Secondary sector:	
Years 7 & 8 (age 11 & 12)	1,740.02
Year 9 (age 13)	1,871.56
Years 10 & 11 (age 14 & 15)	2,163.75
Year 12 (age 16)	2,263.16
Year 13 (age 17)	2,789.34
Additional educational need	
Primary sector	
16.01 % - 19.% entitlement	3.05
19.01% and above	9.15
Free school meals	83.932
Secondary sector	
Free meals above 5.01%	0.47
Cognitive attainment test scores 70-79 (2.01% plus)	1.14
Cognitive attainment test scores 80-89 (10.01% plus)	0.14
Site specific	
Weighted floor area: 8 categories per square meter	0.66 to 2.93
Unweighted floor area: 4 categories per square meter	6.76 to 8.29
Condition factor: 6 categories per square meter	0.13 to 6.02
Site area in hectares: primary	667.93
Site area in hectares: secondary	712.44
Split sites: lump sum (8 categories)	1,370.97 to 84,002.53
Split sites: per pupil (4 categories)	8.97 to 18.91
Remote site: primary	598.08
Remote site: secondary	5,075.99
School specific factors (small size)	
Primary sector	
With less than 50 pupils (lump sum: 4 categories)	41,212 to 57,731.65
With 50 to 177 pupils (lump sum: 4 categories)	39,599.59 to 56,671.83
With more than 177 pupils (lump sum: 4 categories)	39,052.45 to 56,120.87
Less than 37 pupils (per pupil)	1,168.11
Average salary costs for schools with less than 9 teachers, excluding head and deputy.	428,000 in total
Secondary sector	
Lump sum (all schools)	5,617.11
With less than 700 pupils (per pupil)	286.94
Year groups of below 90 (5 year group rates)	870.01 to 1,131.58

Source: Devon County Council Section 52 Budget Statement – 1999/2000.

share was allocated in the form of units of account held by the LEA. In this system the school determines how much to spend on staff and on other goods and services but the actual payments are undertaken by the LEA. This means that two sets of accounts are kept – at the school and at the LEA. The implementation of LMS required a considerable investment of personnel time in developing new computerized accounting systems, making them consistent with existing LEA accounting systems and in training school personnel in financial management. If the LEA's financial system does not operate smoothly, enabling schools to receive regular and accurate financial reports from the LEA, schools experience a considerable amount of frustration and are unable to monitor their expenditures accurately.

After a few years of school-based financial management, the government insisted that all secondary schools must be able to operate bank accounts and receive regular deposits of cash. Fair funding is introducing bank accounts for all schools, but this still has to be fully implemented.

Financial management and resource management are distinct activities. Financial management is concerned with ensuring that money is spent as planned, expenditure does not exceed income and money is not used for fraudulent purposes. This requires good systems of financial control and the regular production of accurate financial reports that are used to monitor the budget.

Resource management concerns decisions about how to allocate the budget among different spending alternatives. Resource management is conducted efficiently if the school achieves the best possible educational outcomes from the resources allocated to it via the delegated budget. Since it is difficult to measure educational outcomes or to judge the trade off between different potential outcomes and there is no precise knowledge regarding how school inputs relate to educational outputs, the efficiency criterion for schools is essentially judgmental (Audit Commission, 2000; Vignoles, Levačić, Walker, Machin, & Reynolds, 2000). Efficient resource management relies on the professional judgments of decision-makers in schools, in particular those of the head teacher. Financial management can be properly conducted but this does not guarantee efficient resource management. A school may make poor decisions regarding its use of resources but have good financial controls to ensure the budget is spent as planned.

Following the initial implementation of local management of schools, OFSTED and the Audit Commission have made considerable efforts to educate school decision-makers on how to manage resources efficiently. My own study of LMS indicated that in the early years, head teachers were successful at taking on financial management but did not spontaneously develop beyond this to an explicit consideration of how to use resources to improve educational attainment. From 1993 onwards the government's development of performance management policies has focused schools' attention on educational outcomes. This has included the expectation that schools should manage resources rationally, that is, by deliberately planning budgets to serve educational objectives rather than using the historic method of budgeting. This focuses entirely on the inputs for which spending is to occur with no regard for their effect on outputs, and is limited to incremental adjustments to last year's budget.

The OFSTED inspection framework includes an assessment of the "efficiency of the school" as part of its evaluation of the quality of school management. OFSTED defines efficiency in the standard way:

> An efficient school makes good use of all its available resources to achieve
> the best possible educational outcomes for all its pupils – and in doing so
> provides excellent value for money. (OFSTED, 1995a, 1995b, p.121).

Given the absence of reliable quantitative measures of school output in relation to inputs, the four criteria that inspectors are required to use for assessing the efficiency of school are qualitative. These are:

Criterion 1: Educational developments are supported through careful financial planning;

Criterion 2: Effective use is made of staff, accommodation and learning resources;

Criterion 3: Efficient financial control and school administration;

Criterion 4: The school provides value for money in terms of the educational standards achieved and the quality of education provided in relation toits context and income (OFSTED, 1995a, 1995b, p. 120)

Hence judgments are made about:

- The aggregate relationship between output and inputs – family, peer group and school inputs (Criterion 4).

- The appropriate mix of school resources (Criterion 2 and Criterion 1).

- The quality of decision-making – whether the school sets appropriate priorities for the educational achievement of its pupils and allocates its available resources in the best way to meet these priorities (Criterion 1).

- The extent to which financial control and school administration are efficient (Criterion 3).

Because the technical relationships required for measuring efficiency in terms of output/input are unknown, great emphasis is placed on the existence of rational decision-making processes in the school. In particular, schools are expected to have a medium-term school development plan (usually 3 years) and to state the approximate cost of actions included in the plan. The school development plan should be used when preparing the budget so that school development and budget planning are integrated processes. The best practical advice on budgeting is offered in two joint publications (see Audit Commission & OFSTED, 2000a, 2000b). Additional advice is available on the Audit Commission's website, which includes a facility to compare the spending ratios in one's own school budget with those of similar schools.

There is considerable evidence that while most schools have been successful in adopting sound financial management practices, most have found rational resource management a difficult process to understand and then apply (Bennett, Levačić, Glover, Crawford, & Earley, 2000; Glover, Bennett, Crawford, & Levačić, 1997; Glover, Levačić, Bennett, & Earley, 1996; Levačić & Glover, 1997). However, over time an increasing number of schools are succeeding in adopting these processes. The improved inspection ratings for school efficiency summarized in OFSTED annual reports comparing 1996/97 and 1998/99 are shown in Table 5.

The Audit Commission's (2000) findings are consistent with those of OFSTED:

- More schools are better at financial management than at resource management.

- Although most schools have clear priorities and most have processes in place to set their budgets, they are less proficient at making a link between the two. This is partly attributable to the historic division between the school development plan (SDP), which was originally designed to address only new curriculum developments and the budget over which schools originally had limited control. Some schools have not yet managed to integrate their development planning with their budget setting. The resource management survey revealed that only 50% of head teachers felt that these links were fully in place (para. 20).

- Most schools were successfully monitoring their expenditures. However some schools lacked the expertise to extract clear and meaningful monitoring reports from their financial software (para. 22).

Table 5
The Efficiency of schools in England 1996/97 and 1998/99

	Good	Satisfactory	Unsatisfactory
	%	%	%
Primary schools			
Efficiency*	63 (52)	33 (41)	4 (7)
Financial planning (Criterion 1)	60 (50)	30 (34)	10 (16)
Use of teaching and support staff (Criterion 2)	59 (51)	36 (41)	6 (9)
Use of learning resources and accommodation (Criterion 2)	57 (51)	40 (45)	3 (5)
Efficiency of financial control & administration (Criterion 3)	78 (71)	20 (25)	2 (4)
Value for money (Criterion 4)	50 (39)	43 (52)	8 (8)
Secondary schools			
Efficiency*	65 (61)	29 (32)	6 (7)
Financial planning (Criterion 1)	62 (59)	26 (25)	11 (16)
Use of teaching and support staff (Criterion 2)	57 (55)	33 (35)	10 (10)
Use of learning resources and accommodation (Criterion 2)	60 (58)	37 (36)	3 (6)
Efficiency of financial control & administration (Criterion 3)	85 (82)	13 (15)	2 (3)
Value for money (Criterion 4)	57 (52)	35 (41)	8 (7)

Source: OFSTED, 2000a, App. 3, pp. 74, 79.

* Efficiency is a composite rating for inspection schedule 6.3, the efficiency of the school, derived from ratings for Criteria 1 to 4.

UNRESOLVED ISSUES IN THE SCHOOL-BASED RESOURCE MANAGEMENT

In the course of the development of school-based resource management in England a number of important issues have emerged and persisted. These are also likely to arise in other national contexts implementing this form of SBM.

Funding of schools

The transparency of formula funding has stimulated debate about the distribution of resources to schools and whether the historic patterns revealed are efficient and equitable. The main issues are:

- The relatively low funding for primary compared to secondary pupils (see Figure 8 below). In recent years the government has been increasing the relative funding of primary schools and LEAs have also sought to restore the balance.

- The amount of additional funding that it is appropriate to give schools for educating pupils with special educational needs and how this should be distributed (Hill & Ross, 1999; Marsh, 1995, 1997).

- The apparent horizontal inequity, meaning that pupils in similar schools in different LEAs can be funded differently because of the system of local authority grant determination and the discretion LEAs have to determine their own education spending and its distribution. Head teachers' associations favor a national funding formula but the government is reluctant to remove an element of LEA discretion (Department of Environment, 2000; Downes, 2000; West & Pennell, 2000).

- LEA funding formulae are still too dependent on historic funding patterns and are not sufficiently needs-based (Audit Commission, 2000).

- Financial uncertainty makes rational and medium-term planning difficult for schools. Many schools have accumulated surpluses, which they justify as a safeguard against future funding cuts but which others (e.g., the Audit Commission) regard as indicative of inefficiency if the funds are not earmarked for a specific project. Other schools have been unable to foresee or plan for budget cuts, e.g., due to a falling roll, and have accumulated deficits[11].

Management issues

- Some question whether budget devolution has gone too far and placed too heavy a burden on primary head teachers and governing bodies who do not have the administrative support staff available in secondary schools. The Audit Commission (2000) expressed reservations as to whether the latest extension of

---

11   In the Audit Commission (2000) study 10% of schools had accumulated budget deficits and 10% had surpluses in excess of 10% of their annual budget.

delegation under Fair Funding has yielded benefits. It recommends that LEAs need to be given a clearer role and the resources they need for it should be allocated, rather than requiring even further percentage delegation targets. In contrast, the Conservative Party is advocating greater budget delegation and "freeing" schools from the LEA.

- The role of head teachers has fundamentally changed with the development of regulated SBM. They are required both to manage the school as a business and to secure high educational standards through effective instructional leadership. In the more complex school environment, where competition is ever-present, head teachers must also strategically manage the boundaries between the school and its environment.

  The new demands on head teachers are reflected in the government's promotion of the new National Professional Qualification for Headship, professional development programs – the Leadership Program for Serving Head Teachers – and a new National School Leadership College. Head teacher pay has risen and now includes a performance element. However, the increased demands of the job are reflected in the increasing difficulties schools are currently experiencing in recruiting head teachers.

- Concern has also been expressed at the growing management demands on school governing bodies. Increasingly the governing body is treated as an agent of government policy. Lay people have limited time and expertise for carrying out the heavy responsibilities that are legally theirs. With an effective head teacher, the governing body is assured that the duties they are ultimately responsible for are carried out properly. Without this, a serious breakdown in management can occur, if neither the LEA nor the governing body have sufficient capacity to cope with poor school leadership. Currently the DfEE is reviewing the responsibilities of the governing body with a view to placing more responsibilities for staffing, for example, solely on the head teacher, though this is not supported by school governor national organizations.

AND FINALLY: IS IT WORKING?

When we examine performance indicators over time for the English education system, any changes can only be attributed to the joint effects of performance regulation and school-based management. Indicators of key stage test results and GCSE examination results, displayed in Figures 5, 6 and 7, show more or less steady improvement over time[12].

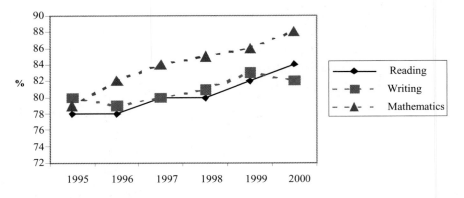

Figure 5. Percentage of 7 years olds achieving level 2 or above at Key Stage 1

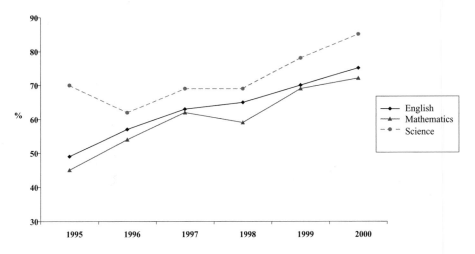

Figure 6. Percentage of children aged 11 achieving KS2 level 4 and above

---

12 In this interpretation it has to be assumed that the level of difficulty of the tests has not decreased. So far there is no clear evidence that this is the case, and QCA insists that standards are comparable from year to year.

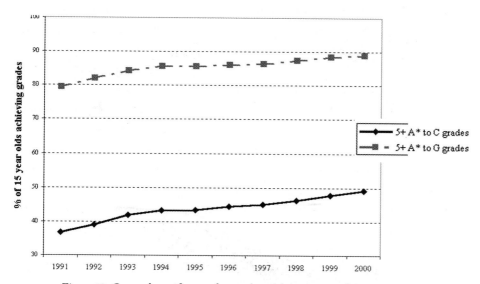

Figure 7. General certificate of secondary education results 1991-2000

In the same period, as shown in Figure 8, education expenditure per pupil in real terms rose between 1988/89 and 1992/3 – the early years of local management of schools – but then declined until 1998/9. Only in the last year has expenditure been raised by the government as part of its plans to increase education spending by 5.4%.

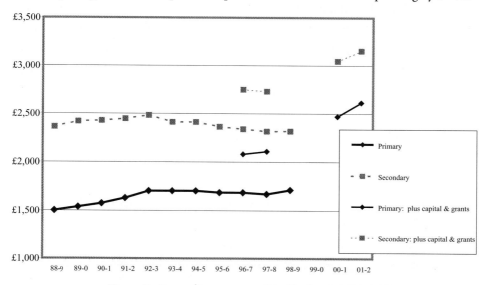

Figure 8. Expenditure per pupil in England, 1988-2001

Sources: 1993/4 – 1998/9: LEA-maintained schools unit costs in England, DfEE Departmental Reports, 1999 & 2000. 1988/9, 1992/3: UK average public spending per school pupil, Table 1.3 Education Statistics, DfEE. 1996/7 – 2001/2: Standard spending assessment and special and specific grants per pupil, House of Commons Hansard Written Answers, Dec. 15, 2000. The three series have been expressed in a common base year price (1996/7). For 1988/9 – 1992/3, the UK average public spending per pupil has been adjusted downward to make it consistent with the English LEA-maintained schools data, which are plotted in Figure 8.

The rise in educational attainment in the primary sector since 1995 has been achieved without any real per capita increase in spending, while the more recent improvements in GCSE results have occurred during a period of declining real per-pupil funding in the secondary sector. Taken together, this is indicative of a general increase in efficiency in the school system as a whole.

However, squeezing out inefficiency may come at a price. As well as increasing difficulties in head teacher recruitment, there is currently a considerable teacher shortage in England, particularly in areas where the cost of living is relatively high. It has been estimated that there are currently 10,000 vacancies for secondary teachers (Dean, 2001), which is about 5% of the total staffing complement. Although pay in real terms has increased, teaching is perceived as being a more demanding job requiring longer hours than prior to the 1990 education reforms. The government is being forced to offer various inducements for people to train as teachers and to take posts in difficult schools or expensive areas. The trade-off between an efficient system and a cheap system was well understood by Robert Lowe, president of the Board of Education in the 1860s, who pronounced of state schooling, "If it shall not be efficient it shall be cheap, and if it is not cheap it shall be efficient."

REFERENCES

Association of Metropolitan Authorities (1994). *Local management of schools review.* London: AMA.

Audit Commission (1993). *Adding up the sums: Schools' management of their finances.* London: HMSO.

Audit Commission, & OFSTED (2000a). *Getting the best from your budget: A guide to the effective management of school resources.* London: Audit Commission.

Audit Commission, & OFSTED (2000b). *Keeping your balance: Standards for financial management in schools.* London: Audit Commission.

Audit Commission, & OFSTED (2000c). *Money matters: School funding and resource management.* London: Audit Commission.

Bennett, N., Levačić, R., Glover, D., Crawford, M., & Earley, P. (2000). The reality of school development planning in the effective primary school: Technicist or guiding plan? *School Leadership and Management, 20*(3).

Berka, W. (2000). The legal and philosophical meaning of autonomy in education. In W. Berka & H. Penneman (Eds.), *Autonomy in education: Yearbook of European Association for Education Law and Policy, Vol. III.* The Hague: Kluwer Law International.

Bullock, A., & Thomas, H. (1994). *The impact of local management on schools.* Birmingham: National Association of Head Teachers and the University of Birmingham.

Bullock, A., & Thomas, H. (1997). *Schools at the center.* London: Routledge.

Caldwell, B. (1990). Educational reform through school-site management: An international perspective on restructuring education. *Advances in Research and Theories of School Management and Educational Policy, 1,* 303-333.

Chandler, A. (1966). *Strategy and structure: Changes in the history of industrial enterprise.* New York: Doubleday Anchor Books.

David, J. (1989). Synthesis of research on site-based management. *Educational Leadership, 48*(8), 45-53.

Dean (2001, March 2). Morale plummets as shortages rise. *Times Educational Supplement,* p. 6.

Department for Education (1992). *Choice and diversity: A new framework for schools.* London: DFE.

Department for Education (1994). *Local management of schools: Circular 2/94.* London: DFE.

Department for Education and Employment (1997). *Excellence in Schools.* London: Stationery Office.

Department for Education and Employment (1998a). £75 million boosts radical Education Action Zones to raise standards. *DfEE News 318/98.*

Department for Education and Employment (1998b). Blunkett issues tough challenge to Education Authorities. London: DfEE Press Release.

Department for Education and Employment (1998c). *Statistics of education schools in England.* London: DfEE.

Department for Education and Employment (2000a). *A Guide to the Law for School Governors.* London: DfEE.

Department for Education and Employment (2000b). *Performance management in schools.* DfEE 0051/2000. London: DfEE.

Department for Education and Employment (2000c). *Performance management: Guidance for governors.* London: DfEE.

Department for Education and Employment (2001a). *Public private partnerships: A guide for governors.* London: DfEE (available at www.dfee.gov.uk/ppp).

Department for Education and Employment (2001b). *Schools – building on success: Raising standards, promoting diversity and achieving results* (a green paper). London: DfEE.

Department of Environment. (2000). *Modernizing local government finance* (a green paper). London: DETR.

Douma, S., & Schreuder, H. (1998). *Economic approaches to organizations.* New York: Prentice Hall.

Downes, P. (2000). *Fairer funding.* Secondary Head Teachers Association.

Glover, D., Bennett, N., Crawford, M., & Levačić, R. (1997). Strategic and resource management in primary schools: Evidence from OFSTED inspection reports. *School Leadership and Management, 17*(3), 357-374.

Glover, D., Levačić, R., Bennett, N., & Earley, P. (1996). Leadership, planning and resource management in four very effective schools. *School Organization, 16*(2-3).

Gorard, S., & Fitz, J. (1998). The more things change... The missing impact of marketization. *British Journal of Sociology of Education, 19*(3), 365-376.

Gorard, S., & Fitz, J. (1999a). *Do markets cause segregation? The results of ten years of school choice in England and Wales.* Mimeo, University of Cardiff.

Gorard, S. & Fitz, J. (1999b). Investigating the determinants of segregation between schools. *Research Papers in Education.*

Gray, J. (2000). Causing concern but improving: A review of schools' experiences. *DfEE Research Report RR188.* London: DfEE.

Hill, P., & Ross, K. (1999) Issues in funding pupil-specific factors related to supplementary educational need. In K. Ross & R. Levačić (Eds.), *Needs-based resource allocation in education via formula funding of schools.* Paris: International Institute of Educational Planning.

Hill, P. T., Pierce, L. C., & Guthrie, J. W. (1997). *Reinventing public education: How contracting can transform America's schools.* Chicago: University of Chicago Press.

Kelly, J. (1999, December 14). Ministers boost school services outsourcing. *Financial Times.*

Le Grand, J. (1990). *Quasi-markets and social policy.* University of Bristol, School of Advanced Urban Studies.

Levačić, R. (1992). The LEA and its schools: The decentralized organization and the internal market. In G. Wallace (Ed.), *Local management of schools: Research and experience* (pp. 82-101). Clevedon and Philadelphia: BERA Dialogues, *Multilingual Matters.*

Levačić, R. (1993). Local management of schools as an organizational form: Theory and application. *Journal of Educational Policy, 8*(2), 123-141.

Levačić, R. (1995a). *Local management of schools: Analysis and practice.* Buckingham: Open University Press.

Levačić, R. (1995b). School governing bodies: Management boards or supporters' clubs? *Public Management and Money, 15*(2), 35-40.

Levačić, R. (1998). Local management of schools: Results after six years. *Journal of Educational Policy, 13*(3), 331-350.

Levačić, R. (1999). Formula funding of schools in England and Wales. In K. Ross & R. Levačić (Eds.), *Needs-based resource allocation in education via formula funding of schools.* Paris: International Institute of Educational Planning.

Levačić, R., & Glover, D. (1997). Value for money as a school improvement strategy: Evidence from the new inspection system in England. *School Effectiveness and Improvement, 8*(2).

Levačić, R., & Hardman, J. (1998). Competing for resources: The impact of social disadvantage and other factors on English secondary schools' financial performance. *Oxford Review of Education, 24*(3), 303-328.

Levačić, R., & Ross, K. (1999). Principles for designing needs-based funding formulae. In K. Ross & R. Levačić (Eds.), *Needs-based resource allocation in education via formula funding of schools.* Paris: International Institute of Educational Planning.

Levin, H. (1990). The theory of choice applied to education. In W. H. Clune & J. F. Witte (Eds.), *Choice and control in American Education: Volume 1.* New York: Falmer Press.

Levin, H. (1991). The economics of educational choice. *Economics of Education Review, 10*(2), 137-158.

Levin, H. M. (1997). Raising school productivity: An x-efficiency approach. *Economics of Education Review, 16*(3), 303-311.

Mansell, W. (2000, July 14). Private firms to share £5 billion. *Times Educational Supplement.*

Marsh, A. (1995). The effect on school budgets of different non-statemented special education needs indicators within a common funding formula. *British Educational Research Journal, 21*(1), 99-116.

Marsh, A. (1997). *Survey of current practice for resourcing additional educational needs in LEAs.* Slough: Education Management Information Exchange, NFER.

Maychell, K. (1994). *Counting the cost: The impact of LMS on schools' patterns of spending.* Slough: NFER.

Noden, P. (2000). Rediscovering the impact of marketization: Dimensions of social segregation in England's secondary schools, 1994-99. *British Journal of Sociology of Education, 21*(3), 371-390.

Office for Standards in Education (1995a). *Guidance on the inspection of nursery and primary Schools.* London: HMSO.

Office for Standards in Education (1995b). *Guidance on the inspection of secondary schools.* London: HMSO.

Office for Standards in Education (1998). *The annual report of Her Majesty's Chief Inspector of Schools.* London: The Stationery Office.

Office for Standards in Education (2000a). *The annual report of Her Majesty's Chief Inspector of Schools.* London: The Stationery Office.

Office for Standards in Education (2000b). *Improving city schools: Strategies to promote educational inclusion,* London: OFSTED.

Parsons, C. (1996). Permanent exclusions from schools in England: Trends, causes and responses. *Children in Society, 10,* 177-186.

Stevens, J. (1993). *The economics of collective choice.* Boulder, CO: Westview Press.

Targett, S. (1999, September 6). Outsourcing companies to fight for £500 million education market. *Financial Times.*

Thompson, G., Mitchell, J., Levačić, R. & Frances, J. (Eds.). (1991). *Markets, hierarchies and networks: The coordination of social life.* London: Sage.

Vignoles, A., Levačić, R., Walker, J., Machin, S., & Reynolds, D. (2000). *The relationship between resource allocation and pupil attainment: A review.* London: DfEE.

West, A., Noden, P., Kleinman, M., & Whitehead, C. (2000). *Examining the impact of the specialist schools program* (Research Report RR196). London: DfEE.

West, A., & Pennell, H. (2000). New Labor and school-based expenditure in England: Changing the system of funding? *British Educational Research Journal*, 26(4), 523-536.

Williamson, O. (1975). *Markets and hierarchies: Analysis and anti-trust implications.* New York and London: Free Press/Collier Macmillan.

Willms, J. D., Nash, G., & Stern, D. (1997). Alert and inert clients: The Scottish experience of parental choice of schools. In E. Cohn (Ed.), *Market approaches to education*. Oxford: Elsevier Science Ltd.

Wohlstetter, P., Van Kirk, A., Robertson, P., & Mohrman, S. (1997). *Organizing for successful school-based management*. Virginia: Association for Supervision and Curriculum Development.

SCHOOL-BASED MANAGEMENT:
THE UNITED STATES EXPERIENCE

Michael W. Kirst

INTRODUCTION AND OVERVIEW

The education system of the United States was founded from the bottom up between 1830 and 1900, based on 120,000 small and rural local districts. When the education system was instituted, elected school boards performed the executive, legislative, and judicial functions, including hiring teachers, building schools, and suspending unruly pupils. The U.S. school site has never been the prime focus of school policy and management. School-based management (SBM) has taken a back seat to district-wide concerns, and the many attempts to introduce SBM have had a marginal impact and have little to do with improving classroom instruction.

The nature of district governance and management is such that they resist school-based management. In 2001, 95,000 school board members in 14,500 districts are still formally in charge of local elements of the public school system. SBM reformers attempt to overcome district-wide policies, such as union contracts, but often meet with resistance. However, the technology and design of SBM continues to improve as we learn how to do it better. Uncertainty over who should control site policies is another crucial issue.

There have been some positive trends recently regarding school-based management, such as comprehensive school reform (e.g., "Success for All"), school site budget formats, charter schools, and school-based accountability. But absolute SBM eludes policymakers in most districts. Education reform in the United States has been characterized as "tinkering towards utopia," so SBM keeps inching forward. Improving the relationship between student achievement and SBM would help realize more widespread implementation, but governance/management changes like SBM have only an indirect impact upon pupil learning.

Management and organizational changes rise and fall as a major U.S. education policy issue. From 1900 to 1920, American cities created centralized districts that established uniform policies for all schools. This "one best system" ended much of the autonomy at each school and introduced budgets, personnel and curricula that were standardized throughout the entire district. School-based management was lost in this centralized efficiency model that persists to this day in both large and small cities/suburbs. Small towns and rural areas feel their small school districts do not require school-based management because district school boards are already close to the people they represent.

School-based management has also been hampered by a lack of confidence in site-level educators to manage education well. Opponents contend there is not much site-level talent waiting to be unleashed through SBM. Extensive capacity building is needed before SBM can be introduced, but few districts have been able or willing to invest in more site capacity, including information systems and rethinking the principal's ubiquitous role. Recently, state governments have been taking over failing schools and "reconstituting them." But such pro-active school-based management policy is limited to extreme cases where schools have failed for many years. "Restructuring" and SBM as the symbols of school reform peaked in the 1990's, but little remains of these efforts.

American scholars do have good plans on how to make SBM work, but there is a lack of agreement regarding who should control school-based management – teachers, parents, administrators, or all three of them? The 1960's featured community control by parents and citizens, but by the 1980's the teachers were given priority in Los Angeles. In 1990, Chicago went back to parent control, and by 2000, Los Angeles moved to geographic decentralization with sub-units of 60,000 pupils.

There have been successful cases of school-based management in the United States, but the extent of school improvement has not been overwhelming. This is partly due to the difficulty in measuring change. U.S. researchers have completed detailed site-based budget designs, but budgets are just the beginning of successful implementation. Briggs and Wohlstetter (in press) found eight elements that were associated with successful school-based management.

1. A vision focused on teaching and learning that is coordinated with student performance standards;

2. Decision-making authority used to change the core areas of schooling;

3. Power distributed throughout the school;

4. Developing teachers' knowledge and skills oriented towards change, a professional learning community, and shared knowledge;

5. Mechanisms for collecting and communicating information related to school priorities;

6.   Financial and other types of incentives to acknowledge progress toward school goals;

7.   Shared school leadership among administrators and teachers;

8.   Resources from outside the school.

"Institutional choice" provides a partial framework for this paper. Often, educational policy debates focus more on what should be done, than on which institutions should be authorized to make and implement policy. One crucial policy decision is the choice of a decision-maker; this determines to a large extent the balance of education governance. (For example, courts have been reluctant to delegate civil rights protection to local school districts in Mississippi.) Another type of institutional choice is whether to place certain functions in the hands of markets (e.g., vouchers) or politics (e.g., school board elections). Recent state reform movements, for example, included an institutional choice to enhance the curricular and testing role of state government at the expense of local control.

Clune stresses two important characteristics of available institutions: agreement on substantive goals and the capacity to achieve those goals. Substantive goals are crucial because of the need to ensure support for a policy. Courts may be more enthusiastic about civil rights goals than school principals in Mississippi, but support must be bolstered by institutional capacity. For example, courts cannot run school districts on a weekly basis. One method of choosing institutions can be called comparative institutional advantage, which begins with distrust or criticism of a particular institution. Since no decision-maker is perfect, the distrust directed at one decision-maker must be carefully weighed against the advantages of that decision-maker, and both the advantages and disadvantages of alternative decision-makers. In other words, although institutional choice typically begins with distrust, distrust itself offers nothing in the absence of a superior alternative. The logic of comparative institutional advantage also implies the futility of seeking perfect or ideal implementation of a policy. The real world offers a "least worst choice" of imperfect institutions (Clune, 1987).

One problem with institutional choice analyses is the tendency to confuse predictive with normative applications. In education, policy correlations between new institutional choices and education are often unclear. For instance, how much of an increase in SBM will lead to improved teacher morale or better classroom instruction? How does parent control of school choice through vouchers lead to increased learning?

The rate of substitution is equally unclear, for example, at what point will increased national influence in education lead to a decline in the state role? It is possible to avoid zero-sum properties through various win-win scenarios, such as state curriculum content guidelines that help teachers communicate higher order thinking and do not interfere with local teacher professionalism or site autonomy. Overall, institutional choice is complex, uncertain, and subject to continual political change. The accumulation of policies over many years embodies a set of preferences about which institutions should govern what components of a policy area. For example, from 1960 to 1990 states in the U.S. drastically increased their control of local school budgeting in order to provide more equal spending.

Although most countries have established school systems based on national control, the United States has always emphasized local control based predominantly on small districts. SBM has not been part of this governance history. In 1948 the U.S. had 89,000 school districts, and it now has 15,020. Moreover, unlike most countries, American school governance is detached from the general government (e.g. cities, counties) that provides other services for children. Changes in governance over the years have challenged these original institutional choices concerning who should run U.S. schools. A key thesis of this paper is how the evolution of institutional choice and governance in the U.S. has hindered SBM and makes it difficult today. As this paper will demonstrate, reform of educational governance that results in different educational choices is often motivated by a desire to change school priorities and policies (Tyack, 1974). Replacing those in power with those who are out of power is one way to attempt policy changes. Moreover, directly changing the objectives of schools may be more difficult politically than indirectly changing local school policies by "reforming" governance. Institutional choice, such as SBM, becomes another policy tool to temporarily resolve the debates among the numerous and conflicting goals the public has for education. For example, reformers at the turn of the twentieth century wanted a unitary curriculum across cities and an end to SBM bilingual education in German, Polish, and other languages. The 1983 report, *A Nation At Risk,* implied that school-based control of curriculum standards was not optimal and therefore, state government should assume more control of local curricular policies (U.S. Department of Education, 1983)

Recent critics of educational governance have alleged that democratic government is inappropriate and dysfunctional for schools. These critics want to replace institutional choice with reliance upon the market, through vouchers and individual choice (Chubb

& Moe, 1990). Typically, changes in institutional choice are the result of agreement concerning goals, as well as widespread dissatisfaction and loss of confidence in the quality of educational outcomes. So far, SBM is not perceived as the solution to U.S. concerns over low achievement and test scores.

THE HISTORIC DOMINANCE OF LOCAL CONTROL BY SCHOOL DISTRICTS

The concept of the local school board originated in New England, where citizens controlled the schools directly through town meetings. By 1826, however, Massachusetts had already created a separate school committee divorced from the rest of local government, and the Massachusetts model spread throughout the nation. Horace Mann, one of the founders of the American school system, proclaimed that "the common school was to be free, financed by local and state government, controlled by lay boards of education, and mixing all social groups under one roof" (Kirst, 1991). The school board was to be nonpartisan and nonsectarian.

In the 1800s, schools were grouped into districts and controlled by hundreds of thousands of local board members. As late as 1890, 71% of Americans lived in rural areas, where the one-room school was typical (Tyack, 1974). By the turn of the 20th century, however, as society moved into the modern era, significant changes were in store for school boards. A pressing public education issue during the period from 1890 to 1910 was the role of the alleged unscrupulous party politician (Tyack, 1964). It was not uncommon in large cities for teachers to use political influence to get positions and, sometimes, to be fired later on when their political patron lost an election. Frequently, members of the board of education were supported by major parties and elected on a decentralized ward basis. (A "ward" in the U.S. is equivalent to a small neighborhood.) In 1910, for instance, Pittsburgh had 222 local board members, while Boston had 30 sub-committees with a total membership of 142 elected on a political ward basis (Tyack, 1974). The Board of Education was often used as a political stepping stone and consequently, party nominations for school board were hotly contested. To gain control of the situation, reformers wanted to divorce policy-making and management from the politician through centralization under a professional superintendent. This implied an end to SBM. Moreover, teachers wanted to see an end to the spoils system in determining their careers, and they wanted hiring and personnel decisions to be determined by the central district rather than through SBM.

Urban school reform was part of a broader pattern of the social elite galvanizing municipal change at the turn of the century (Hays, 1963). Although the surface rhetoric pitted the corrupt politician against the community-oriented citizen, the reformers' underlying motives have been questioned by several historians. The reform resulted in a professional culture that tends to be less diverse than the cultures represented in the neighborhood boards. Tyack (1974) expressed this viewpoint in stronger language:

> Underlying much of the reform movement was an elitist assumption that prosperous, native-born, Protestant Anglo-Saxons were superior to other groups and thus should determine the curriculum and the allocation of jobs. It was the mission of the schools to imbue the children of the immigrants and the poor with uniformly WASP ideals.

Here we clearly see the change in institutional choices being used as a way of changing policy. The watchwords of the reform movement in the city schools became "centralization," "expertise," "professionalization", "non-political control," and "efficiency." The most attractive models of organization for education were the large-scale industrial bureaucracies rapidly emerging in the 1880-1910 Age of Consolidation (ibid.). The school sites and SBM were part of a discredited regime of excessive decentralization.

The reformers contended that the board members elected by neighborhoods advanced parochial and special interests at the expense of the needs of the school district as a whole. What was needed to counter this atomization of interest was election-at-large, or one board for the whole city. Professional expertise rested upon the assumption that scientific school administration would be independent of the particularistic values of particular groups. A good school system is one that benefits everyone, not just one segment of the community or a particular site. This unitary community idea would help protect schools from the influence of local political parties and interest groups (Salisbury, 1967).

The reformers of 1900-1920 charged, moreover, that since the neighborhood school boards worked through numerous sub-committees, their executive authority was splintered. No topic was too trivial for a school site or a separate sub-committee, ranging from ways to teach reading to the purchase of doorknobs. At one time, Chicago had 79 school board sub-committees and Cincinnati had 74 (Tyack, 1974). The primary requirement for better management was thought to be centralization of power in the hands of a chief executive who had considerable authority, delegated by a board with seven to nine members who had been elected from the entire city. Only under such a system could someone make large-scale improvements and be held accountable.

It was sometimes a very small and elite group that secured new charters from state legislatures and thereby reorganized the urban schools without a popular vote in the cities (ibid.). This turn of the century school reform was implemented by a network of policy-makers comprised of successful businessmen, university leaders, and municipal reformers; this network later created concepts like the city manager.

The realignment in influence further enhanced what Callahan called the "cult of efficiency" in school operation (Callahan, 1962). This "cult" played down the desirability of SBM decisions, political influence, conflict, or pressure groups and favored scientific management. Leading academicians, for example, concentrated on finding a specific set of tools for the administrative aspects of school management and created a merit system bureaucracy based on university certificates. They were not interested in SBM. This closed system operated within a value system of leadership, ranging from politically neutral competence through certified, central office professional administrators. To keep political parties out of deciding school policy, school elections remained unaligned with political parties and ballots were nonpartisan. Moreover, board members were elected at-large as "trustees" rather than from sub-districts or school sites as "representatives."

THE EVOLUTION OF THE ROLE OF THE DISTRICT SCHOOL BOARD

Before the mid-1960s, a description of the role of the district-wide school board would have sounded something like this: School boards most often mediate major policy conflicts, leaving the determination of important policy issues to the central district professional staff; even in mediating, they might do little. In the process, they often simply legitimized the proposals made by the professional staff, making only marginal changes (Boyd, 1976). School boards paid scant attention to SBM or any other decentralization scheme.

Although board members spent the bulk of their time on details, they did establish a policy "zone of consent" that made clear to the superintendent what was, and what was not, acceptable. For example, a superintendent who tried in 1960 to introduce bilingual education in a rural, conservative California district would discover that this program was outside the board's zone of consent.

207

The centralization that occurred in school boards did not have an impact on rural boards. Rural boards, however, were greatly affected by a rapid process of school consolidation that created larger schools with the capacity to offer a wide range of curriculum options. What was once an archipelago of districts in America - with each island having a board and community in harmony - was combined into a system of larger, more varied districts. The 89,000 districts of 1948 became 55,000 five years later, 31,000 by 1961, and 15,020 by 1991. During the 1970s, on any given day, three districts disappeared forever between breakfast and dinner. Earlier, in the 1960s, that many had evaporated between breakfast and the morning coffee break, with another seven gone by dinner. SBM in small districts gave way to centralized decisions in large school districts.

THE EFFECTS OF TEACHER COLLECTIVE BARGAINING AND CONTRACTS

The late 1960s saw the beginning of an intense period of collective bargaining based on the industrial union model. Between 1965 and 1980, in most states except those in the Southeast and Mountain regions, teachers realized that they needed collective bargaining. This was a major movement away from administrative dominance of governance.

The outcome of collective bargaining is a written and time-bound agreement covering wages, hours, and conditions of employment. Unions want centralized agreements with school districts rather than having to negotiate with each school, so unions are very wary of SBM. At the school site, the language of the central school board's union contract must be interpreted so as to apply to specific circumstances. This means that the school's principal, teachers, and union building representative must become very familiar with the terms of the central district contract. Yet even familiarity does not forestall many disputes over specific teaching arrangements. These disputes can lead to grievances whose settlement can help clarify the contract at the central district level.

What happens to administrator authority, particularly among principals, when contracts filter down through the loosely coupled school system? A major study found that although some provisions tightly restrict the principal's freedom of action, others are redefined to fit the particular requirements at the school site. That is, "such factors as teacher interests, educational outcomes, administrative leadership, and staff allegiance were balanced and counterbalanced" (Johnson, 1984). How the principal works with the union contract also affects teachers' respect for administrators. In short, setting standards and expecting much of teachers can help principals earn tolerance – and even respect – from teachers in interpreting the contract. For teachers, a good school is more important than union membership, close observance of a contract, or control of the schools. As one administrator observed, "Teachers like to be part of a winning team" (ibid., p. 163). But the central district teacher contract remains an impediment to SBM, and forces the principals to react to centralized policies.

In the 1960s, the push for structural changes was termed "community control." Now, four decades later, many of its supporters have faded, though some changes have taken place. Community control seeks to create several sub-systems within one large school system such as New York or Los Angeles, moving decision-making from the center and relocating it within several new community-based school boards of lay members (Levin, 1972). Particularly favored by minority groups who lacked influence on central administrators, this new concept envisioned a neighborhood board with the power to remove personnel hired by the old centralized board and having complete discretion to reallocate budget priorities. Of course, little support for this existed among school professionals.

Decentralization, on the other hand, was supported by teachers, principals, and administrators who found the urban centralized system cumbersome. Decentralization created sub-districts of many schools within the geographic area of a city. Educators complained they could not get supplies and personnel from the central office and were prevented by overall regulations from implementing needed curricular changes and teaching reforms. They assumed that better education would be possible if more professional educators had greater decision-making power. In effect, field administrators would gain authority from central administrators, similar to an army command situation. Under community control however, lay board members and citizens (particularly minorities) would gain more influence than they now had when confronting all the professionals, as well as citywide voting constituencies. In retrospect, there was little community control, but widespread decentralization in big city schools throughout the 1970s (LaNoue & Smith, 1973).

The increasing complexity of school policy-making tends to offer more influence to those who control detailed information and assessments of policy alternatives. The control of information highlights the role of the school bureaucracy vis-à-vis the superintendent. At this point, research in rural districts has not progressed enough to differentiate the influence of the superintendent from his or her own staff. However, we do know a great deal about this pattern in the urban schools. There, the central office staff has accumulated so much decision-making authority regarding such areas as curriculum, personnel assignment, and facilities, that the roles of outlying district administrators and building principals are restricted. Under present conditions, the principal is too involved with day-to-day management of the school to participate effectively in broad policy-making. District superintendents, in turn, are primarily concerned with assuring that policies set down by central headquarters are followed by the schools in their districts. The superintendent's impact derives, in part, from an orchestrating or choreographing role that cultivates a sense of mission for the bureaucracy and establishes a particular climate. Top officials at the central office are traditionally chosen from within the system by the superintendent or superintendent's committee. In some districts the board must ratify his or her recommendations, but a new superintendent cannot always bring in a new team of top administrators.

SCHOOL-BASED MANAGEMENT IN THE U.S.A.: 1960-1990

A major debate surrounds the relative policy autonomy that SBM and school sites should have compared with the central office. SBM schemes from 1960 to 1990 have gone through several phases and variations (Guthrie, 1986; Meyer, 1979). In the 1960s, the focus was on school-site budgeting, and increased amounts of unrestricted funds (about 10%) were provided at the school building level. In most school districts, only very small amounts (less than 3% per pupil) are earmarked for flexible decision-making by the school. This flexibility has been broadened to include the ability to exchange teachers for teaching aids and to change the standard, centrally determined, personnel formulas. Indeed, school districts typically use allocation formulas for each school based on the number of pupils. Some states, such as California, have directed small amounts of unrestricted aid to the school sites from state school improvement programs.

The question then becomes, "Who should control policy and practice at the school level?" Four viewpoints have been advanced:

1. Under the concept of the principal as a site manager, the principal should control these resources and be held accountable for the success of the school. Success can be measured through school-site performance reports that encompass pupil achievement scores, as well as the allocation choices made by the principal. This view of the principal as the site manager was reinforced by the school effectiveness literature's focus on strong site leadership.

2. Parents should control site policy because they are the consumers and care most deeply about policies at the schools their children attend. Parents are less interested in central district policies that have no easily-discernible impact on their children. The American philosophy of lay leadership implies that parent school site councils should deliberate and decide school-level policy and SBM.

3. Teachers should form a school site senate and allocate funds and personnel, as well as decide instructional issues. Teachers cannot be held accountable for pupil performance if they do not control resource allocations but must instead follow standardized instructional procedures. SBM by teachers would also enhance the professional status and self-image of teachers.

4. None of these rationales is sufficiently compelling to make it the norm. Consequently, SBM should have a "parity" of membership among teachers, administration, and parents ensuring that they reach an agreement through bargaining and coalitions. At the secondary school level, pupils may be included. All factions deserve a place at the table, and the best arguments should prevail.

While this SBM debate has been intellectually stimulating, few districts have permitted much school site flexibility.

Another and more serious problem exists with site-based management reforms in the years between 1960 and 1990. The outcome policy-makers were focused on whether SBM was being implemented at a site, not whether pupils learned more. This supports the thesis that SBM may be an adult-oriented game that appears regularly in democratic policy conflict. Such games are a struggle over the power to decide highly political goals, namely:

1. What symbols will dominate among policy-making players, often a form of "symbolic politics" (Edelman, 1967). Thus, SBM will increase educational and economic "productivity."

2. How public resources will be allocated among these players, both vertically (revenue supplements provided by the states) as well as horizontally (allocation of funds within an SBM school).

3. What structure for decision-making will control both the symbolic and resource sides of the decentralization struggle. Thus, both decentralized as well as centralized reforms are about desirable decision-making systems.

4. Which historical forces will influence SBM. Thus history is but another form

of adult influence created by preceding generations that shapes the adult game today.

Fundamentally then, this set of interactions is perceived as political because SBM is a struggle over the power to decide dominant symbols, to secure resources, to employ facilitative structures, and to express historical influences. If politics is, in Harold Lasswell's classic formulation, "the study of who gets what, when, and how," then SBM reforms clearly share those political qualities.

However, SBM interactions should be distinguished from child-oriented games, namely, those that focus on what happens to pupils in the learning environment. The essence of this game is not explicitly centered on power, hence it is not overtly political. Rather, it focuses on leading children to learn, so it is primarily educational. This kind of game:

1. Focuses on the curriculum and instructional aspects of the teaching profession.

2. Begins with, operates, and concludes with an assessment mode to determine whether these efforts actually do increase learning.

This assessment component of the child-oriented game should be central to SBM, and its frequent absence in American approaches to SBM distinguishes it from the adult-oriented game of policy-making. Historically, pupil assessment has built a complex testing and measurement concern into an established field of pedagogy. Recently, assessment has also widely demonstrated the inability of many schools to increase scholastic achievement. But assessment is a sword that cuts two ways. The final section will examine the U.S. experience with SBM in the last decade, including some hopeful signs on its relationship to changes in classroom instruction and enhanced pupil attainment.

KEY ELEMENTS OF SUCCESSFUL SCHOOL-BASED MANAGEMENT

Between 1960 and 1990, U.S. schools generally viewed the implementation of SBM as the end result. But the increased workload upon teachers and administrators caused by SBM generated a more serious questioning of SBM goals: Can an organizational change such as SBM lead to increased student achievement? How can SBM be included as part of an overall school improvement program, and not merely a stand-alone "management innovation?" Wohlstetter's review (Briggs & Wohlstetter, in press) concluded:

The empirical evidence supporting the claims that SBM can generate improvement has not been overwhelming. While varied, the reasons for the lack of evidence include: a) difficulties in measuring change and outcomes associated with SBM; b) complexities in implementing a management model that requires significant efforts from teachers, principals, and district personnel to alter work practices; and c) the challenge of working in an environment that is shaped by local, state, and national politics. Nevertheless, there are studies which conclude that SBM leads to changes in school culture, classroom practices, and student achievement.

Many SBM adherents contend that changes in school culture and classroom practice are necessary requirements for better pupil achievement. But SBM must have some causal link to improved instruction, not just a focus on redistributing decision-making power and resources. If SBM leads to a greater sense of community among teachers, how does this "community" translate into instructional change? Organizational changes like SBM may be similar to changing the shell of a turtle, while classroom instruction is what lies underneath the turtle's shell.

This concern has led U.S. policy-makers to link SBM with an instructional control mechanism at the state, district, or school level. For example, SBM can operate within and reinforce curriculum content standards established by the State of California. SBM can focus on the "how" rather than the "what" of instruction under some American SBM models. But other SBM approaches allow the school site to determine both the "how" and "what" of instruction. In either case, the key is to generate a schoolwide sense of purpose with regard to teaching, learning, and pupil achievement standards before SBM can be implemented.

For SBM to work effectively, key decision-making areas must be located at the site level. These include extensive or complete discretion in such spheres as finance, curriculum, personnel, supplies, and facility modifications. But this level of discretion is precisely what has been so difficult to achieve in the American context. The unions want centralized labor contracts and do not want to bargain with school sites. Central administrators traditionally hire and assign principals. School boards play a major role in facilities. Public concern over low test scores in the last several years has led to a return to curriculum supervision at the state or district level. For example, Chicago uses standard content and pedagogical "scripts" in many of its schools, despite having site councils that select the principal.

The best SBM sites have a carefully crafted role reserved for the central office in order to enhance the implementation of SBM at the school. These effective districts do not assume that all the talent, experience, and enthusiasm already exists at the school level and only needs to be liberated by SBM in order to be successful. Key district roles include:

- Creating a school-based information system that allows the central level to accept accountability for educational outcomes (e.g., "what"), while loosening up its control of the "how." The U.S. has rarely created a school-based information system and some states have only recently produced school site test scores.

- Preparing site personnel to understand and make budget decisions that have traditionally been made at the district level.

- Helping to recruit qualified teachers for site selection.

- Enhancing site capacity to plan and execute teaching improvements.

- Offering whole-school instructional models that can be adapted by the site. Prominent U.S. models include "Success for All," "Core Knowledge" and "Accelerated Schools."

A crucial problem that must be overcome involves the excessive role of the chief site administrator – the principal. U.S. principals have too many roles, and the job has become impossible to do well. Principals rarely have sufficient support staff and are overwhelmed by day-to-day details. They cannot lead or oversee all of their existing responsibilities, much less take on new ones involving SBM. The central district must rethink the principal's role and provide flexibility by hiring more site administrators. A key characteristic of successful SBM is the ability to delegate power throughout the school and create networks of decision-making teams. These would include working teams and ad hoc committees responsible for areas such as curriculum, technology, etc. As Wohlstetter notes (Briggs & Wohlstetter, in press):

> In successful SBM schools, school leadership is shared among administrators and teachers. Principals often take on the role of manager and facilitator of change, while teacher leaders often take on responsibilities around issues of teaching and learning[1].

The U.S. is moving towards a new school-based system of accountability. But progress is uneven among states, and the tight/loose model is not fully implemented. This model allocates "tight" accountability for pupil performance to central officials, but allows for "loose" site methods to achieve student results. It is the "loose" part that is proceeding more slowly, as well as the use of financial and other types of incentives to

---

1   See also: Goertz & Odden (1999) and Robertson et al. (1995).

motivate both individual teachers and school faculties towards the school's goals. Few U.S. schools use financial incentives for SBM other than additional compensation for extra work. There are only a few school districts that reward teachers for acquiring new knowledge and skills related to SBM.

U.S. schools provide teachers with very little time for working together, so the school day must be restructured. If all the decision-making activity is concentrated within a site council, this body may become overloaded. Part of the problem is enabling parents to help make decisions and not just be symbolic participants. Professional development may be necessary to ensure the success of SBM, and should include decision-making and management skills. Parent and community members should be involved in a training program aimed at achieving collective goals. Successful professional development is most effective when it is sustained, intensive, and has follow-up guidance. Other effective practices include leadership by site councils, sub-committees, department heads, and informal leaders. The principal's role, however, is crucial and he/she must be able to work in a shared decision-making environment.

CONCLUSION

The U.S. knows how to implement effective school-based management. Now it needs the commitment and political coalition to ensure that these effective practices are carried out. The spread of charter schools, however, is providing impetus and examples of both productive and non-productive SBM. State governments are taking over failing schools and providing more insights for successful SBM. But progress may be slow and uneven across the U.S., given the nation's tradition of district administration.

REFERENCES

Boyd, W. (1976). The public, the professionals and educational policy: Who governs? *Teachers' College Record, 77*, 556-558.

Briggs, K., & Wohlstetter, P. (in press). Key elements of a successful school-based management strategy. *Journal of Educational Finance.*

Callahan, R. (1962). *Education and the cult of efficiency.* Chicago: University of Chicago Press.

Chubb, J., & Moe, T. (1990). *Politics, markets and America's Schools.* Washington, DC: Brookings Institution.

Clune, W. (1987). *Institutional choice as a theoretical framework.* New Brunswick, NJ: Center for Policy Research in Education.

Edelman, M. (1967). *The symbolic uses of politics.* Urbana, IL: University of Illinois Press.

Goertz, M. E., & Odden, A. (Eds.). (1999). *School-based financing.* Thousand Oaks, CA: Corwin Publishing.

Guthrie, J. (1986, December). School-based management: The next needed education reform. *Phi Delta Kappa, 68,* 305-309.

Hays, S. (1963). The politics of reform in municipal government in the Progressive Era. *Pacific Northwest Quarterly, 55,* (163).

Johnson, S. M. (1984). *Teachers in schools.* Philadelphia: Temple University Press.

Kirst, M. (1991, November). School board: Evolution of an American Institution [special issue]. *American School Board Journal,* (11-13).

La Noue, G. R., & Smith, B. L. (1973). *The politics of school decentralization.* Lexington, MA: Lexington Books.

Levin, H. (Ed.). (1972). *Community control of schools.* Washington, DC: Brookings Institution.

Meyer, J. (1979). *The impact of centralization.* Stanford, CA: Institute of Educational Finance and Governance.

Robertson, P. J. et al. (1995). Generating curriculum and instructional innovations through school-based management. *Educational Administration Quarterly, 31*(3), 375-404.

Salisbury, R. (1967, Summer). Schools and politics in the big city. *Harvard Education Review, 37,* 408-424.

Tyack, D. (1964). Needed: The reform of a reform. In *New Dimensions of School Board Leadership.* Evanston, IL: National School Boards Association.

Tyack, D. (1974). *One best system.* Cambridge, MA: Harvard University Press.

U.S. Department of Education (1983). *A nation at risk.* Washington, DC: U.S. Government Printing Office.

FROM EXPERIMENT TO EDUCATIONAL POLICY: THE TRANSITION TO SCHOOL-BASED MANAGEMENT IN ISRAELI SCHOOLS

Ami Volansky

The Compulsory Education Law (1949) established, to a large extent, the authority of the educational institutions in Israel. While elementary education (and later on, lower secondary education as well) developed by creating an increasing dependence on the central government, by virtue of its being a compulsory education that the government was required to provide to everyone, the secondary education system (high school and vocational school) developed by creating different organizational and management patterns that gave these institutions greater pedagogic and administrative independence.

Being "compulsory" education, a pattern of government involvement in all the school's spheres of activity developed gradually and systematically. The state determined – by law, regulation, circulars and procedures – all matters and concerns, including pedagogic issues such as, curricula, class structure and organization; procedures for preparing homework; how pupils should write in their notebooks; school climate; and other areas as well, for example, physical planning of schools – the schoolyard, the width of hallways, size of the classroom, and where the light in the classroom should fall on the pupils' desks. In 1953, all teachers working in the official education system became employees of the public service sector. This move increased the involvement of the Ministry of Education in all aspects of personnel management. Now, the Ministry was required to regulate the movement of teachers between cities, between schools and between the State and State-religious education systems; but no less than this, to engage in issuing authorizations for in-service training, retirement, vacations, transfers, disciplinary warnings, firing of teachers, etc. As stated, these process developed gradually, and the pattern of involvement by the Ministry of Education and the local authority within the school continued to grow. Such patterns defined the authority (which was slowly expanded) of the Ministry's district office and its inspectors, the various units of the Ministry – which were increasing in number, and the local authorities. But it was only natural that the greater the authority of such external agencies, the less importance was given to any consideration of those who were directly responsible for teaching the children – the principals and teachers.

Although the secondary education system, and especially the upper-secondary schools, enjoyed greater freedom in the administrative sphere due to the fact that the teachers were not public servants but rather employees of corporations, including local authority workers, it was given almost no leeway for pedagogic initiative or growth because the system was entirely dictated by policies of external and centralized matriculation examinations.

It is no wonder, therefore, that teachers themselves claimed that the extreme centralization that developed took away all their pedagogic initiative and ability to think differently from the ways dictated by the central authority, and they were the ones who began to call for granting greater autonomy to school personnel. The 1970s saw the start of the shift towards pedagogic autonomy.

PEDAGOGIC AUTONOMY

The feeling that patterns of centralization that had developed made management clumsy, slowed down the decision-making processes and led to faulty supervision of the entire system were among the factors that led to the appointment of the Commission "To Encourage Teacher Initiative" in 1971, by Minister of Education at the time, Mr. Yigal Alon. The report's introductory remarks stated:

> In recent years we have seen signs of weariness, apathy, and even bitterness, among teachers. The present state of affairs in the Israeli education system has also led to these feelings. Even the most dedicated teacher is liable, in a centralized educational regime, to become tired, lose interest, and avoid taking personal responsibility for his educational activities. Teachers cannot escape fatigue, apathy and bitterness if they are not given autonomy in certain spheres (Volansky, 1999).

Submission of this report to the Education Minister sowed the initial seeds for the concept of educational autonomy, which continued to gain momentum during the 1970s and 1980s.

The main premise tended to encourage initiative among teachers in the schools. A formula was devised whereby elective classes constituted 25% of the official curriculum, and recommendations were made that teachers be given pedagogic autonomy concerning the organization of three class hours according to their own judgment, rotation in job positions, etc. During these two decades, Director-General's

Circulars were issued to encourage initiative and independence in the schools, committees were established to promote this, and a joint planning team was formed by the Ministry of Education and Tel Aviv University to advance this concept of school autonomy. The underlying assumption of the program is that an autonomous school is one that satisfies its own needs, and therefore, the school must adopt its own educational philosophy, determine operative goals in the academic sphere, including selecting educational materials and content, and carry out evaluation and feedback processes. Reshef (1984), one of the organizers behind the concept of school autonomy, expanded on these aspects and added that as an organization, the autonomous school would also engage in teacher training.

The policy of the Ministry of Education to encourage initiative, flexible methods and, in practice, greater pedagogic and administrative autonomy, encountered problems during the latter half of the 1980s. Heavy budget cutbacks meant that between 1979-1985, the number of classrooms hours declined by 9.2% in elementary education, and by 20% in the lower secondary schools. These cutbacks actually reversed the freedom and flexibility that had been given to schools on the basis of pedagogic autonomy, and schools no longer had the ability to implement programs for elective and optional subjects, which were the very essence behind the idea of autonomy. One more problem, which was no less important, was the fact that the desire to empower schools was carried out without the central authority being ready to relinquish its control. The schools' ability to implement activities was made contingent upon their receiving prior approval from the inspectorate (Inbar, 1987). These conditions left the schools dependent upon the bureaucracies that constituted the Education Ministry's network of decision-makers and inspectors. Under such circumstances, school-based initiatives, formulation of new programs and ideas generated by the teaching personnel clashed with bureaucratic efforts to preserve the central authority until "grassroots" programs developed, which offered schools theoretical rights, but not any real opportunity for implementation (Inbar, 1987).

CONCEPTUAL BACKGROUND BEHIND THE TRANSITION TO SCHOOL-BASED MANAGEMENT

Difficulties in implementing school autonomy and the disparity between hope and reality were carefully studied by the Ministry of Education in the early 1990s, and were among the motives for starting to formulate a school-based management approach in Israel. Three developments contributed towards this trend, based on academic findings on the one hand, and the implementation of reforms on the other hand. These were: Devising a new perspective on the role of school leadership; a wealth of research findings regarding the characteristics of effective schools; structural reforms, whose goal was to reduce the level of alienation between the citizen receiving services and the institution, primarily by delegating authority to units in the field that were in direct contact with those receiving the services and by finding a new balance between centralization and decentralization. This issue also included the desire to reduce social gaps and increase equality via a new policy for allocating resources.

The concepts of commitment and accountability are key ideas for understanding the new perspectives being articulated in the leadership sphere, and they are the first step towards understanding the background behind the transition to school-based management. The question before us, which is both theoretical and practical, is: What are the conditions needed to maximize teachers' accountability and their commitment to the pedagogic objectives that have been decided? There has been development in the theoretical realm, and the most interesting indication of this is McGregor's Theory X and Theory Y (McGregor, 1985). According to Theory X, the average person lacks ambition, tends not to assume responsibility, prefers to be led by others, will make every effort to avoid fulfilling his obligation and opposes change; therefore, people need to be controlled, directed and forced to make the efforts necessary to fulfill the organization's objectives. In contrast with this approach, according to Theory Y, work is the source of the satisfaction sought by all people. When certain conditions prevail, the average person learns to seek out responsibility, will use his imagination, originality and creativity to solve the problems facing the organization, and the most meaningful compensation for him will be the satisfaction of his ego and self-fulfillment within the context of his performance. But this does not happen by itself, rather these events take place against the background of the organization's particular management style and conditions, and therefore it is management's responsibility to allow people to cultivate and develop their individual abilities. Such individual growth will also constitute the organization's growth. An extensive range of publications and studies on leadership in general, and educational leadership in particular, support the approach based on Theory Y, and among these are the studies conducted by Cheng (1996), Handy (1988), Leithwood et al. (1996), Peters and Waterman (1982), Sergiovanni and Starratt (1993), and Williams (1995, 1998).

Transferring the locus of control from an external source of authority to the school, and formulating a new approach and perspective regarding the individual's place within the organization (the teacher, in the case of an educational organization) is being developed and its implementation has begun; this is also the result of conditions in the field. The school has become a complex working environment, with aspects involving planning and implementation. The variety and increase in the number of subjects; the constant development of new curricula; the use of information technologies; the introduction of computers for teaching, learning and evaluation; the change in the teacher's role by directing pupils towards sources of information, rather than serving as their sole source of information; expanding on the approach of the child in the center; the pressure placed on the school to meet children's needs "in real time"; the transition to a multi-cultural student population (immigrants, foreign workers); the tension and competition between different religious groups and streams in the education system; the flight of the public from public education; opportunities for working in the home; the use of outsourcing by schools; the expectation to improve scholastic achievement; striving towards a school climate free of drug abuse and violence – all of these are just some of the expectations placed on the school principal and his staff. It is no wonder, then, that as the complexities of running a school became more apparent, the more we understood that administrative methods and management styles had to change and that administrative authority had to be located where the main educational processes were taking place – that is, in the school. Furthermore, it was understood that technically transferring authority was not enough, rather it would be necessary to create conditions for including teachers in the planning and implementation – with the goal of intensifying the commitment and accountability of the teaching personnel for the planned outcomes.

A second source of inspiration for the development of self-managed schools are the studies concerning effective schools. These studies asked: Under what conditions are schools more effective in achieving their educational objectives as compared with other schools with similar socio-economic backgrounds? A common denominator was found in a series of studies pointing to the fact that in schools that clearly define their goals with staff members and derive those goals from the school's educational vision; make decisions with very little dependence upon bureaucratic procedures; work under maximum flexibility; focus on the needs of the pupils; are flexible with regard to class and lesson structure; employ feedback to evaluate educational accomplishments and goals; are constantly on the lookout for obstacles that might prevent or impede their ability to improve achievement; have teachers who are deeply involved in all aspects of the curriculum; delegate authority among staff members; have an "open door" policy where the principal is more of a consultant, providing the staff with support (even when they fail) and guidance; are less concerned with their formal authority – there is an increase in the school's level of achievement and the level of satisfaction of all those involved: pupils, teachers and parents (Beare, Caldwell, & Millikan, 1989; Caldwell & Spinks, 1998; Cheng, 1996; Dimmock, 1993; Hopkins, 1987; Reynolds & Cuttance, 1993; Volansky, 1995, 1997). Thus, it is clear that if certain working conditions exist, a school can become more effective in achieving its pedagogic goals.

The third factor, and a background for the transition to school-based management, was worldwide reform that began to take place in the early 1980s, motivated by the feeling that centralized management, through organizations that commanded most of the operational components, was not sensitive enough to individual needs. The approach developed, and a need was felt, for creating a new balance between the central power and the power of the periphery (the schools). These ideas were based on the claim that creating uniformity through greater centralization of the education system does not enhance equality. Rather the opposite, such uniformity leads to the development of complex bureaucracies and "organizational giants" which, instead of serving the individual citizen, lead to feelings of alienation, organizational complexity and lack of control. Critics argue that the larger the organization grows and the more cumbersome its scope, the greater the internal contradiction involved in its management. Different units within the organization overlap, and sometimes they even operate in conflict with components of the official or unofficial policy. Not only does the tendency to departmentalize a centralized educational system tend to complicate things, it is also a burden on the structure of the curriculum and makes it difficult for the school to fulfill its defined educational goals. Professional committees, public committees, public and private associations, and local and national officials attempt to influence the structure of the curricula and training programs. Political and administrative pressures for rapid achievement encourage the administration to adopt a "project-oriented" mentality. This reality places a heavy burden on the school and creates conflicts in expectations and time tables. Without the ability to focus on long-term educational goals, centralized organizations operating in this manner for a long time are only fooling themselves that by coordinating and supervising all parts of the system they will enable them to resolve these contradictions. It is only an illusion, critics say (Volansky, 1994, 2003).

These three factors, based on both theoretical elements and applied reforms, inspired the initial planning for the transition to school-based management in Israel, and the creation of a new system of balances between the central authority and the schools.

THE TRANSITION TO SCHOOL-BASED MANAGEMENT IN ISRAEL

In 1992 the Ministry of Education formulated an initial planning document to examine structural reforms that had been implemented in school systems around the world, in order to enable the transition to school-based management. The report also examined the difficulties facing the education system in carrying out school autonomy in Israel, and the correlation between studies conducted around the world on effective schools and findings on school-based management (Volansky, 1992). The report was presented to a committee appointed by the Education Minister at that time, Ms. Shulamit Aloni. The committee's job was to recommend principles for the transition by schools to school-based management.

The committee, which presented its conclusions in 1993, recommended decentralization of authority to the schools via a transition to self-management. The main recommendations were: (1) The school will be funded according to a "pupil basket of services," which would include most of the budget items and would be equitable and made public. There would be a differential "basket" for special needs pupils. (2) The school will operate as a closed financial system. (3) Self-managed schools will define clear goals (work plans). (4) The school will operate a system for feedback and evaluation. (5) Authority concerning personnel will be delegated to the school. (6) The role of the inspector in self-managed schools will focus on consulting, support and direction for the school on the ways and means by which its goals can be achieved.

The report included two additional recommendations that were rejected in light of the public debate that followed its publication. These recommendations included establishing an executive committee for the school, and giving school principals the authority to recommend teacher dismissals. The practical significance of these recommendations was a structural change in the official education system and an overall change in the culture of running elementary and lower-secondary schools. According to the approach that had been devised, the future role of the Ministry of Education would focus mainly in the area of defining overall policies, while schools would be in charge of practical implementation of those policies. Schools would be given maximum authority to carry out policy with maximum flexibility. According to

223

this approach, the Ministry would deal with establishing the government curriculum; setting budget criteria in order to reinforce the foundations of equality; determining standards for assessing scholastic achievement; and official supervision over fulfilling and attaining the central values and national goals as defined by law and in accordance with Education Ministry policy.

In order to realize these recommendations, it was necessary to give schools implementational authority which, up to now, had been in the hands of the Ministry of Education, as well as powers that previously belonged to the local authorities. A further significance is that changes would be needed in the division of authority within the school, because now the school faculty was expected to carry the main burden of the authority and accountability, both for the pedagogic work, planning and budgeting, and monitoring (feedback) the educational outcomes defined in the school's work plan.

Launching this undertaking involved an experiment that was introduced in nine schools at the beginning of the 1995-96 academic year, and was expanded to include 43 schools in 1996-97. Findings of the research that accompanied the experiments point to the fact that schools that participated in the experiment underwent two key changes: (A) In the organizational-pedagogic sphere – the schools improved their pedagogic goals; curricula were implemented so as to be more appropriate to the goals they had set; school-based feedback developed gradually. (B) In the operational resources sphere – the school's authority was increased with regard to personnel; the school had greater independence to manage its own budget; the school succeeded in rallying many significant creative forces. Summarizing this phase of the experiment (Friedman & Barma, 1998; Friedman, Barma, & Toren, 1997) researchers claim that in reality "a new culture of management and independent thinking in the school" had developed and that principals were unwilling to return to their previous work methods. It was further found that the transition to school-based management aroused certain fears and some local authorities strengthened their hold on the school in order to ensure their continued influence on the school's educational activities while increasing their demands for feedback data concerning achievement and parent satisfaction.

The experimental stage uncovered additional difficulties in implementation, which led to new decisions. It became apparent how deep the gaps in allocations between local authorities were. There were differences in allocations between schools within the same local authority. Regarding the transition to school-based management for a single school or only a small number of schools in a particular locality, the local authority did not feel obligated to transfer all budgetary resources to the schools using direct allocations based on criteria. And the most complex issue of all was the fact that the transition to school-based management had created a "new management language." Without joint training to enable creation of a dialogue based on the new language – between decision-makers in the local authority, inspectors and school principals – the chances of realizing expectations for changing the structure of the school's authority were small.

In practice, inspectors and local authority employees who took part in the experiment saw this as just another project, one of many, undertaken by the Ministry of Education, while the transition to school-based management necessitated new organizational and management behaviors that were almost in total contradiction with the procedures they had used to run the schools up to now.

Therefore, a resolution began to emerge for solving two issues: the signing of an agreement with the local authorities for the transition of all schools in their jurisdiction to school-based management; and training for all schools, from key officials in the local authority and local school inspectors, in order to ensure the creation of a new management language that would be shared by all those involved in the process.

At the end of the 1996-97 school year, the first agreement was signed with the Jerusalem municipality, and a year later, with the cities of Haifa, Kiryat Shemona, Netivot and Kiryat Malachi. During 1999-2000, another 30 cities joined this move, including Tel Aviv, and in 2001 ten more communities were added.

The agreements signed with the local authorities include four principles:

1. Defining the program's pedagogic goals;

2. The obligation of the local authority to transfer to the schools in its jurisdiction all the budgetary resources designated for the pupils, teachers and the school;

3. The obligation of the Ministry of Education to an identical transfer of budgetary resources;

4. The right of the school to decide whether it wants to join the program at all, and if so, during what year.

The agreement also defined the goals of the transition to school-based management and the commitment of both sides to carry this out, and the obligation by all parties (principals, authority representatives including the treasurer, inspectors) to undergo in-service training for the purpose of fostering the common language needed to implement the new management culture.

The new phase, which is presently underway, created several advantages, but new difficulties were encountered. The advantages lie in the fact that for the first time schools could engage in pedagogic planning for the school year, and even beyond, while knowing in advance all the resources they had available as a result of the transition to a public and transparent (clear) budget formula, based on funding from both the Ministry of Education and the local authority. Although schools were exposed to a sphere that had been unfamiliar to them before, namely, budgetary planning, the advantages for the pedagogic staffs were many and satisfying, and made up for the disadvantages of having to deal with this new area. For the first time, schools realized that they were no longer dependent on the inspector's allocation of hours based on the number of classes – they now had the freedom to organize studies, hours and class structure as a result of the transition to a pupil-based standard rather than a standard based on hours per class. Now, principals were permitted to decide, and the new allocation of hours even allowed this, whether to split classes in subjects they preferred and needed, whether to add a class at a particular age level, to add a therapeutic assistant to a class, to add consulting hours or a librarian's position, to purchase books, computers or equipment – all based on the school's work plan and the budgetary framework at the school's disposal. Several schools used their budgetary surplus to acquire 30, 40 and even 50 new computers, to set up a botanical garden, to purchase an "ecological bubble" and to implement activities they had never undertaken because these had not been within their authority, or because certain procedures did not allow them the flexibility and consideration regarding the pedagogic use of the system's resources. This flexibility now gave the schools plenty of leeway, but this flexible operation also presented the school with numerous problems with the two other parts of the triad – the Ministry of Education and the local authority.

So long as the program operated on an experimental basis, its impact on Education Ministry budgets was minimal. Once the transition was made from experiment to policy and was expanded to over one-third of the elementary schools (around 650 elementary schools and another 40 secondary schools in various stages of the transition process), it became clear to decision-makers at the Ministry of Education that the transition to school-based management meant a serious reduction in the authority held by the Ministry's various officials. The move towards a formula for public budget allocations left officials with much less freedom than they previously enjoyed. Around one-third of their operating budgets now had to be transferred to the schools based on certain criteria, and nobody, except for school personnel, had the right to determine how those resources would be utilized. This step created tremendous internal pressure within the Education Ministry, and between the Ministry and the schools. In several localities the inspectors asked to continue deciding on the internal allocation of hours, which were given to the school in light of criteria-based allocations and in contradiction to the opinion of the school principal and faculty. Attempts were made to reduce the scope of formula-based allocations in order to allow the Ministry of Education to keep more authority (and budget) than it had decided, by agreement, to relinquish. In reality, we witnessed a syndrome as serious as the one that destroyed the idea of school autonomy in the 1980s – systemic difficulties within the Education Ministry in relinquishing its authority and budgets, and switching to the school's authority and considerations. In several cases, these difficulties led to a crisis of faith with the school principals. These problems, which were usually discovered too late, left a bitter taste with those participating in the process – the principals, the local authorities, and several agencies within the Ministry of Education.

Problems were also discovered within the local authorities. The transition to school-based management obligated local authorities to define a "basket of pupil services." The basket was defined on the basis of an economic assessment of all the local authority's budgetary resources earmarked for the school.

The results of this assessment led, for the first time, to setting a ceiling or public rate for local pupil budgets by the local authority. The schools' advantage began to weaken even in the early stage when the local authority declared the actual level of service it was making available to its residents (i.e., its pupils). This public declaration was significant because, for the first time, the school was being given an anchor – however minimal it was – and budgetary basis for pedagogic planning which was difficult to reverse without paying some price, and perhaps, would only add to it.

Along with the advantage of defining a "pupil basket," the process of changing to school-based management exposed the serious disparities that existed within Israeli society in the educational sphere. The budgetary basket for services ranged from NIS 280 per pupil to NIS 800 per pupil – a difference of some 300%. Furthermore, following the budgetary assessment it was clear that some local authorities were suffering from budgetary crises and serious deficits that prevented them from transferring the funds that were earmarked for the "pupil basket." Budgets from government sources, such as the Ministry of Education or the Ministry of the Interior, or from other agencies outside the local authority, were seized by various suppliers without being able to transfer them to their rightful destination. School personnel in some locations, and usually those in the weakest areas in Israeli society, do not benefit from operating budgets that include auxiliary services, such as maintenance, renovations, equipment, therapeutic assistance, etc., because of this reality. Therefore, the gaps between local authorities prior to the transition to self-based management sometimes reached 1,000%.

THE END OF THE STORY OR THE BEGINNING?

The transition to self-based management for schools in Israel is beginning to take shape. This is a slow and gradual process of change, and we can learn from it on two levels. In the pedagogic sphere, we can already identify findings similar in direction to those of effective schools. Defining clear goals for the pedagogic staff, flexible operations, the ability to respond to pupil needs in real time, school-based feedback, flexible organization of studies and class work, delegating authority to school personnel, changing the principal's administrative style and an "open door" policy – all these, as the early indicators of changes in the administrative and organizational culture stemming from school-based management, have a positive influence on the school. The research accompanying the process has not studied, nor was it asked to, changes in academic achievement under school-based management. The only evidence we have is the satisfaction expressed by those schools that have undergone the process to the fullest. This satisfaction is expressed for the most part by the teachers, but also by pupils (in those schools where the process has "trickled down" to the student body), parents and inspectors.

In the coming years it will be necessary to raise research questions in the pedagogic sphere, such as: Does school-based management work to promote weaker pupils? Was there a change in the quality of training and instruction in the school? What is the pedagogic significance of preparing school work plans, and whom do they serve? Did the school's ability for pedagogic endeavors increase as a result of adopting a policy of direct budgetary allocations? Was there a change in the management style? Did the transition to school-based management encourage other school principals, or expose hidden personality traits principals already had? Did teachers' status improve as a result of giving the school direct authority? Did the transition to school-based management expose the gaps that exist between local authorities which they could not reduce on their own? What steps must the government take so that a child living in Israel's peripheral communities will benefit from the same, if not better, service resources in comparison with a child living in the center of the country? These are just some of the pedagogic questions that have emerged as a result of the transition to school-based management.

Another sphere for which we have only partial information at this point, and which must be studied, relates to the ability of the education system to switch from centralization to decentralization. Here, too, theories concerning the behavior of systems and organizations undergoing change can shed some light on what we have seen in the field. The Ministry of Education and the local authorities, two components of the system that are supposed to transfer some of their power to the local schools and, in essence, relinquish some of that power, do not constitute a single entity. Some prominent parts of the system are reluctant to accept this policy of change in the structure of their authority and the transition to school-based management, and are attempting to forestall the process. Even if their behavior did not constitute a single entity, we could say that this pattern, which was fully seen in 2000, is similar to that which prevented the processes of school autonomy in the 1970s and 1980s, even though the circumstances are different. If, in the 1980s, school autonomy was aimed at delegating pedagogic authority, the switch to school-based management assumes that pedagogic autonomy is possible and can be realized only if accompanied by real authority over operating budgets for pedagogic planning, and thus, implementation as well. If there is no connection between these two components there can be no autonomy – claim the initiators of the transition to school-based management. While in the 1980s the Ministry spoiled the foundations for the autonomy it had itself initiated through bureaucratic demands for "operational approval" for every initiative or idea put forth by the school, in 2000 they are attempting, even if only in some parts of the system, to undermine the allocations formula and reduce the budgets themselves in order to keep a greater degree of authority in the hands of the inspectors. The local authorities are not a single entity. Some of them have led the process admirably and with determination, while in other cases, we have witnessed a syndrome similar to the one we saw in the Ministry of Education – attempts to delay and prevent school-based management. The different theoretical approaches with regard to systems theory, the psychology of change, sociology and political science – shed light on this pattern of behavior and explain why these systems straddle the fence between centralization and decentralization (Buckley, 1967; Prigogine, 1976; Sungaila, 1990; Volansky, 2003).

Thus we are faced with a clash between the values of different organizations. On the one hand, we have both research and theoretical knowledge indicating that under conditions of self-based management, the school – and therefore, the education system – has a good chance of reaching higher academic achievement; on the other hand, the systems tend to preserve the power they have.

The tension described herein has led to four developments: One, in August 2000, the legislature passed preliminary legislation regarding the obligation of the local authority to transfer all funds earmarked for the pupil, the teacher and the school to their destination, without allowing the authority to utilize these funds at all. The law also states that the head of the local authority shall bear personal, criminal responsibility if the instructions contained in the law are not carried out, making him also subject to possible monetary fine. The second development is that in September 2000, there was a discussion held in the Ministry of Education, in order to prevent continued attempts to undermine the formulae for school allocations. The purpose and the significance of these attempts is to give the Ministry of Education greater leeway by reducing the authority of the school switching to school-based management. The third development is reflected in the formulation of a new organizational model, known as the "local district" whose main purpose is to empower the school by merging the authority of the Education Ministry district and those of the local authority and creating a single, unified organizational entity (district), while at the same time developing a method of operation that will reduce the disparities in budget allocations between the different local authorities. The fourth development is that the Teachers' Federation and the Ministry of Education have published a joint position paper calling for schools to switch to school-based management. This position paper closes the door on seven years of serious disagreement and creates a commitment, not only by the Education Ministry to implement the process, but also by the Teachers' Federation. These four developments, each one of which can stand on its own, join together in a single purpose – to reinforce the status, power, authority and responsibility of the school and its teaching faculty.

We can summarize by saying that we are witnessing a process that has both progressive and conservative elements – conflicts between agents wanting to instill change and those who wish to maintain the organization's status quo. The transition to school-based management in the year 2000 is, therefore, the end of the chapter, but it is not the end of the story.

REFERENCES

Beare, J., Caldwell, B. J., & Millikan, R. (1989). *Creating an excellent school.* London: Routledge.

Buckley, W. (1967). *Sociology and modern systems theory.* New Jersey: Prentice Hall.

Caldwell, B. J. & Spinks J. M. (1998). *Beyond the self-managing school.* London: Falmer Press.

Cheng, Y. C. (1996). *School effectiveness and school-based management.* London: Falmer Press.

Dimmock, C. (Ed.). (1993). *School-based management and school effectiveness.* London: Routledge.

Friedman, I., & Barma, R. (1998). *The transition to school-based management.* Jerusalem: Szold Institute (in Hebrew).

Friedman, I., Barma, Y., & Toren, S. (1997). *School-based management: Changing the school's management culture.* Jerusalem: Szold Institute (in Hebrew).

Handy, C. B. (1988) *Understanding organisations.* London: Penguin Press.

Hopkins, D. (Ed.). (1987). *Improving the quality of schooling.* London: Falmer Press.

Inbar, D. (1987). Is autonomy possible in a centralized education system? In I. Friedman (Ed.), *Autonomy in education: Conceptual frameworks and implementation processes* (pp. 53-71). Jerusalem: Szold Institute (in Hebrew).

Leithwood, K., Chapman, J., Corson, D., Hallinger, P., & Hart, A. (Eds.). (1996). *International handbook of educational leadership and administration.* Dordrecht, The Netherlands: Kluwer Academic Publishers.

McGregor, D. (1985). *The human side of enterprise.* New York: McGraw-Hill.

Ministry of Education and Culture. (1993). *Recommendations of the steering committee on school-based management.* Second draft (interim report). Jerusalem (in Hebrew).

Peters, T., & Waterman, R. (1982). *In search of excellence.* New York: Harper & Row.

Prigogine, I. (1976). Order through fluctuation: Self-organisation and social system. In E. Jantsch & C. Waddington (Eds.), *Evolution and consciousness: Human system in transition.* London: Addison-Wesley.

Reshef, S. (1984). *Autonomy in education – Background, chances and principles for implementation.* Tel Aviv: Ministry of Education and Culture and Tel Aviv University (in Hebrew).

Reynolds, D., & Cuttance, P. (1993). *School effectiveness - Research, policy and practice.* New York: Cassell.

Sergiovanni, T. J., & Starratt, R. J. (1993): *Supervision*. New York: McGraw-Hill.

Sungaila, H. (1990). The new science of chaos: Making a new science of leadership? *Journal of Educational Administration, 28*(2).

Volansky, A. (1992). *Proposal for a program of changes in the education system* (Planning Document No. 1). Jerusalem: Ministry of Education (in Hebrew).

Volansky, A. (1994). Individualism, collectivism and market forces in education – Is the social cost necessary? *Megamot (Trends) 36*(2-3), 238-252 (in Hebrew).

Volansky, A. (1995). *Development trends in the American education system.* Jerusalem: Ministry of Education (in Hebrew).

Volansky, A. (1997). *Between the center and the periphery in Canada's education system – Historical background, theoretical models and developments in the 1990s.* Tel Aviv University, School of Education (in Hebrew).

Volansky, A. (1999). The dialectic between centralization and decentralization. In E. Peled (Ed.), *Ministry of Education Jubilee Annual.* Tel Aviv: Ministry of Defense (in Hebrew).

Volansky, A. (2003). *The 'Pendulum Syndrome' of centralization and decentralization processes in education - The case of England and Wales.* Tel Aviv: Ramot Publishing, Tel Aviv University.

Williams, V. (Ed.). (1995). *Towards self-managing schools.* London: Cassell.

Williams, V. (Ed.). (1998). *Conceptual and practical issues in school leadership - Insights and innovations from the U.S. and abroad.* San Francisco: Jossey-Bass.

THE THEORY AND PRACTICE OF SCHOOL-BASED MANAGEMENT FOR SCHOOL EFFECTIVENESS: AN INTERNATIONAL PERSPECTIVE*

Yin Cheong Cheng

DIRECTIONS OF SCHOOL REFORMS IN INTERNATIONAL CONTEXTS: TOWARDS SBM

Due to the rapid changes and developments in technology, economy, and political climate in the 1980s and 1990s, educational environments in the Asia-Pacific region, as well as in Western countries, have undergone rapid changes. In the new century, educational goals will become more uncertain and complex; educational tasks will be more demanding; expectations from the public will be more diverse, and school accountability to the public will be more serious than at any time before. In order to cope with the challenges arising in the 1990s and the 21st century, numerous educational reforms and school restructuring movements have been undertaken to pursue educational effectiveness and school development not only in Canada, the USA, and the UK in the west, but also in Asia-Pacific regions such as Australia, New Zealand, Mainland China, Singapore, Malaysia and Hong Kong.

The search for effective schools, the shift to school-based management, the emphasis on development planning in schools, the assurance of a quality education, the implementation of new curricula and the application of information technology in education are typical examples of the efforts of reform movements (Caldwell & Hayward, 1998; Caldwell & Spinks, 1992; 1998; Cheng, 1996a, 1996b, 1999; Hargreaves & Hopkins, 1991; MacGilchrist, Mortimore, Savage, & Beresford, 1995; Murphy & Beck, 1995; Reynolds & Cuttance, 1992; Scheerens, 1992; Stringfield, Ross, & Smith, 1997).

The major developments of educational changes and school reforms in international contexts can be summarized as shown in Figure 1.

---

*   This paper is one of the reports from the research project on school-based management that is supported by a competitive earmarked research grant of the Research Grants Council of Hong Kong. The author would like to acknowledge the award of the Council to this project. A major part of the materials in this paper draw heavily on earlier works (Cheng 1996a, 1997a, 1998).

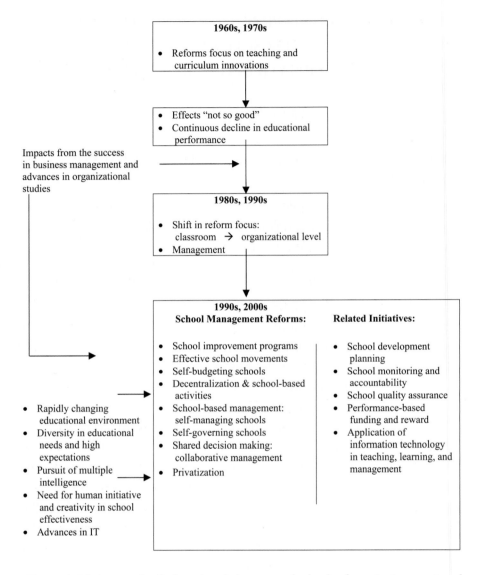

Figure 1. Major trends of educational changes and school reforms in international contexts (particularly in Western countries)

In the 1960s and 1970s, educational changes focused primarily on the improvement of teaching methods, curriculum design, and learning aids, particularly in some advanced western countries. But unfortunately, the effects of these changes were often insignificant, if they existed at all. In the USA, for example, even though great efforts were put into instructional innovations and school facilities, pupils' learning performance and outcomes seemed to show no significant improvement. People doubted that the effectiveness of schools influenced students' performance (Averch, Carroll, Donaldson, Kiesling, & Pincus, 1974; Coleman et al., 1966; Gross & Gross, 1985). In the 1980s, following advances in organizational and management sciences and the success of management development in business and industry, people began to believe that if they wanted to enhance quality of education, they would have to shift their focus from the classroom level to the organizational level, and improve the education system and school management. From the late 1980s and throughout the 1990s, there have been different types of school reforms in many parts of the world. Due to the rapid changes in educational environment, the diverse and high expectations on school education, the need for human initiative and creativity in processes of teaching and management, and the advances in information technology particularly in the new century, the shift towards school-based management (SBM) seemed to be inevitable and has become mainstream.

From these developments, several trends of school reforms for school effectiveness can be observed in international contexts (Cheng, 1996a, 1999).

From improvement to development

There is a shift in emphasis from school improvement to school development. In the school improvement tradition, it is often assumed that school goals are clear and static and schools should be improved if they cannot achieve these goals successfully. But now educational environments are changing very quickly and school goals are not so clear and rigid anymore. In order to adapt to changing environments, there is a strong need to continuously develop nearly every important aspect of the school, including school goals, curriculum, personnel, organizational structure, school process, and technology in management, teaching and learning. Continuous school development is necessary for long-term school effectiveness. Conceptually, school improvement is a narrow, short-term and remedial concept. In contrast with this, school development is a comprehensive, long-term, and formative concept. The strong support for the planning of school development in international school reforms truly reflects the emphasis of the school development concept.

From quantity to quality

A clear shift can be seen from educational quantity to educational quality. People are not satisfied merely with the quantity of educational service provided in the school. They are more concerned about the quality. Whether the quality of school education can meet the high and diverse expectations of school constituencies, and how it can be enhanced and ensured have become key issues in most of the current educational reforms. This is the major reason why quality assurance and quality inspection in school education are key elements in school reform.

From maintenance to effectiveness and accountability

Traditionally, people are more concerned about problems happening in schools, and they invest a great deal of effort to avoid problems and maintain normal school functioning. They often ignore whether schools are effective or not. But now there is a shift of emphasis from school maintenance to school effectiveness. Maintaining daily functioning is not sufficient to satisfy the need for high quality education. The present school reforms aim at maximizing school effectiveness and keeping schools accountable to serve diverse educational needs. Therefore, school monitoring and performance reviews are important components to ensure school accountability and effectiveness. Developing performance indicators, and training school principals and teachers to use them for school improvement and development, become a critical part of school reform efforts.

From external structural control to school-based management and human initiative

The shift in school management from external structural control to school-based management or self-management is evident. The traditional, centralized management often ignores school-based needs and human initiatives, and it is ineffective and too rigid for developing school-based initiative and meeting changing school-based needs. In current school reforms, devolution of power from the central authority to the school level, school autonomy and self-management, and participation of different school constituencies (e.g. principal, teachers, parents, alumni, students, and even the community) are strongly encouraged to facilitate the school-based initiative for school development and effectiveness.

From simplistic techniques to sophisticated technology in management, teaching and learning

In present school reforms, a clear shift of emphasis from the use of simplistic techniques to the application of sophisticated technology in school management or planning can be observed. Traditionally, it is often assumed that school goals are obvious, static and standard, handed down by the central education authority. Schools are all under external control and are dependent on the management of the central authority. Therefore, there is no strong need to use any sophisticated management technology to deal with the impact of changing environments. But today, following the aforementioned shifts and reforms, the use of sophisticated technologies such as strategic management, development planning, participative management and quality assurance, is strongly emphasized and promoted in schools. In particular, rapid developments in information technology have a tremendous impact, and may lead to changes in the options and patterns of education. Widespread use of such technologies in teaching, learning and management in order to enhance school effectiveness is necessary and inevitable in ongoing educational reforms.

Obviously, these trends represent some of the advances in knowledge, research, practice and policy, particularly in the areas of school effectiveness and school-based management in recent years. But compared with the huge scale of the ongoing educational reforms involving numerous schools, staff and pupils, these advances are still too insignificant and insufficient to support the formulation and implementation of effective reforms. Particularly, the traditional ideas and beliefs about school goals and functions and school-based management are still quite simplistic and cannot provide a clear direction for educational reforms in schools (Cheng, 1996c; Cheung & Cheng, 1996). It is not surprising that many reforms with positive intentions have failed and have been met with frustration. There is a strong need for more empirical research and theory-building to support the practice of school-based management and ongoing educational reforms.

Based on the experiences from current school reforms in international contexts, as well as the author's research, this paper aims to highlight a new knowledge base for the practice of school-based management for the pursuit of school effectiveness and educational quality.

SCHOOL FUNCTIONS / GOALS AND INTERNAL SCHOOL PROCESSES FOR SCHOOL-BASED MANAGEMENT

In thinking about school-based management and effectiveness, we should consider the following basic questions:

1. Knowledge and relevance of school functions/goals. *In the new century, what are the functions and goals schools should assume in order to meet the challenges and expectations from a changing and demanding educational environment?* This question is closely related to the direction of school reform and the practice of school effectiveness. Without a clear understanding of school functions and goals, we do not know how effective schools are in performing their functions and goals and in what direction we should improve them. We foresee that the educational environment will be even more changing and demanding and our schools will have multiple goals and functions to meet the challenges of the new century (Beare & Slaughter, 1993; Cheng, 1997a; Dalin & Rust, 1996). But many ongoing educational reforms are often conducted with a very narrow perception about school goals. Ignorance of multiple and complex school functions in educational reforms cannot bring out effective strategies to support school development (Cheng, 1996a). To a great extent, school effectiveness will depend on the relevance of existing school goals and functions to the needs and challenges of the changing educational environment.

2. Knowledge of internal school process. *How can the internal school process be re-engineered such that the school as a whole can perform the aforementioned functions and goals successfully?* This question is related to the internal effectiveness of schools. As we know, the schools are often strictly bounded by limited input of resources, a tight time frame for implementation, poor knowledge and technology in education and management, and rigid external and internal structural controls. They are not empowered and they lack opportunities to learn, develop, and adapt in the changing and diverse environment. To a great extent, the current school-based management movements try to make it easy for schools to overcome these constraints. But, due to simplistic decentralization at the site-level without support of more sophisticated knowledge and technology of management and education, the effects of these reforms are often problematic (Cheng & Cheung, 1997). How can schools be re-engineered to maximize their internal effectiveness regarding school process within the context of different constraints, and maximize their capacity for multiple school functions in a changing educational environment?

These two questions are critical to the formulation and implementation of school-based management reforms in order to enhance school effectiveness and educational quality. But their answers demand a new set of principles to re-engineer our schools instead of fragmentary remedial measures. Based on the author's recent research and thinking on school effectiveness and school-based management (Cheng, 1996a, 1996b, 1996c, 1997a), a framework can be proposed for developing a new knowledge base of school functions and internal process for practicing school-based management in international contexts.

This framework for school-based management will be explained in the following three parts: (1) "value added" and "value created" in school effectiveness; (2) knowledge framework of multiple school functions and goal relevance; (3) knowledge framework of internal process.

"VALUE ADDED" AND "VALUE CREATED" IN SCHOOL EFFECTIVENESS

As explained above, school effectiveness is mainly determined by the relevance of school goals and functions and the internal school process. Improving these two aspects should be a key target of school-based management with the aim of enhancing school effectiveness. The commonly used term school's value added can be further expanded into two types, value added and value created, as illustrated in Figure 2.

Value added in school effectiveness: This represents the idea that for given school goals and functions, the school can improve its internal process to achieve a greater extent of the given goals and functions such that it adds value in school effectiveness from time t1 to time t2, as shown in area A in Figure 2.

Value created in school effectiveness: This refers to the concept that when improving internal process, the school can enhance the relevance of its goals and functions, or create new goal relevance and achieve these goals such that it creates value (different from old goals and functions) in school effectiveness from time t1 to time t2, as shown in area B in Figure 2. (It is assumed that enhancement of goal relevance or development of new goals will only occur by improving the internal process.)

Value reduced in school effectiveness: There are two types of value reduced: one due to loss in internal process (Area A) and the other due to loss of goal relevance from time t1 to time t2 (Area B), as shown in Figure 3.

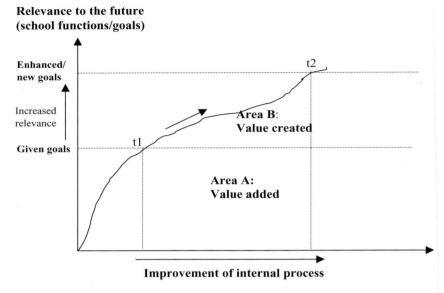

Figure 2. "Value added" and "value created" in school effectiveness

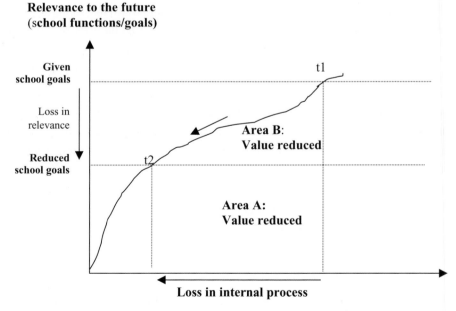

Figure 3. "Value reduced" in school effectiveness

240

KNOWLEDGE FRAMEWORK FOR SCHOOL GOAL RELEVANCE AND MULTIPLE SCHOOL FUNCTIONS

In order to enhance value created and value added, it is necessary to establish and increase the relevance of school goals and functions and create relevant new school goals. But how should this be accomplished? It is a critical issue. We must have comprehensive knowledge of school functions and goals in the new century when implementing school-based management.

Borrowing from the knowledge of disciplines such as psychology, sociology, political science, economics, futurism, and organizational studies, the potential school functions may be classified into five types, particularly in the new century: technical/economic functions, human/social functions, political functions, cultural functions, and educational functions, at the individual, institutional, community, societal, and international levels, as shown in Table 1 (Cheng, 1996a).

New knowledge of technical/economic functions. When planning school reform, we need the new knowledge about what schools can contribute to technical or economic development and needs at different levels. We can expect schools to help pupils acquire knowledge and skills necessary to survive and participate in a competitive economy, and provide staff with job training and opportunities. Schools are service organizations providing quality service; they also serve as a life place and a place of work for faculty and other relevant personnel. In addition, schools serve the economic and instrumental needs of the local community, supply quality labor forces to the economic system, modify or shape economic behaviors of pupils (McMahon, 1987), and contribute to the development and stability of the economy's manpower structure (Hinchcliffe, 1987). At the international level, education supplies the high quality manpower necessary in international competition, economic cooperation, protecting the earth, and technology and information exchange.

Yin Cheong Cheng

Table 1

Knowledge framework of multiple school functions

	Knowledge of Technical/Economic Functions	Knowledge of Human/Social Functions	Knowledge of Political Functions	Knowledge of Cultural Functions	Knowledge of Educational Functions
Individual (students, staff, etc.)	• Knowledge & skills training • Career training • Job for staff	• Psychological developments • Social developments • Potential developments	• Development of civic attitudes and skills	• Acculturation • Socialization with values, norms, & beliefs	• Learning how to learn & develop • Learning how to teach & help • Professional development
Institutional	• As a life place • As a work place • As a service organization	• As a social entity/system • As a human relationship	• As a place for political socialization • As a political coalition • As a place for political discourse or criticism	• As a center for cultural transmission & reproduction • As a place for cultural revitalization & integration	• As a place for learning & teaching • As a center for disseminating knowledge • As a center for educational changes & developments
Community	• Serving the economic or instrumental needs of the community	• Serving the social needs of the community	• Serving the political needs of the community	• Serving the cultural needs of the community	• Serving the educational needs of the community
Society	• Providing quality labor forces • Modifying economic behavior • Contributing to the manpower structure	• Social integration • Social mobility / social class perpetuation • Social equality • Selection & allocation of human resources • Social development & change	• Political legitimization • Political structure maintenance & continuity • Promoting democracy • Facilitating political developments & reforms	• Cultural integration & continuity • Cultural reproduction • Production of cultural capital • Cultural revitalization	• Development of the education professions • Development of education structures • Dissemination of knowledge & information • Learning society
International	• International competition • Economic cooperation • International trade • Technology exchange • Earth protection • Sharing information	• Global village • International friendship • Social cooperation • International exchanges • Elimination of national / regional/racial/gender biases	• International coalition • International understanding • Peace/against war • Common interests • Elimination of conflicts	• Appreciation of cultural diversity • Cultural acceptance across countries/regions • Development of global culture	• Development of global education • International education exchanges & cooperation • Education for the whole world

Adapted from Cheng (1996a).

New knowledge of human/social functions. We need new knowledge regarding the contribution of schools to human development and social relationships at different levels of society. Schools can be expected to assist students in developing themselves psychologically, socially and physically, and help them develop their full potential. A school is a social entity or social system composed of different human relationships. Moreover, schools serve the social functions of the local community, support social integration of multiple and diverse constituencies of society, facilitate social mobility within the existing class structure, select and allocate competent people to appropriate roles and positions, and contribute to long-term social change and development (Cheng, 1995). It is possible that schools reproduce the existing social class structure and perpetuate social inequality (Blackledge & Hunt, 1985). Due to the growing global consciousness (Beare & Slaughter, 1993), schools are expected to play an important role in preparing students for international harmony, social cooperation, global human relationships, and elimination of national, regional, racial and gender biases at the international level.

New knowledge of political functions. New knowledge on the contribution of schools to political development at different levels of society is also necessary in formulating school reform policy. Schools are expected to help students develop positive civic attitudes and skills and exercise the rights and responsibilities of citizenship. Schools act as a place for systematically socializing students into a set of political norms, values and beliefs, or for critically discussing and reflecting on existing political events. Schools play an important role by serving the political needs of the local community and society, legitimizing the authority of the existing government, maintaining the stability of the political structure, promoting awareness of democratic movements, and facilitating planned political developments and changes (Thomas, 1983). The growing awareness of international dependence reinforces the need for education to contribute towards international understanding, global common interest, international coalitions, peace movements against war, and elimination of conflicts between regions and nations.

New knowledge of cultural functions. School re-engineering requires new knowledge of the contribution schools can make to the transmission and development of culture at different levels of society. Schools are expected to help students develop their creativity and aesthetic awareness and to be socialized with the important norms, values and beliefs of society. Schools act as a place for the systematic transmission and

243

reproduction of culture for the next generation, cultural integration among multiple and diverse constituencies, and cultural revitalization of outdated and weak traditions. In addition, schools often serve as a cultural unit to carry the explicit norms and expectations of the local community, transmit all the important values and artifacts of society to students, integrate diverse subcultures from different backgrounds, and revitalize the strengths of the existing culture. But it is also possible that schools reproduce and perpetuate cultural inequality within society (Apple, 1982; Cheng, 1995; Collins, 1971; Giroux, 1981). Schools can be expected to encourage appreciation of cultural diversity and acceptance of different norms, traditions, values and beliefs in various countries and regions and ultimately, to contribute towards the development of a global culture through the integration of diverse cultures.

New knowledge of education functions. Traditionally, schools are assumed to play the major role as education providers. Inevitably, new knowledge as to the contribution of schools towards the development and maintenance of education at different levels of society is necessary for school reform. Due to the rapid development and change in nearly every aspect of the world, people have begun to accept education as an important value or goal in and of itself (Chapman, 1996). Schools are expected to help students learn how to learn, and help teachers learn how to teach. Similarly, facilitating teachers' professional development is another of education's key functions. Schools serve as a place for systematic learning, teaching and disseminating knowledge, and as a center for systematically experimenting and implementing educational changes and developments (Cousins, 1996). Schools provide service for different educational needs within the local community, facilitate development of education professions and education structures, disseminate knowledge and information to the next generation, and contribute to the formation of a learning society. In order to encourage mutual understanding among nations and establish "a global family" for the younger generation, schools can contribute towards the development of global education, international exchange and cooperation in education.

Knowledge of long-term and short-term functions. In formulating policy on school reform, we need to know what time span is to be used for considering school functions. The above school functions may be further divided into two types: long-term functions and short-term functions. Long-term functions refer to the contributions or effects of schools that take place and continue over a long period of time (e.g., more than a few years). These functions are often very important, though people may not necessarily perceive them as such. Short-term functions refer to those contributions or effects of schools that occur explicitly within in a short period of time (e.g., a few months or less than a few years). In general, for each type of technical/economic, human/social, political, cultural and educational function, there may exist both long-term and short-term functions. The knowledge of both long-term and short-term school functions and their relationships, particularly in a changing environment, is necessary for considering the priorities, strategies and policies of school reforms.

Knowledge about diverse emphases on school functions. For different people or constituencies, the expectations of school functions are often different and diverse. Some people may be more concerned with technical and economic functions, while others may concentrate on political functions. Some people may pay attention to the functions at the individual levels but others may focus more on the functions at the community level or society level. Even though in the past school functions at the international level might not have attracted much attention, there seems to be a growing concern with this in recent years (Beare & Slaughter, 1993). The understanding of the diverse emphases on school functions among school stakeholders can provide the knowledge base necessary for developing strategies and policies to manage the potential conflicts and dilemmas from diverse interests, and the potential resistance from various constituencies to school reforms.

Interdisciplinary knowledge about school functions. For different academic disciplines, the emphasis on types and levels of school functions may be different, too. For example, school functions at the individual level may receive more attention in educational psychology. For sociology of education, school functions at the society level, particularly those related to social mobility, equality and class stratification, may attract more concern. Economics of education often focuses on the economic functions of schools at different levels. In the field of school management or organizational behavior, school functions at the institutional level are inevitably the major topic of school reform. Obviously, different academic disciplines have different foci when they are used to support policy formulation for school reform. In order to achieve a comprehensive knowledge base for understanding multiple school functions and supporting policy-making on school restructuring, an interdisciplinary approach, if not multiple disciplines, should be encouraged to develop knowledge.

New knowledge of multiple school effectiveness and their relations. In general, school restructuring aims at enhancing school effectiveness for achieving expected school functions. The concept and knowledge of school effectiveness are critically important when formulating policies on school reform. Taking the above school functions, we may define school effectiveness as the capacity of the school to maximize school functions or the degree to which the school can perform school functions, when given a fixed amount of school input. Since there are five types of school functions, school effectiveness may be further classified into five types: technical/economic effectiveness, human/social effectiveness, political effectiveness, cultural effectiveness, and educational effectiveness. Moreover, since there are five levels of school functions, school effectiveness may be classified into five levels: school effectiveness at the individual level, at the institutional level, at the community level, at the society level, and at the international level.

From an input-output perspective, when the discussion is mainly in terms of non-monetary inputs or processes (e.g., number of textbooks, classroom organization, etc.), the comparison of output function to non-monetary input (or process) may be called school effectiveness. If the discussion is mainly in terms of monetary input (e.g., $3,000 input per student, cost of books, salary, etc.), then the comparison between school output function and monetary input may be referred to as school efficiency.

It is important to note that the relationship between the five types of school effectiveness, between the five levels of school effectiveness, and even between effectiveness and efficiency may be very complicated, and not necessarily positive. A school with a high technical effectiveness at the individual level does not necessarily promise high technical effectiveness or social effectiveness at the society level, although people often assume the existence of such a positive relationship (Grosin, 1994). Furthermore, many studies from radical perspectives challenge the traditional belief of schools' "positive" functions on social equalization by pointing out that schools do not promote social equality, but probably perpetuate the inequality of social class (Blackledge & Hunt, 1985; Cheng, 1995). Therefore, even though schools have higher technical effectiveness at the institutional level, they do not necessarily have the effectiveness of promoting social equality as expected. To a great extent, the relationship of technical effectiveness to social effectiveness or cultural effectiveness is very controversial in the field of sociology of education. In addition, the relationship between technical effectiveness and technical efficiency may not be simple. It is often a hot topic for research in the field of economics of education (Cheng & Ng, 1997; McMahon, 1987).

In general, enhancing one type of school effectiveness does not necessarily promise an increase in the other four types. Similarly, increasing school effectiveness at one level does not certainly result in improved effectiveness at the other levels. There are no studies concerning the inter-effectiveness of relationships. In order to develop effective policy for school restructuring, there is an urgent need to develop a new knowledge base about the relationship between different models of school effectiveness.

Shift to a new knowledge base on school functions. From the above conception of school effectiveness for multiple functions at multiple levels, a shift to a new knowledge base on school functions proposed for consideration in future research, policy-making and practice is summarized in Table 2, below.

Traditionally, the discussion of school restructuring or school-based management is often based on the simplistic conception of school functions, involving technical/economic effectiveness and social effectiveness at the individual or institutional levels only. Neglecting the multiplicity and complexity of school functions and effectiveness inevitably limits school restructuring. Therefore, in school-based management, we need a new knowledge base to cover a wider spectrum of school functions and effectiveness including technical/economic, human/social, political, cultural and educational dimensions. What's more, not only are the issues at the individual and institutional levels strongly emphasized, but those at the community, society and international levels should be given sufficient attention as well. Traditionally, short-term effectiveness is often the major focus of school reforms. With the new knowledge base, both the school's short-term and long-term effects should be important for school-based management.

Usually, with the traditional knowledge base, people primarily emphasize technical/economic or human/social effectiveness, and they assume there is no great difference in the expectations of different constituencies at various levels (e.g., parents, students, teachers, administrators, community, economic sector, social service sector, policy-makers, the public, etc.). They have ignored the potential dilemmas from differences in the constituencies' expectations regarding effectiveness. If we agree that schools have multiple functions and that constituencies at different levels have diverse expectations, what kind of management should we employ to enhance school effectiveness? The study and management of these dilemmas should be one of the key concerns in current movements for school reform. Obviously, how to decrease these dilemmas and allow schools to acquire the greatest congruence between levels and between categories of effectiveness is a crucial issue in this new knowledge framework.

Table 2

New knowledge framework and traditional knowledge framework of school effectiveness in school reforms

	New knowledge framework on school function and effectiveness	Traditional knowledge framework on school function and effectiveness
Nature of school functions and effectiveness	• Based on multiple concept of school functions: technical, social, political, cultural and educational • Conception at five levels: individual, institutional, society community, and international • Both short-term and long-term considerations	• Based on simplistic concept of school functions, particularly on technical and social functions only • Conception only at one or two levels, particularly at the individual or institutional levels • Mainly short-term considerations
Expectation of school effectiveness	• For different constituencies, different types of school effectiveness are expected • Dilemmas exist	• Emphasizing mainly technical or social effectiveness, assuming no major differences in expectations • Dilemmas are ignored
Assumption about relationships	• Complicated relationship between types • Complicated relationship between levels • Complicated relationship between effectiveness and efficiency • Inter-relationships not necessarily positive, need to be studied and managed	• Positive relationship between types • Positive relationship between levels • Positive relationship between effectiveness and efficiency • No strong need to study and manage inter-relationships
Disciplinary knowledge to be used in reform	• Interdisciplinary cooperation and efforts are needed	• Mainly single discipline is used; separate efforts are made
Focus of school reform effort	• Multiple types of effectiveness • Multiple levels of effectiveness • Relationship between types • Relationship between levels • Relationship between effectiveness and efficiency	• Separate/single type of effectiveness • Separate/single level of effectiveness
Implications for management and policy in school reform	• To maximize effectiveness in multiple types at multiple levels • To maximize efficiency in multiple types at multiple levels • Need to ensure congruence between types and levels • Need to ensure congruence between effectiveness and efficiency	• Mainly to maximize effectiveness in separate type at single level • Mainly to maximize efficiency in separate type at single level • No need to ensure congruence between types and levels • No need to ensure congruence between effectiveness and efficiency

The traditional knowledge base often assumes that there is a positive relationship between categories of effectiveness, between levels of effectiveness, or between effectiveness and efficiency, and it is not necessary to manage these inter-relationships in the process of policy-making and school restructuring. As we have discussed, this assumption is very problematic. The inter-relationships may be very complicated, and not necessarily positive. The increase in school effectiveness in one category does not promise a concomitant increase in the other. Therefore, in the new knowledge framework, it is important to study these inter-relationships if we want to make reasonable efforts in pursuing school effectiveness. Traditionally, school reform may involve a single key discipline (e.g., educational psychology), or depend on separate efforts of each discipline. Obviously, this is not sufficient to understand the complexity of school functions and effectiveness and to support policy formulation on school restructuring. With the new knowledge framework, we should encourage interdisciplinary cooperation (e.g., involving educational psychology, economics of education, sociology of education, anthropology, organizational theories, etc.) and efforts towards understanding and enhancing school effectiveness. The focus of school reforms should include multiple categories of effectiveness at multiple levels, the relationship between categories, the relationship between levels, and the relationship between effectiveness and efficiency. Meanwhile, we need to develop a comprehensive theory to explain each inter-relationship and provide practical guidelines for enhancing school effectiveness.

In the traditional knowledge framework, only some categories of school effectiveness or efficiency at one or two levels are stressed; the rest are neglected and little is known about the importance of congruence between levels and the congruence between effectiveness and efficiency. No wonder many policy efforts seem to be less-than-successful at enhancing school effectiveness, if not total failures. If we understand that there is a multiplicity in school effectiveness, then school-based management should aim to maximize school effectiveness and efficiency of multiple categories at multiple levels.

How to ensure congruence among categories, levels, and between effectiveness and efficiency, how to enhance overall school effectiveness at all levels without stressing a particular category, and how to solve the dilemmas arising from the different expectations of various constituencies should be critical issues for further investigation in the current school reform and school-based management movements in the new knowledge framework.

KNOWLEDGE FRAMEWORK OF INTERNAL SCHOOL PROCESS FOR SCHOOL-BASED MANAGEMENT

As mentioned previously, "How can the internal school process be re-engineered such that the school as a whole can perform the aforementioned functions and roles or can add value in school effectiveness?" is another basic question in formulating school reform policy and implementing school-based management. The answer to this question needs a new knowledge base regarding the internal school process that can enlighten us regarding:

1) How a school can maximize the use of the internal resources to achieve optimal conditions for operation and continuous development in management, teaching and learning;

2) How a school can recognize the multiple school functions and effectiveness and successfully mobilize all possible efforts to achieve them in such a changing environment, particularly in the new century.

There is a need for knowledge about how schools can continuously develop themselves, pursue broad and new school functions, and enhance effectiveness to serve the needs of development of individuals, local community, society, and international communities (for a discussion of the knowledge framework needed by self-managing schools, see Cheng's article found in Part I, pp. 32-34 - Ed.).

Principles of school-based management

School-based management is one of the most salient worldwide educational reforms. School-based management means that the school management tasks are set according to the characteristics and needs of the school itself and therefore, school personnel and schools themselves have much greater autonomy and responsibility for the use of resources to solve problems and carry out effective educational activities for the long-term development of the school. School-based management and traditional external control management reflect different management principles used by the central authority to manage the school system (Caldwell & Spinks, 1988; Mohrman, Wohlstetter et al., 1994; Murphy & Beck, 1995). The major differences in the principles concerning education and management are summarized in Table 3 (Cheng, 1993).

Assumptions about education. In school-based management, we assume multiple educational goals based on the expectations of multiple school constituencies, and the educational environment is believed to be complex and changing. Therefore, educational reforms or changes in school are inevitably needed to adapt to the changing environment, to enhance effectiveness, and achieve multiple educational goals.

Principle of equifinality. School-based management is based on the principle of equifinality, which assumes that there may be different ways to achieve goals. Flexibility is emphasized and schools have ample leeway to develop and work out their unique strategies for effective teaching and management in their schools.

Principle of decentralization. In the changing educational environment, school management and teaching activities are inevitably faced with difficulties and problems. Therefore, supported by the principle of decentralization, schools should be given the power and responsibility to solve problems effectively wherever the problems occur as soon as possible, and make a greater contribution to the effectiveness of teaching and learning activities.

Principle of self-managing system. With the support of the above principles, it is necessary to enable schools to become self-managing systems under some major policies and structures, with considerable autonomy to develop teaching objectives and management strategies, deploy manpower and resources, solve problems and accomplish goals according to their own conditions.

Principle of human initiative. Due to the existing multiplicity and complexity of educational work, it is impossible to pursue new school functions and enhance educational quality without the initiative and creativity of school personnel. Therefore, school-based management aims at building up a suitable environment for school staff to participate widely, develop their potential, and contribute their initiative and competence to educational quality and school development.

These principles of school-based management can be used to guide school reforms and help schools shift from an external control management mode to a school-based management mode.

Yin Cheong Cheng

Table 3

The principles of school-based management

	Knowledge base of school-based management	Knowledge base of external control management
Assumptions about education	• Multiplicity of educational goals • Complex and changing educational environment • Need for educational reforms • Effectiveness and adaptation oriented • Pursuit of quality	• Unification of educational goals • Simple and nearly static educational environment • No need for educational reforms • Standardization & stability oriented • Pursuit of quantity
Principles used to manage schools	*Principle of equifinality*: • Many different ways to achieve goals • Emphasizes flexibility *Principle of decentralization*: • Problems are inevitable, should be solved when they happen in real time • Looks for efficiency and problem-solving *Principle of self-managing system*: • Self-managing • Actively exploitative • Responsible *Principle of human initiative*: • Develops internal human resources • Wide participation of school members	*Principle of standard structure*: • Standard methods and procedures to achieve goals • Emphasizes generalizability *Principle of centralization*: • Both big or small issues are carefully controlled to avoid problems • Pursues procedural control *Principle of implementing system*: • Externally controlled • Passively receptive • Not accountable *Principle of structural control*: • Enforces external supervision • Expansion of bureaucratic system

Adapted from Cheng (1993).

Knowledge of healthy school functioning profile for school-based management

The school reforms should draw heavily from the strengths of new knowledge and technology. In school-based management, schools should be encouraged to develop and achieve healthy functioning in management and education. According to the advances in research and knowledge about education and management, the characteristics of a healthy school functioning profile can be summarized in terms of school mission, nature of activities, management strategies, use of resources, roles of different constituencies, human relationship, quality of administrators, and evaluation indicators, as shown in Table 4 (Cheng, 1993, 1996a). This profile can provide a new knowledge base to guide changes in some important features of the internal school process.

In school-based management, schools should develop a clear school mission statement, strong organizational culture and school-based educational activities. In these schools, management strategies encourage participation and give full play to staff initiatives. There is also considerable autonomy regarding the use and acquisition of resources. The role of people concerned is active and developmental. Human relationships are open and cooperative with mutual commitment. Administrators should be of high quality and always willing to learn. Evaluation of school effectiveness and monitoring equality should include multi-level and multi-facet indicators with regard to input, process and output in order to help the school learn to improve.

Recently, there has been a strong emphasis on the development and application of knowledge and technology to monitoring and evaluating educational quality in school, whether for purposes of school accountability or development. MacBeath, Boyd, Rand and Bell (1997) and Cheng (1997b, 1997c) can provide examples of a comprehensive framework for employing indicators to evaluate and monitor different aspects of school functioning. The effective use of monitoring and evaluative technology will bring out the information and knowledge needed to develop and ensure the healthy profile of school process. Therefore, knowledge of monitoring and evaluating should be necessary in school-based management.

Knowledge of strategic management in school-based management

In facing challenges from the rapidly changing environment in the new century, it is important in school-based management to create conditions so that schools can be responsive to the changing internal and external environments, develop and achieve their goals and have organizational development and learning. Therefore, a knowledge of strategic management is very important for school-based management to help schools establish a management system to support their continuous organizational learning and development. The strategic management process can be illustrated as shown in Figure 4. It is a cyclical process which consists of five stages: environmental analysis, planning and structuring, staffing and directing, implementing, and monitoring and evaluating (Cheng & Ng, 1994; Cheng, 1996c). Participation and leadership are necessary and crucial for initiating and maintaining the entire strategic management process.

Table 4
Knowledge of school functioning profiles in school-based management

Characteristics of internal functioning	Profile based on new knowledge	Profile based on traditional knowledge
School mission	• Mission clear, shared, developed and willingly actualized by members • Emphasize participation in developing educational mission • Strong and unique organizational culture exists	• Mission unclear, imposed by external sources, not developed and accepted by school personnel • Emphasize keeping and implementing external mission • Weak and vague organizational culture exists
Nature of school activities	• School-based activities: managing and educating according to characteristics and needs of school	• Non school-based activities: content and style of education and management determined by external authority
Management strategies Concept of human nature	• Theory Y • Complex Man • Participation and development regarded as important	• Theory X • Rational Economic Man • Supervision and control regarded as important
Concept of school organization	• School is a place students, teachers and administrators live, everybody has the right to development	• School is a tool, teacher is employee, kept when needed, out when not needed
Style of decision-making	• Decentralization • Participation of teachers, parents and even students	• Centralization • Administrators make decisions
Leadership style	• Multi-level leadership: symbolic, cultural and educational leadership in addition to technical and human leadership	• Low level leadership: mainly technical and human leadership
Use of power	• Mainly expert and reference power	• Mainly legitimate, reward and coercive power
Managing techniques	• Sophisticated scientific techniques	• Simple techniques or experiences
Use of resources	• Autonomy; self-budgeting • According to school needs • In time to solve problems • Tend to broaden sources of education resources	• Tightly restricted by the central • According to external rules • Apply and wait for permission • Tend to avoid troublesome procedures for more resources

Table 4 (continued)

Characteristics of internal functioning	Profile based on new knowledge	Profile based on traditional knowledge
Role differences		
Role of school	• Active-developing style: exploit all possibilities for development of the school, teachers, and students • Problem-solving	• Passive-receptive style: implement centralized mission, follow administration procedure • Avoid making mistakes
Role of central authority	• Supporter and advisor	• Strict supervisor and controller
Role of administrator	• Goal developer and leader • Manpower starter and coordinator • Resource developer	• Watcher of static goals • Personnel supervisor • Resources controller
Role of teacher	• Partner • Decision-maker • Developer • Implementer	• Employee • Follower • Order receiver • Implementer
Role of parent	• Receiver of quality services • Partner: positive participation and cooperation • School supporter	• Receiver of quantity services • Outsider: not eligible for participation and cooperation
Human relations	• Partnership • Team spirit, open and cooperative • Shared commitment • Organizational climate: commitment style	• Hierarchical • Superior - subordinates, closed and defensive • Conflict of interest • Organizational climate: headless disengagement, or control style
Quality of administrator	• Possess knowledge/techniques of modern management • Continue to learn and grow, discover and solve problems • Open-minded	• Possess considerable administrative experience • Work according to ordinances and rules, avoid problems • Familiar with current ordinances
Evaluating effectiveness and monitoring quality	• Multi-leveled and multi-faceted, including input, process and output; academic achievement being only one of them • Evaluation is a learning process for school improvement	• Pay much attention to academic achievement or a few final outcomes, neglect the process and development • Evaluation is a means of administrative supervision

Adapted from Cheng (1993).

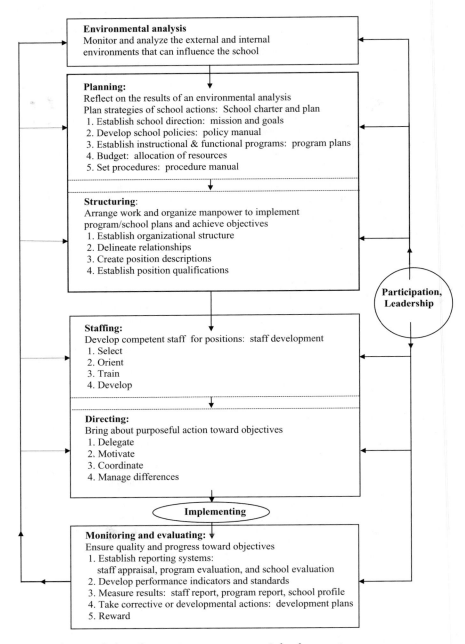

Figure 4. Knowledge of strategic management: School strategic management process

The strategic management system can support continuous learning and development of the whole school to face challenges and pursue multiple school functions in a changing environment. In other words, it provides a necessary linkage between internal school process and external environment, and facilitates and adapts the internal school process to achieve multiple school functions at different levels. Therefore, in the shift towards school-based management, there should be a clear knowledge of strategic management to help schools establish the necessary mechanism to be responsive to the changing environment, to learn, and to develop.

Knowledge of multi-level self management in school-based management

In school-based management, developing self management at the individual and group levels should also be an important element of new educational reforms (Cheung & Cheng, 1996). Under the major framework of school policy, individual staff members and groups can have appropriate autonomy to plan, manage, and carry out their work. Multi-level self-management is an important approach to encouraging and developing the necessary human initiative for the pursuit of school effectiveness and educational quality.

An overview of multi-level self-management in school is summarized in Table 5. The group self-management process, similar to strategic management at the school level, includes environmental analysis, planning and structuring, staffing and directing, implementing, monitoring and evaluating. For individual self-management, the process is only slightly different in "planning and affiliating" and "developing and directing." Within the framework of school strategic management, both individual and group self-management processes provide appropriate autonomy, as well as a systematic and cyclical process for individuals and groups to reflect on their environment, plan their work, allocate human resources, develop teams, cooperate with colleagues, monitor and evaluate their own progress and output. During these cycles, individuals and groups can learn and develop themselves continuously and carry out their work effectively, even in a changing environment.

There may be mutual influence and support as part of this self-management process, at individual, group, and school levels. On one hand, strategic management at the school level can affect the quality of self-management at the group and individual levels. On the other hand, individual self-management can be the primary building block for group self-management which, in turn, is the cornerstone of self-management or strategic management at the school level. As a whole, through continuous learning and development in self-management at multiple levels, the necessary human initiative, competence, and commitment can be developed for the pursuit of multiple school functions and effectiveness.

Knowledge of a dynamic process for multiple effectiveness

A school may try to be effective by relying on multiple functions for its survival. Since the available resources are often limited, it is very difficult for a school to maximize the effectiveness for all functions and achieve all its goals at the same time. A school may experience different pressures from multiple and conflicting environmental constraints and constituencies in the process of pursuing multiple functions. Based on the intensity of these pressures, the school develops different priorities for functions and goals to be pursued. The importance and priority of functions may vary over time and across circumstances. A school may be assumed to be effective if it is aware of the different pressures from internal and external environments and can show adaptability and flexibility in setting up a new priority for functions to be pursued in the near future. It pursues dynamic effectiveness among these multiple and conflicting pressures. Even though it cannot maximize the effectiveness of all school functions or criteria at the same time, it can do so in the long run if it has a strategic management system and leadership within the framework of school-based management.

The dynamic perspective of maximizing the effectiveness of multiple school functions supports the importance of school's organizational learning and development in a changing environment (Chapman, 1996). Therefore, in school-based management, the knowledge of a dynamic process for maximizing multiple school effectiveness should be developed and applied to understanding and managing the complicated and longitudinal nature of school behavior.

Knowledge of layer management in school-based management

Holistic education is one of the major trends in educational reforms. Recently, school education has often been emphasized as a holistic process, in which students as individuals and groups can receive maximum opportunity to learn and develop themselves to be multifaceted individuals. But unfortunately, the concept of the whole school approach and how it can maximize learning opportunities is often unclear. There is an urgent need for a new knowledge framework of whole school education for implementing school-based management.

Table 5

Knowledge of multiple self-management

Stages of self management	Process at the School Level	Process at the Group Level	Stages of self management	Process at Individual Level
Environmental analysis	▪ Reflect on the school's internal and external environment, crucial to its existence ▪ Focus on its strength, weakness, opportunities and threats as a school	▪ Reflect on the group's internal and external environment crucial, to its existence ▪ Focus on its strength and weakness, opportunities and threats as a group	*Environmental analysis*	▪ Reflect on personal attributes and external environment ▪ Focus on personal strength, weakness, opportunities and threats as a member in the group and school
Planning and structuring	▪ Develop school mission, policies and action plans ▪ Negotiation and compromise in decision ▪ Focus on structural issues such as organizational structure, budgeting and allocation of resources.	▪ Develop group's direction and action plans consistent with the school's mission and policies ▪ Negotiation and compromise in decisions ▪ Focus on issues like work designs, relationship delineation, and communication flows	*Planning and affiliating*	▪ Develop personal goals and action plans within the frames delineated by the school and the group ▪ Focus on the technical aspects of planning and designing of educational programs ▪ Establish affiliation and relationship with colleagues, students, parents and community
Staffing and directing	▪ Recruitment and deployment of staff ▪ Focus on human resource aspects of management such as staff development and delegation	▪ Deployment of members ▪ Focus on professional development of members and group learning	*Developing and directing*	▪ Develop personal professional competence ▪ Allocate personal resources and attention ▪ Focus on self-learning
Implementing	▪ Ensure the availability of necessary resources, guidance and support ▪ Focus on issues related to actual launching of all programs	▪ Ensure the proper allocation of resources ▪ Ensure mutual guidance and support among members to facilitate effective problem solving ▪ Focus on program implementation by the group	*Implementing*	▪ Ensure effective use of allocated resources ▪ Frequent rehearsal ▪ Focus on personal performance in the program or group
Monitoring and evaluating	▪ Set up work standards, monitor and control system for groups or programs ▪ Monitor and regulate pace of program implementation ▪ Evaluate the whole school performance ▪ Focus on ensuring quality of programs ▪ Use information to initiate next cycle of school self management	▪ Set up work standards for members, self monitor and regulate work pace of the group ▪ Evaluate performance of the group as a whole ▪ Focus on ensuring the group performance in delivering programs ▪ Use information to initiate the next cycle of group self management	*Monitoring and evaluating*	▪ Set up personal performance standards ▪ Self-observation, monitor and regulate personal work pace ▪ Evaluate personal performance ▪ Focus on ensuring personal performance ▪ Use information to initiate the next cycle of individual self management

Adapted from Cheung & Cheng (1996).

This knowledge framework can be developed from the concept of layer management previously proposed by this author (Cheng, 1996a, 1996b, 1996e). The school process may be divided into the following processes: the management process – a process wherein principal and administrators influence teachers in terms of leadership, management, and staff development; the teaching process – a process where teachers influence students in terms of leadership, teacher-student relationships, and teaching strategies; and the learning process – a process by which student(s) learn in terms of cognitive, affective, and behavioral change and development. From this line of thinking, the school process can be illustrated as a matrix comprised of three dimensions: categories of actors, levels of processes, and domains of effects.

Based on this matrix of school process a broader concept, layer management, can be introduced for managing the school process. The matrix of school process can be separated into actor layers such as the administrator layer, the teacher layer, and the student layer, as shown in Figure 5. The management unit of school process is based on the layer instead of the cell of the matrix. This can provide a more comprehensive unit for thinking about the holistic nature of the school process. In order to maximize the effectiveness of the teaching process, the teacher layer should influence the student layer as a whole (Cheng & Tsui, 1996). In other words, teachers at different levels should influence their students through all their behavioral, affective and cognitive performance. They influence not only individual students but also students in groups and the whole school. They influence not only students' behaviors but also their affective and cognitive development. This is holistic teaching. Similarly, the administrator layer should influence or support the teacher layer as a whole in order to maximize the effectiveness of the management process. A development cycle in terms of staff training programs or student activities programs can be established in each layer in order to support the needs of administrators, teachers, and students to learn and develop continuously at individual, group, school levels (Cheng & Tam, 1994).

The above layer concept can be used as the building block for re-engineering schools to provide holistic education and maximize opportunity for effective teaching and learning. Therefore, in ongoing and future educational reforms towards school-based management, the knowledge of layer management should be useful for schools to conduct holistic education and provide quality services.

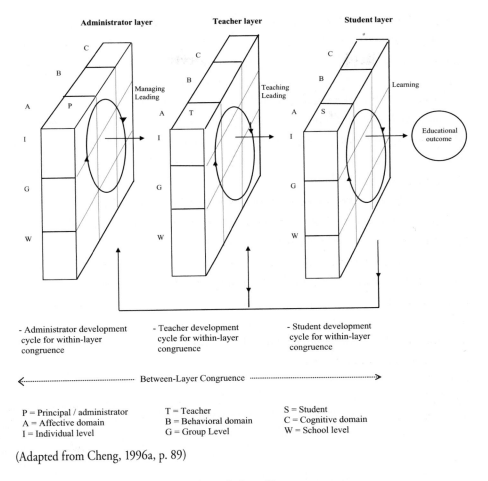

- Administrator development
cycle for within-layer
congruence

- Teacher development
cycle for within-layer
congruence

- Student development
cycle for within-layer
congruence

⟵·· Between-Layer Congruence ··⟶

P = Principal / administrator   T = Teacher   S = Student
A = Affective domain   B = Behavioral domain   C = Cognitive domain
I = Individual level   G = Group Level   W = School level

(Adapted from Cheng, 1996a, p. 89)

Figure 5. The knowledge of layer management

Knowledge of congruence in implementing school-based management

Congruence in school process. The school process generally involves numerous staff members and students in managing, teaching, and learning at different levels. Congruence in internal school process is critical to the effectiveness of school functioning. It can reduce internal wastage and negative conflict, and produce the necessary synergy to support the school and to develop and pursue new and multiple school functions. Many educational reforms often ignore the congruence between

261

different types of activities in managing, teaching and learning and focus on changes in only fragmentary aspects without taking into account their impact on other aspects. The results of such reforms are often limited, if not harmful. Therefore, school-based management needs knowledge about congruence in school process.

Based on the previous writings of this author (Cheng, 1987, 1996a), a principle of congruence can be proposed to predict the relationship between internal school effectiveness and school process, as follows: The greater the congruence in the school process, the higher the internal school effectiveness. There are three basic types of congruence in the school process:

- Congruence across domains: This means that the effects of the school process produced or received are mutually consistent in the behavioral, affective and cognitive domains of each actor at each level.

- Congruence across actors: This suggests that the performances of the principal, administrators, teachers and students are mutually consistent in each domain at each level.

- Congruence across levels: This implies that the characteristics of activities at the individual level, the group level and the whole school level are mutually consistent for each actor in each affective domain.

According to the layer management concept, the basic types of congruence described above can be further expressed in two forms of layer congruence:

- Within-layer congruence: This refers to the congruence within a given layer. For example, within teacher-layer congruence represents consistency within the teacher layer in terms of domain congruence (i.e., consistency across the affective, behavioral and cognitive domains) and level congruence (i.e., consistency across the individual, group and school levels) of teachers.

- Between-layer congruence: This indicates the congruence between any given layers. For example, between administrator-teacher layer congruence represents congruence between the administrator layer and teacher layer in terms of consistency in the affective, behavioral and cognitive performance of administrators and teachers at the different levels.

Using the principle of congruence, we can predict that the greater the between-layer congruence and the within-layer congruence, the higher the internal school effectiveness.

Congruence in technology. The technology used in a school can be classified into management technology, pedagogic technology and learning technology. In order to bring about positive educational results, the three types of technology should be congruent with each other. Management technology should be used to support the nature and process of teaching and learning. Pedagogic technology should facilitate learning activities and provide the best opportunity for all students to learn according to the expected educational content. Learning technology should fit the expected educational experiences and goals and facilitate learning by pupils with different personal characteristics and learning styles. There are two types of technology congruence that can influence the effectiveness of the internal school process:

- Between-type congruence of technology: This refers to the congruence between management technology, pedagogic technology and learning technology in terms of mutual support and assistance in operation.

- Within-type congruence of technology: This relates to the congruence between the components of one type of technology in terms of mutual support and assistance in operation. For example, whether curriculum arrangement, teaching strategies, teaching methods, instructional media, classroom management and educational evaluation are mutually supported and facilitated may have an impact on the effectiveness of pedagogic technology.

Congruence in school culture. The cognitive and affective congruence of school actors at the individual level, the group level and the school level is a hidden part of process congruence that is often related to school culture. To a great extent, the sharing of beliefs, values and assumptions about education, management, morality and citizenship should be the core part of school culture because it can shape and determine the major characteristics of overt processes and artifacts in school. The values and beliefs about morality, citizenship, education and management in school may or may not be mutually consistent (Bottery, 1993; Cheng, 1987). There may be two kinds of congruence in values and beliefs:

- Between-type congruence of values and beliefs: This refers to the congruence between different types of values and beliefs of education, management and morality/citizenship.

- Within-type congruence of values and beliefs: This relates to the congruence of values and beliefs within the same type. For example, the congruence across the educational values and beliefs (about aims, curriculum, methods, roles of teacher and student, and ideals of education outcomes) belongs to within-type congruence, and this may shape the educational process in a consistent pattern and impinge on its effectiveness.

In school-based management, the above knowledge of congruence in school process, technology, and culture can provide a basic guiding principle for directing internal school activities of management, teaching, and learning. In general, the greater the congruence in school process, technology, and culture, the greater the internal synergy and effectiveness.

Knowledge of total home-school cooperation and community support

In order to face the uncertainties and challenges of a changing education environment and pursue new school functions and effectiveness, parental cooperation and community support is necessary for school-based management in terms of education, resources, management and legitimacy (Cheung, Cheng, & Tam, 1995). To conceptualize home-school cooperation and community support and effectively develop them requires a new knowledge base for this sphere.

According to Tam, Cheng and Cheung (1997), there are two implications to total home-school cooperation. First, cooperation means that the families are involved in school education and support the school through various means (Cheng, 1991a). On the other hand, it also means that the school empowers or facilitates the families to strengthen their family education and to participate in school education. The knowledge framework of total home-school cooperation and community support is illustrated in Figure 6.

The school education includes a holistic educational process from the teacher/ administrator layer to the student layer involving the affective, behavioral, and cognitive domains at the individual, group and school levels (Figure 6). In order to facilitate school education and maximize its effectiveness, parents should be encouraged to become involved in this holistic process. Parental involvement in school education may include four different levels: participation in educating individual students, participation in parents' organizations, participation in the daily operations of the school, and participation in school decision-making.

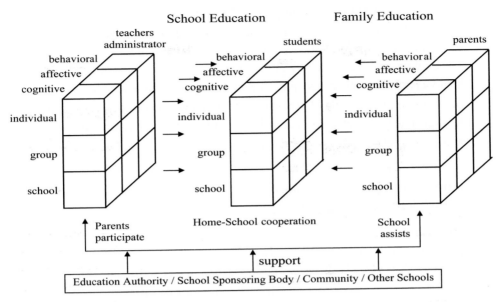

Adapted from Tam, Cheng, & Cheung, 1997.

Figure 6. Knowledge of total home-school cooperation and community support

As shown in Figure 6, family education should be conceptualized as a strong partner alongside school education, and involving multiple levels and multiple domains as well. Family education at the individual family level may include parents supervising the studies of their own children, spending time with them, listening to what they think and feel, developing a close relationship, analyzing problems with them, discussing family matters with them, and sharing their values and beliefs with them. Family education at the group level may include families within the same school in the same district, or parents of students of the same class or in the same grade joining together to organize activities for educating children. Some examples of these activities may be forming a support network, organizing study groups, seminars and workshops, sharing childcare experiences and insights among parents, learning new concepts and techniques for family education, etc. All these activities are helpful in supporting family education instrumentally and affectively. Family education activities at the group level may be expanded to the school level, so that all parents in the school can participate. Family education activities conducted at multiple levels can help parents become a strong synergetic force and a large resource pool for themselves and the school in educating their children (Tam, Cheng, & Cheung 1997).

265

Under the constraints of limited resources, tight schedules, multiple constituencies and a changing environment, the support and involvement of the community (including the education authority, the school's sponsoring body, professional agencies, and local organizations) are very important to the school's efforts in developing total home-school cooperation and pursuing multiple school functions for serving local communities, society and international communities (Goldring & Sullivan, 1996). In sum, knowledge of total home-school collaboration and community support is necessary in school-based management.

Knowledge of transformational leadership for practicing school-based management

The challenges resulting from a changing education environment, the implementation of educational reforms and the pursuit of new school functions and effectiveness demands that our school leaders possess a new set of leadership beliefs and the competence to transform former, traditional constraints, facilitate educational changes, and develop an appropriate school environment where teachers and students can work, learn and develop effectively. Therefore, new knowledge of transformational leadership should be an important component of the knowledge base for school-based management in the new century.

During the past decade, some important studies were conducted on principals' leadership in Hong Kong schools. The major findings of ten studies are summarized in Table 6. Nearly all the findings of these studies support the importance and contribution of a principal's leadership to school performance, teacher work performance, and student educational performance. Specifically, the following insights can be summarized from these research projects (Cheng, 1997d):

1. School leaders can encourage an open school climate or positive principal-teacher relationship.

2. School leadership can develop teachers' professionalism, esprit de corps and sense of community.

3. School leaders can influence teachers' organizational commitment, job satisfaction and work attitudes.

4. School leadership can make a difference in pupils' learning attitudes and affective and academic learning outcomes, even in a school of "low academic achievers."

5. A strong and balanced leadership in the structural, human, political, cultural and educational dimensions is critical for school effectiveness.

6. School leaders need strong support in leadership training and development for professional growth.

Table 6

Research on principals' leadership in Hong Kong schools

Research Project	Samples	Principal's Leadership studied	Key Findings
Cheng (1991b)	• 64 aided secondary schools • 627 teachers	• Relationship • Initiating structure	• Principal's leadership is strongly related to organizational climate and organizational effectiveness. • Higher relationship and higher initiating structure is preferable.
Yuen & Cheng (1991)	• 50 aided secondary schools • 306 teachers	• Eight types of management behaviors	• Both supportive leadership and instrumental leadership are related to teacher's affective commitment to school. • This relationship can be moderated by the teacher's professional orientation and task significance.
Chan, Cheng, & Hau (1991)	• 197 aided sec. schools • 2,000 teachers	• 20 management behaviors	• Nearly all of the management behaviors are strongly related to teachers' and principals' satisfaction with the principal-teacher relationships in school.
Chan & Cheng (1993)	• 60 aided secondary schools • 756 teachers	• Instructional leadership with 12 dimensions	• Instructional leadership of principals is characterized by providing incentives for learning, enforcing academic standards, and maintaining high visibility. • All the 12 instructional leadership dimensions are correlated with teachers' sense of efficacy, sense of community, and professional interest. • Public examination results are better in schools with effective instructional leadership.
Cheng, et al. (1994)	• 53 aided secondary schools • 1,500 teachers • 35,000 students	• Instructional leadership with 12 dimensions	• Most instructional leadership dimensions are strongly related to students' academic achievements (standardized tests and public exams) and social and personal developments, longitudinally.
Cheng (1994)	• 190 primary schools • 678 classes • 21,600 students • 3,877 teachers	• Five dimensions of leadership: structural, human, political, cultural, & educational	• Strong leadership in the five dimensions is closely related to: •Organizational performance; •Teachers' individual and group performance; •Students' individual and class performance.
Kwok, Lo, Ng, & Cheng (1997)	• 152 aided secondary school principals	• Five dimensions of leadership • Management difficulties • Confidence, efficacy, & satisfaction	• There seem to be three stages of principal development: new (1-2yrs), less experienced (3-5), and experienced (6 or above). • The development patterns of these 3 groups of principals are different in terms of leadership dimensions, management difficulties, confidence, efficacy, and satisfaction. • The less experienced principals might encounter more problems in leadership.
Chan, Cheng, & Yip (1994)	• 3 "low academic achiever" schools	• Contribution of the five leadership dimensions to school improvement	• A strong and balanced leadership can make a difference in low academic achiever schools.
Shum & Cheng (1997)	• 39 female principals • 321 teachers	• Five dimensions of leadership • Sex-role orientation	• The five leadership dimensions and androgynous orientation are positive and strong predictors for teachers' work attitudes.
Chui (in press)	• 48 secondary schools • 548 teachers	• Relationship of vision to five leadership behaviors	• There is a strong relationship between vision and communicating values, empowering teachers, people orientation, teacher professional development, & structural leadership.

Adapted from Cheng (1997d).

Some of the above research findings indicate a shift in the leadership concept, from a simplistic model to a more comprehensive and dynamic concept. Recently, transformational leadership has been strongly emphasized (Bass, 1985; Bass & Avolio, 1994; Silins, 1992, 1993). It is believed that a school leader is one who not only adapts his/her behavior to the situation but also transforms it. School leadership is not only a process to influence the behavior of school staff members but also their attitudes, values, and beliefs; not only of individual members but throughout the entire school; not only goal achievement but also goal development and culture building in school (Cheng, 1996d; Cheng & Yuen, 1996; Leithwood, Tomlinson, & Genge, 1996).

The traditional concept – duality of leadership with the concern for people and the concern for task – may be too simplistic and insufficient to institute transformational leadership. Based on Bolman and Deal (1991a, 1991b), Cheng (1994) and Sergiovanni (1984), a comprehensive model of five dimensions of school leadership – human leadership, structural leadership, political leadership, cultural leadership, and educational leadership – can be proposed for developing the transformational leadership needed to re-engineer schools (Cheng & Yuen, 1996). In school-based management, the knowledge of transformational leadership and five dimensions of leadership should be emphasized.

CONCLUSIONS

Numerous educational changes and school reforms have been introduced in the pursuit of school effectiveness and educational quality in different parts of the world. Unfortunately, most of the past educational reforms that have focused on fragmentary improvement and remedial treatment are not sufficient to bring about holistic school development and long-term effectiveness, and inevitably many of them have experienced serious frustration, if not failure.

The failure of past international school reforms and educational practices is often due to (1) a failure to recognize the relevance of school goals on the rapidly changing environment; and (2) a lack of understanding of the internal school process. Based on the experiences from ongoing school reforms in international contexts and the author's research, this chapter has highlighted a new knowledge base for the practice of school-based management for school effectiveness and educational quality.

Depending on the relevance of school goals and functions and the internal school process, the basic concepts of value added and value created in school effectiveness can be clarified and employed to direct the implementation of school reform. Therefore, the relevance of school goals and the improvement of internal school process should be considered as the two key elements for introducing school-based management and enhancing school effectiveness.

In order to enhance value created and value added in school effectiveness, new knowledge concerning multiple school functions including technical/economic, human/social, political, cultural, and educational functions at different levels is necessary for policy formulation to re-engineer schools and enhance their effectiveness in a changing educational environment. Furthermore, new knowledge about the internal school process can be used to enhance internal effectiveness and efficiency and contribute to the school's value added and created. The necessary knowledge base for school-based management should include the principles of school-based management, the knowledge of healthy school profile, the technology of strategic management, the dynamic concept of maximizing multiple effectiveness, the idea of layer management, the theory of congruence in school, the knowledge of total home-school cooperation and community support, and the new paradigm of school leadership.

In order to assess and monitor school effectiveness as a whole, certain models have been developed and they can also be used to direct the implementation of school-based management (see Cheng, 1996a for details). They include the goal model, the resource-input model, the process model, the satisfaction model, the legitimacy model, the organizational model, the ineffectiveness model, and the total management model. The basic characteristics of the models are summarized in Table 7.

The goal model is very often used in evaluating school performance or studying school effectiveness. Many people believe that the formally stated goals should be the basic requirements for schools to fulfill, and therefore they should be used to assess school effectiveness. The model assumes that there are clearly stated and generally accepted goals for measuring school effectiveness, and that a school is effective if it can accomplish its stated goals with given inputs. This model is useful if school outcomes are clear, and effectiveness criteria commonly accepted by all involved constituencies are available. Indicators of school effectiveness are often the objectives listed in school plans and programs, particularly those related to quality of learning and teaching environment, academic achievement in public examinations, etc.

Table 7

Models for monitoring school effectiveness

	Concept of school effectiveness	Conditions for model usefulness	Evaluation indicators / key areas (e.g.)
Goal model	• Achievement of stated goals	• Goals are clear, consensual, time-bound, and measurable; resources are sufficient	• Objectives listed in the school/program plans, e.g. achievements
Resource-input model	• Achievement of needed resources & inputs	• There is a clear relationship between inputs and outputs; resources are scarce	• Resources procured, e.g. quality of student intake, facilities, financial support, etc.
Process model	• Smooth & "healthy" internal process	• There is a clear relationship between process and outcome	• Leadership, communication, participation, coordination, social interaction, etc.
Satisfaction model	• Satisfaction of all powerful constituencies	• The demands of the constituencies are compatible and cannot be ignored	• Satisfaction of Education Authorities, management board, administrators, teachers, parents, students, etc.
Legitimacy model	• Successful legitimate or marketing activities for school survival	• The survival and demise among schools must be assessed	• Public relations, marketing, public image, reputation, status in the community, accountability, etc.
Ineffectiveness model	• Absence of characteristics of ineffectiveness in school	• There is no consensual criteria of effectiveness but strategies for school improvement are needed	• Existing conflicts, dysfunctions, difficulties, defects, weaknesses, etc.
Organizational learning model	• Adaptation to environmental changes and internal barriers	• Schools are new or changing; the environmental changes cannot be ignored	• Awareness of external needs and changes, internal process monitoring, program evaluation, development planning
Total quality management model	• Total management of internal people and process to meet strategic constituencies' needs	• The constituencies' needs are compatible; the technology and resources are available for total management	• Leadership, people management, strategic planning, process management, quality results, constituencies' satisfaction, impact on society, etc.

Due to the existing pressure of different expectations from multiple and powerful constituencies, schools often need to pursue multiple, but often inconsistent goals. Resources become the critical element in school functioning. The resource-input model assumes that more scarce and valued resource inputs are needed for schools to become more effective. A school is effective if it can acquire its needed resources. Therefore, inputs and acquisition of resources become the primary criteria of effectiveness. Quality of student intake, facilities, resources, and financial support procured from the central education authority, alumni, parents, sponsoring bodies or any outside agents are important indicators of effectiveness.

The nature and quality of the school process often determine the quality of output and the degree to which the school goals can be achieved. Particularly in education, experience in school process is often taken in the form of educational aims and outcomes. The process model assumes that a school is effective if its internal functioning is smooth and "healthy." Thus the selection of indicators may be based on these processes, classified as management effectiveness indicators (e.g. leadership, decision-making), teaching effectiveness indicators (e.g., teaching efficacy, teaching methods), and learning effectiveness indicators (e.g., learning attitudes, attendance rate).

School effectiveness may be a relative concept, depending on the expectations of concerned constituencies or parties. Therefore, satisfaction of powerful and strategic constituencies, rather than some form of objective criteria, is often used as the critical element to assess school effectiveness. Recently, there has been a strong emphasis on quality in school education. The concept of quality is, in fact, closely related to the satisfaction of clients' (customers' or constituencies') needs, or conformance to the clients' requirements and expectations. The satisfaction model defines that a school is effective if all its strategic constituencies are at least minimally satisfied.

Under the impact of rapid changes and developments in the local community as well as in the global context, the educational environment for schools becomes more challenging and competitive. On the one hand, schools have to compete seriously for resources and overcome internal barriers; on other hand, they have to face the external challenges and demands for accountability and value for money. Along this line of thinking, the legitimacy model suggests that a school is effective if it can survive as a result of engaging in legitimate or marketing activities. Therefore, the indicators of effectiveness are often related to the activities and achievements in public relations, marketing and accountability, and the school's public image, reputation, or status in the community, etc.

The ineffectiveness model describes school effectiveness from a "negative" side and defines a school as being basically effective if there is an absence of characteristics of ineffectiveness in the school. The model assumes that it is easier for the concerned school constituencies to identify and agree on criteria for school ineffectiveness than criteria for school effectiveness. In addition, strategies for improving school effectiveness can be more precisely identified by analyzing school ineffectiveness as opposed to school effectiveness. The indicators of ineffectiveness may include existing conflicts, problems, difficulties, defects, weaknesses, and poor performance. It seems that "no ineffectiveness" may be the basic requirement for effectiveness.

The organizational learning model assumes that the impact of environmental changes and the existence of internal barriers to school functioning are inevitable and therefore, a school is effective if it can learn how to make improvements and adapt to its environment. Whether the school and its personnel (particularly, the administrators and teachers) can learn to deal with change and reduce internal barriers is very important. The indicators of school effectiveness may include awareness of community needs and changes, internal process monitoring, program evaluation, environmental analysis, and development planning, etc.

For long-term success, quality performance or effectiveness, total management of the internal environment and process to meet the customers' (or clients' and strategic constituencies') needs is the key. The critical elements of total quality management in school include focusing on strategic constituencies (e.g., parents, students, etc.), continuous process improvement, and total involvement and empowerment of school personnel. According to the total quality management model, a school is effective if it can involve and empower all of its members in school functioning, conduct continuous improvement in different aspects of the school process, and satisfy the requirements, needs and expectations of the school's powerful constituencies – both external and internal – even in a changing environment. To a great extent, the total quality management model of school effectiveness is an integration of the above models, particularly the organizational learning model, the satisfaction model, and the process model.

As discussed above, each of the eight models has its own strengths and limitations in assessing school effectiveness and directing school practice. In various situations and given a variety of time frames, different models may be useful for studying school effectiveness. Comparatively, the organizational learning model and the total quality management model seem to be more promising for achieving multiple school functions at different levels.

With any luck, the above knowledge base, as well as the multiple models, can contribute to the implementation of school-based management for school effectiveness in different parts of the world in the new century.

REFERENCES

Apple, M. (1982). *Cultural and economic reproduction in education*. London: Routledge and Kegan Paul.

Averch, H. A., Carroll, S. J., Donaldson, T. S., Kiesling, H. J., & Pincus, J. (1974). *How effective is schooling? A critical review of research*. Englewood Cliffs, NJ: Educational Technology Publications.

Bass, B. M. (1985). *Leadership and performance beyond expectations*. New York: Free Press.

Bass, B. M., & Avolio, B. J. (1994). *Improving organizational effectiveness through transformational leadership*. Thousand Oaks, CA: Sage.

Beare, H., & Slaughter, R. (1993). *Education for the twenty-first century*. London: Routledge.

Blackledge, D., & Hunt, B. (1985). *Sociological interpretations of education*. Sydney: Croom Helm.

Bolman, L. G., & Deal, T. E. (1991a). *Reframing organizations*. San Francisco, CA: Jossey-Bass.

Bolman, L. G., & Deal, T. E. (1991b). *Images of leadership* (Occasional Paper No. 20, pp. 1–21). Cambridge, MA: Harvard University, National Center for Educational Leadership.

Bottery, M. (1993). *The ethics of educational management*. London: Cassell.

Caldwell, B., & Hayward, D. K. (1998). *The future of schools*. London: Falmer.

Caldwell, B., & Spinks, J. (1988). *The self-managing school*. London: Falmer.

Caldwell, B., & Spinks, J. (1992). *Leading a self management school*. London: Falmer.

Caldwell, B., & Spinks, J. (1998). *Beyond the self managing school*. London: Falmer.

Chan, B., Cheng, Y. C., & Hau, K. T. (1991). *A technical report on the study of principal-teacher relationships in Hong Kong secondary schools*. Hong Kong: The Chinese University of Hong Kong.

Chan, S. H., Cheng, T. S., & Yip, S. T. (1994). *Leading low academic achiever schools: Group research report*. Hong Kong: CUHK, Department of Educational Administration and Policy, Y. C. & Cheng.

Chan, Y. C., & Cheng, Y. C. (1993). A study of principals' instructional leadership in secondary schools. *Educational Research Journal, 8*, 55–67.

Chapman, J. (1996). A new agenda for a new society. In K. Leithwood, J. Chapman, D. Corson, P. Hallinger, & A. Hart (Eds.), *International handbook of educational leadership and administration* (pp. 27-60). Dordrecht, The Netherlands: Kluwer Academic Publisher.

Cheng, Y. C. (1987). School processes and effectiveness of civic education. *Education Journal, 15*(2), 11-17.

Cheng, Y. C. (1991a, May). The meaning and function of parental involvement in schools. *ICAC Periodical for Schools*, pp. 1-2.

Cheng, Y. C. (1991b). Leadership style of principals and organizational process in Hong Kong secondary schools. *Journal of Educational Administration, 29*(2), 25–37.

Cheng, Y. C. (1993). The theory and characteristics of school-based management. *International Journal of Educational Management, 7*(6), 6–17.

Cheng, Y. C. (1994). Principal's leadership as a critical indicator of school performance: Evidence from multi-levels of primary schools. *School Effectiveness and School Improvement: An International Journal of Research, Policy, and Practice, 5*(3), 299–317.

Cheng, Y. C. et al. (1994, November). Instructional leadership and students' educational outcomes in Hong Kong secondary schools. Presentation at the annual conference of the Hong Kong Educational Research Association.

Cheng, Y. C. (1995). *Function and effectiveness of education.* Hong Kong: Wide Angle Press.

Cheng, Y. C. (1996a). *School effectiveness and school-based management: A mechanism for development.* London: Falmer.

Cheng, Y. C. (1996b). *The pursuit of school effectiveness: Research, management, and policy.* Hong Kong: The Hong Kong Institute of Educational Research of the Chinese University of Hong Kong.

Cheng, Y. C. (1996c). *The improvement of school management: Theory, reform, and practice.* Hong Kong: The Hong Kong Institute of Educational Research of the Chinese University of Hong Kong.

Cheng, Y. C. (1996d, June). The transformational leadership for pursuit of school effectiveness in Hong Kong schools. Keynote address presented at the annual conference of the Hong Kong Association of Heads of Secondary Schools, The Chinese University of Hong Kong.

Cheng, Y. C. (1996e). A school-based management mechanism for school effectiveness and development. *School Effectiveness and School Improvement: An International Journal of Research, Policy, and Practice, 7*(1), 35-61.

Cheng, Y. C. (1996g). Multiplicity of school functions: A new direction for school effectiveness research. *Educational Research Journal, 11*(2), 175-184

Cheng, Y. C. (1997a). School re-engineering in the new century: An organizational perspective. *Educational Research Journal, 12*(1), 73-95.

Cheng, Y. C. (1997b). *Monitoring school effectiveness: Conceptual and practical possibilities and dilemmas in developing a framework.* In Report on School-based indicators of effectiveness of the Asia-Pacific Economic Cooperation (APEC) Education Forum. Eugene, OR: Clearinghouse on Educational Management. (ERIC Document Reproduction Service No. EA028359).

Cheng, Y. C. (1997c). *A framework of indicators of education quality in Hong Kong primary schools: Development and application.* In Report on school-based indicators of effectiveness of the Asia-Pacific Economic Cooperation (APEC) Education Forum. Eugene, OR: Clearinghouse on Educational Management. (ERIC Document Reproduction Service No. EA028358).

Cheng, Y. C. (1997d). *The transformational leadership for school effectiveness and development in the new century.* Eugene, OR: Clearinghouse on Educational Management. (ERIC Document Reproduction Service No. EA028356)

Cheng, Y. C. (Ed.). (1999). Recent education developments in Southeast Asia [Special issue] *School Effectiveness and School Improvement, 10*(1), 3-124.

Cheng, Y. C., & Cheung, W. M. (1997). Multi-models of educational quality and multi-levels of self management. *Educational Management and Administration, 24*(4), 451-462.

Cheng, Y. C., & Ng, K. H. (1994). School management initiative and strategic management. *Journal of Primary Education, 4*(2), 1-16.

Cheng, Y. C., & Ng, K. H. (1997). Conception and management of school crisis: A multi-perspective analysis. *Education Journal, 25*(1), 1-23.

Cheng, Y. C., & Tam, W. M. (1997). Multi-models of quality in education. *Quality Assurance in Education, 5*(1), 22-31.

Cheng, Y. C., & Tsui, K. T. (1996). Total teacher effectiveness: Conception and improvement. *International Journal of Educational Management, 10*(6), 7-17.

Cheng, Y. C., & Yuen, B. Y. (1996, August). Strategic leadership in school: Multi-functions for strategic management. Paper presented at the Eighth Regional/International Conference of the Commonwealth Council on Educational Administration, Kuala Lumpur.

Cheung, W. M., & Cheng, Y. C. (1996). A multi-level framework for self management in school. *International Journal of Educational Management, 10* (1), 17-29.

Cheung, W. M., Cheng, Y. C., & Tam, W. M. (1995). Parental involvement in school education: Concept, practice and management. *Journal of Primary Education, 5*(2), 57-66.

Chui, H. S. (in press). Vision and leadership of principals. *Journal of Educational Administration.*

Coleman, J. S., Campbell, E. Q., Hobson, C. J., McPartland, J., Mood, A. M., Weinfeld, F. D., & York, R. L. (Eds.). (1966). *Equality of educational opportunity.* Washington, DC: US Government Printing Office.

Collins, R. (1971). Functional and conflict: Theories of educational stratification. *American Sociological Review, 36,* 1002-1019.

Cousins, J. B. (1996). Understanding organizational learning for educational leadership and school reform. In K. Leithwood, J. Chapman, D. Corson, P. Hallinger, & A. Hart (Eds.), *International handbook of educational leadership and administration* (pp. 589-652). Dordrecht, The Netherlands: Kluwer Academic Publisher.

Dalin, P., & Rust, V. D. (1996). *Towards schooling for the twenty-first century.* London: Cassell.

Giroux, H. (1981). *Ideology, culture, and the process of schooling.* Lewes, UK: Falmer.

Goldring, E. B., & Sullivan, A. V. (1996). Beyond the boundaries: Principals, parents, and communities shaping the school environment. In K. Leithwood, J. Chapman, D. Corson, P. Hallinger, & A. Hart (Eds.), *International handbook of educational leadership and administration* (pp. 195-222). Dordrecht, The Netherlands: Kluwer Academic Publisher.

Grosin, L. (1994, January). Do effective schools contribute to greater equity? Paper presented at the International Congress for School Effectiveness and Improvement, Melbourne, Australia.

Gross, B., & Gross, R. (1985). *The great school debate.* New York: Simon & Schuster.

Hargreaves, D. H., & Hopkins, D. (1991). *The empowered school: The management and practice of development planning.* London: Cassell.

Hinchcliffe, K. (1987). Education and the labor market. In G. Psacharopoulos (Ed.), *Economics of education: Research and studies* (pp. 315-323). Kidlington, UK: Pergamon Press.

Kwok, M. L., Lo, S. K., Ng, M .B., & Cheng, Y. C. (1997). New and experienced secondary school principals: Leadership, management difficulties, confidence, efficacy and satisfaction. *Educational Research Journal, 12*(1), 60-72.

Leithwood, K., Tomlinson, D., & Genge, M. (1996). Transformational school leadership. In K. Leithwood, J. Chapman, D. Corson, P. Hallinger, & A. Hart (Eds.), *International handbook of educational leadership and administration.* (pp. 784-840). Dordrecht, The Netherlands: Kluwer Academic Publisher.

MacBeath, J., Boyd, B., Rand, J., & Bell, S. (1997). *Schools speak for themselves: Towards a framework for self-evaluation.* Scotland, UK: University of Strathchlyde.

MacGilchrist, B., Mortimore, P., Savage, J., & Beresford, C. (1995). *Planning matters: The impact of development planning in primary schools.* London: Paul Chapman Publishing.

McMahon, W. W. (1987). *Consumption and other benefits of education.* In G. Psacharopoulos (Ed.), *Economics of education: Research and studies* (pp. 129-133). Kidlington, UK: Pergamon Press.

Mohrman, S. A., Wohlstetter, P. et al. (1994). *School-based management: Organizing for high performance.* San Francisco: Jossey-Bass.

Murphy, J., & Beck, L. G. (1995). *School-based management as school reform: Taking stock.* Thousand Oaks, CA: Corwin Press.

Reynolds, D., & Cuttance, P. (1992). *School effectiveness: Research, policy, and practice.* London: Cassell.

Scheerens, J. (1992). *Effective schooling: Research, theory, and practice.* London: Cassell.

Sergiovanni, T. J. (1984). Leadership and excellence in schooling. *Educational Leadership, 41*(5), 4–13.

Shum, L. S., & Cheng, Y. C. (1997). Perceptions of women principals' leadership and teachers' work attitudes. *Journal of Educational Administration, 35*(2), 168-188.

Silins, H. C. (1992). Effective leadership for school reform. *The Alberta Journal of Educational Research, 38*(4), 317–334.

Silins, H. C. (1993, April). *The relationship between school leadership and school improvement outcomes.* Paper presented at the annual meeting of the American Educational Research Association, Atlanta, GA.

Stringfield, S., Ross, S., & Smith, L. (Eds.). (1997). *Bold plans for school restructuring: The new American schools designs.* Mahwah, NJ: Lawrence Erlbaum Associates.

Tam, W. M., Cheng, Y. C., & Cheung, W. M. (1997). A re-engineering framework for total home-school partnership. *International Journal of Educational Management, 11*(6), 274-285.

Thomas, R. M. (Ed.). (1983). *Politics and education: Cases from eleven nations.* Kidlington, UK: Pergamon Press.

Yuen, B. Y., & Cheng, Y. C. (1991). A contingency study of principal's leadership behavior and teachers' organizational commitment. *Educational Research Journal*, 6, 53–62.

INDEX